The Deacon Reader

Advance Praise
for *The Deacon Reader*

"*The Deacon Reader,* a compendium of excellent articles on many aspects of diaconal ministry, is a timely and valuable resource for every deacon. The relatively brief experience of almost a half century of the diaconate now provides a rich opportunity for theological, pastoral, and spiritual reflection on this remarkable restoration in the Catholic Church. The authors have captured well the powerful movement of the Holy Spirit in this awesome and exciting development of diaconal ministry."

+*Most Rev. William F. Skylstad*
President of the United States Conference of Catholic Bishops

"In the forty years since Vatican II, permanent deacons have assumed an increasingly important share in the mission of the Church, especially in the United States. This has not happened without some bumps along the way, and some misunderstandings about the diaconal identity and role. Precisely for this reason I welcome this collection of essays edited by Dr. James Keating. The time has come for serious, ongoing study of the key challenges faced by deacons, challenges on personal, pastoral, and theological levels. This book contributes admirably toward this goal. I recommend it especially to deacons and those discerning a vocation to diaconal ministry."

+*Most Rev. Thomas J. Olmsted, DD*
Bishop of Phoenix

"This excellent book of essays is a must read, not only for the diaconal community, but for the entire Church. It provides rich and practical insights about the nature of the restored diaconate and its relevance for contemporary ministry. I recommend *The Deacon Reader* wholeheartedly."

+*Most Rev. Howard J. Hubbard*
Bishop of Albany, New York

"This collection of essays on both an ancient and new Christian Order reveals multiple insights on ministry and sacraments and on the infinite potential of the diaconate in serving society and Church. The group of authors representing the intelligentsia of this emerging Order succeed in articulating the uniqueness and complexity of a vocation born from the *aggiornamento* of Vatican II....The reader will find an attractive and informative portrayal of an identity that has matured through interaction and pain. I began reading the essays in hopes of better understanding the deacons and their wives; however, when I finished, the mission of the Church, the meaning of the Eucharist, the identify of Jesus and his Kingdom were renewed and refreshed…"

+*Most Rev. Felipe J. Estévez*
Auxiliary Bishop of the Archdiocese of Miami

"This book sets out to do what it promises: clarify the fundamental identity of the deacon within the Catholic Church. The authors know their material and present it well. They engage in sound scholarship and provide ample footnotes. The chapters are easy to understand. Despite the number of authors, there is a unity to their presentation. I welcome this publication, as it offers a comprehensive set of articles that will facilitate teaching and discussion."

+*Most Rev. Blase J. Cupich, STD*
Bishop of Rapid City

"*The Deacon Reader* provides the reader with the historical, theological, pastoral, and sociological foundations of the diaconate. The essays demonstrate the importance of the ministry of the deacon in today's Church. This collection of unified essays is a valuable tool for priests, deacons, deacon directors, and aspirants who want to know more about the Order of Deacons. I look forward to the collaboration it will promote among all who are involved in ministry."

+*Most Rev. Daniel R. Jenky, CSC*
Bishop of Peoria

"My prayers have been answered! For years, I've been looking for a book like this. Now, thanks to editor James Keating, it is here. *The Deacon Reader* is a comprehensive, informative, and inspiring overview of the diaconate—and may well prove to be the definitive work on the subject. *The Deacon Reader* should be required reading for anyone with a serious interest in this ministry—the ordained, those hoping to be, or those who are just curious. I know it will be a blessing to me and countless other men who are pursuing this vocation."

Greg Kandra, deacon candidate
Diocese of Brooklyn

The Deacon Reader

Edited by
James Keating

GRACEWING

"Having received the favorable recommendation of Monsignor John Wolf, STD, Censor Librorum for the Diocese of Columbus, regarding the text 'The Deacon Reader' edited by Deacon James Keating, I hereby grant the Imprimatur in accordance with C. 830 § 3. Given at the Chancery Office in Columbus this 16th day of May, 2005."

+ The Most Reverend Frederick F. Campbell, DD, PhD,
Bishop of Columbus

Reverend Monsignor Stephan J. Moloney,
Vicar General / Chancellor

The nihil obstat and imprimatur are official declarations that a book or a pamphlet is free of doctrinal or moral error. No implication is contained therein that those who have granted the nihil obstat and the imprimatur agree with the content, opinions, or statements expressed.

The Scripture quotations contained herein are from the New Revised Standard Version: Catholic Edition Copyright © 1989 and 1993, by the Division of Christian Education of the National Council of the Churches of Christ in the United States of America. Used by permission. All rights reserved.

Extracts from the Documents of the Second Vatican Council are the Author's translation and from Walter Abbot's edition of *The Documents of Vatican II* © 1966 by America Press. Used by kind permission of America Press. Visit: www.americamagazine.org.

Cover Art: Lunette with Saint Lawrence. Early Christian mosaic. Mausoleum of Galla Placidia, Ravenna, Italy. Photo Credit: Scala / Art Resource.

Cover design by Cynthia Dunne
Book design by Lynn Else

First published in 2006
Paulist Press
997 Macarthur Boulevard
Mahwah, New Jersey 07430
USA

First published in England in 2006
Gracewing
2 Southern Avenue, Leominster
Herefordshire HR6 0QF

UK ISBN 0 85244 675 6

Printed and bound in the United States of America

This book is dedicated to the deacon class of 2001,
Diocese of Columbus, Ohio—

Richard Busic
Paul DeShaies
Ken Drummer
Klaus Fricke
James Gorski
Mickey Hawkins
Lyn Houze
Doug Mould
Byron Phillips
Frank Sullivan

—and also to Dcn. Frank Iannarino and Tom Johnston,
in gratitude for their years of commitment to diaconal formation.

Acknowledgments

I want to acknowledge with ever deepening gratitude the work of Elizabeth V. Palmer, MDiv, theology faculty research assistant at the Pontifical College Josephinum, Columbus, Ohio, for her faithful dedication in assisting me with the publication of this book.

Contents

Contents

Contributors

Dcn. Thomas Baker, MBA, has been a deacon since 1994 and serves at Saint David the King Parish in Princeton Junction, New Jersey, in the Diocese of Trenton. He is the author of *The Liturgy Committee Handbook* (Twenty-Third Publications, coauthored with Frank Ferrone) and the *Deacon* volume in Twenty-Third's multi-book series on parish ministries. His articles have appeared in *Commonweal, Today's Parish,* and *Church,* among others. In his secular career, Dcn. Baker is the principal of a management consultancy, Open Field Partners.

Dcn. Charles A. Bobertz, PhD, is professor of theology at St. John's School of Theology and Seminary in Collegeville, Minnesota, and a deacon for the Diocese of Saint Cloud. He has held teaching positions previously at St. Michael's College (Vermont) and Loyola College in Maryland. Professor Bobertz is the editor, with David Brakke, of *Reading in Christian Communities: Essays on Interpretation in the Early Church* (University of Notre Dame Press, 2002). He has published widely in leading theological journals.

Dcn. Owen F. Cummings, DD, is Regents' Professor of Theology at Mount Angel Seminary in St. Benedict, Oregon, and a deacon of the Diocese of Salt Lake City. He has published *Deacons in the Church* (Paulist Press, 2004) and *Saintly Deacons* (Paulist Press, 2005).

Dcn. William T. Ditewig, PhD, is executive director of the United States Conference of Catholic Bishops' Committee on the Diaconate in Washington, D.C. Among other works, he has written *101 Questions and Answers on Deacons* (Paulist Press, 2004).

Contributors

Rev. Edward J. Enright, OSA, STD, is assistant professor of church history and modern historical theology, with a specialization in John Henry Newman, in the Department of Theology and Religious Studies at Villanova University in Villanova, Pennsylvania.

Dcn. James Keating, PhD, is associate professor of moral theology in the School of Theology at the Pontifical College Josephinum in Columbus, Ohio. He is editor of the *Josephinum Journal of Theology* and author of many articles and books, particularly in the area of the convergence of morality and spirituality. He serves as deacon at Saint Andrew Parish in Columbus. His latest book, *The Way of Mystery: Eucharist and Moral Living,* is forthcoming from Paulist Press.

Most Rev. Gerald F. Kicanas, DD, is Bishop of Tucson, Arizona, having served previously as Coadjutor Bishop of Tucson and Auxiliary Bishop of Chicago. Before being ordained bishop, he served in various capacities in the Archdiocese of Chicago's seminary system for more than twenty-five years, including rector of Mundelein Seminary at the University of St. Mary of the Lake in Mundelein, Illinois. He also chaired the U.S. Bishops' Committee on the Diaconate for three years.

Rev. Mark A. Latcovich, PhD, is professor of pastoral theology and academic dean at St. Mary's Seminary in Cleveland, Ohio. For the past twelve years he has also worked in the diocesan diaconate formation program as an instructor and consultant, and he has given retreats and seminars for deacons and their wives.

Rev. William S. McKnight, STD, a priest of the Diocese of Wichita, is assistant professor and director of liturgy in the School of Theology at the Pontifical College Josephinum in Columbus, Ohio. He wrote his doctoral dissertation on the diaconate: *The Latin Rite Deacon: Symbol of Communitas and Social Intermediary among the People of God* (Pontificium Athenaeum S. Anselmi, 2001).

Rev. Paul McPartlan, DPhil, is a priest of the Archdiocese of Westminster. After ten years of teaching systematic theology at

Heythrop College in the University of London, he moved to the Catholic University of America in 2005. He specializes in ecclesiology, ecumenism, and Vatican II, and was appointed as a member of the International Theological Commission in 2004. He was involved in the launch of the permanent diaconate in Westminster in recent years, and he chaired the working party established by the Bishops' Conference of England and Wales that produced the forthcoming *Directory for the Formation of Permanent Deacons in England and Wales.*

Rebecca A. Meehan, PhD, is senior research associate in the Department of Sociology at Case Western Reserve University in Cleveland, Ohio.

Dcn. Ray R. Noll, Doct. ès Sc.Rel., is professor of theology in the Department of Theology and Religious Studies at the University of San Francisco in California. He has served for the past eighteen years as a deacon for the Diocese of Santa Rosa, assigned to Saint James Parish in Petaluma. A regular member of the Diaconate Council, he has also taught theology in the diocesan deacon formation program. Dr. Noll's published works include *Sacraments: A New Understanding for a New Generation* (Twenty-Third, 1999).

Dcn. Michael Ross, PhD, is assistant professor of theology in the School of Theology and academic dean for both the College of Liberal Arts and the School of Theology at the Pontifical College Josephinum in Columbus, Ohio. He serves as a deacon at Saint Mary Parish in the Diocese of Columbus.

INTRODUCTION

Dcn. James Keating, PhD

The essays collected in this book aim to give the reader an overview of the theological and pastoral nature of the diaconate and thus to clarify *the fundamental identity of the deacon,* for those who are discerning such a call as aspirants and those who are already candidates for the office. In so doing, the book assists diaconal students in grasping some of the theological, pastoral, spiritual, sacramental, and sociological aspects present in this vocation, and thus foster the intellectual formation of deacon students. The new *National Directory for the Formation, Ministry, and Life of Permanent Deacons in the United States* states that the intellectual formation of the deacon candidate offers "substantial nourishment" and constitutes a "precious instrument for effective discernment and ministry."[1] Before one can proclaim the gospel of Christ in any public way, a sound education in the identity of diaconal ministry is crucial for the building up of confidence; such knowledge also serves as a resource for spiritual and theological growth. Fidelity to one's vocation depends upon a sure knowledge of the nature of one's call. Thus, to educate oneself with vocational knowledge helps secure a firm foundation for a lifelong commitment to the diaconate. Through study, the mind is prepared to utilize the truths, symbols, and history of the diaconate to embrace confidently the mission of the deacon as understood by the church.

Additionally, to grow in awareness of the nature of the diaconal identity aids in the holiness of such candidates, as wisdom is mediated through the study of doctrine. Studying the theological content of vocation is the necessary precondition for growth in

---

1. National Conference of Catholic Bishops, Congregation for the Clergy and Congregation for Catholic Education, *National Directory for the Formation, Ministry, and Life of Permanent Deacons in the United States* (December 26, 2004), no. 118.

holiness of life. One cannot progress in holiness adrift in only a superficial grasp of ministerial skills. By bearing the intellect down upon the meaning of being called by Christ, the mind accurately receives the truth of this calling, and the affections are stirred to love what one has come to know. In loving one's vocation, the conditions for the possibility of becoming a saint are established. In the end, those called to the diaconate want to be competent ministerial deacons, but more so they want to participate in the holiness of the paschal mystery. My hope is that in a small way the following chapters assist the intellect of the deacon candidate in beginning to so participate.

I have divided the book into three parts: historical and theological foundations, pastoral foundations, and sociological foundations for the diaconate. In Part One, the authors uncover the historical and theological matter of the deacon's identity. This material is crucial to appropriate during the formation period, as it explicates the core elements of the diaconal identity. Part Two, on pastoral foundations, assists the aspirant and/or candidate with glimpses into the meaning of formation and also provides a broad view as to how diaconal identity relates to pastoral activity and relationships. As Part Three, I have included sociological chapters on marriage and the diaconate, since these two vocations intertwine at the heart of the man who is called to nuptial love and ordained ministry. Finally, an epilogue completes our reflections and suggests future theological directions for the diaconate, under the theme of *kenosis*.

It is my hope that this book will be used as a basis for classroom discussion and private reflection in order to deepen a diaconal candidate's appreciation for the depth and breadth of the vocation to which Christ has called him. To grasp the intellectual heritage of the church's doctrine, and of one's own vocation, readies a person to be able to speak a word of hope to a searching world. As Pope John Paul II stated:

> Deacons should not slacken in their studies particularly of sacred doctrine, they should carefully read the Scriptures;

they should devote themselves to ecclesiastical studies in such a way that they can correctly explain Catholic doctrine to others and day by day become better fitted to train and strengthen the souls of the faithful.[2]

---

2. John Paul II, "Deacons Are Called to Life of Holiness" (Catechesis at the General Audience of October 20, 1993), no. 4.

PART ONE

Historical and Theological Foundations for Diaconal Identity

CHAPTER 1

The History of the Diaconate

Rev. Edward J. Enright, OSA, STD

Introduction

"In a higher world it is otherwise, but here below to live is to change, and to be perfect is to have changed often." So wrote the venerable John Henry Newman in his *Essay on the Development of Christian Doctrine,* published in December 1845.[1] In this book he writes about the process of development in great ideas, and a great idea has been and is the ministry of the deacon in the church. Newman's predecessors in Germany at the Catholic Faculty of Theology at the University of Tübingen also spoke of the development of ideas, focusing on the idea of church. Also, like Newman, Drey and Möhler held that all of the aspects of the church are organically interrelated,[2] and so, applied to the diaconate, the church in her wisdom views this distinct office of service to be integral not only to the ministry of the church but to the very

---

1. John Henry Newman, *An Essay on the Development of Christian Doctrine* (Notre Dame: University of Notre Dame Press, 1989), 40.

2. Cf. Johann Sebastian Drey, *Brief Introduction to the Study of Theology with Reference to the Scientific Standpoint and the Catholic System,* trans. Michael J. Himes (Notre Dame: University of Notre Dame Press, 1994); Johann Adam Möhler, *Symbolism: Exposition of the Doctrinal Differences between Catholics and Protestants as Evidenced by Their Symbolical Writings,* trans. James Burton Robertson (New York: Crossroad Publishing Co., 1997); Johann Adam Möhler, *Unity in the Church or the Principle of Catholicism Presented in the Spirit of the Church Fathers of the First Three Centuries,* ed. and trans. Peter C. Erb (Washington, DC: Catholic University of America Press, 1996).

organization and mission of the church. As Newman, Drey, and Möhler would readily admit, the journey of ecclesial development has been a bumpy one over the centuries, but it has been a journey the church has never been unwilling to take. The brief history of the diaconate that is laid out following shows another main point of Newman's view of development, that is, that the historical movement of a great idea is from the implicit to the explicit. Therefore, the following trip through diaconal history starts out by uncovering the implicit roots of the order in the early church. The history of the diaconate is painted in a very organic way by its intimate relationship to Jesus himself, whose whole life was diaconal, "to the point of death—even death on a cross" (Phil 2:8), and to the call made by Jesus to all baptized Christians to be his servants in the world.

The New Testament and the Second Century

Several texts in the New Testament are pertinent to the beginnings of the implicit trajectory that will become the explicit ministry of deacon: one in the Acts of the Apostles, two in undisputed letters of Paul, and a fourth in the first of the pastoral epistles (Acts 6:1–6; Phil 1:1; Rom 16:1–2; 1 Tim 3:13). At first all ministries were verbs, the *doing* of something for the Christian community, but later they became nouns, designated offices. The diaconate starts out as seven men serving the Greek-speaking Jewish Christian widows in Jerusalem, a serving that is to be found at two tables at which these neglected saints would sit, the table of the word and the table of charity, both places of need, the spiritual and the material, but each flowing from the other. To put it another way, serving these two tables meant that these men were engaging in an evangelization of the whole person. In the New Testament there was an emphasis on action rather than office, because all the baptized, with Jesus as their model, were to engage in service to their fellow brethren; it was integral to their call in baptism. Even when a noun is used, the stress in Paul's letters and in 1 Timothy is on the doing of tasks, although it is often difficult to determine in any clear fashion what the tasks are. As Kenan Osborne, OFM, cautions, when it comes to New Testament data about any ecclesial matters, one has to be very careful not to read into texts anachronistically what appears at a later time in the church's history.[3] Although designated offices began to evolve slowly in apostolic Christianity, some form of church order was a concern of the first-century leaders. Of the texts mentioned, 1 Timothy is the clearest with regard to ordered ministry. As it does with the qualifications for the office of bishop-presbyter (these two offices were not distinct during the first century), so does 1 Timothy do with the qualifications for the office of deacon, namely, describe what type of man would best be suited to carry out the ministry of serving in the Christian community: Such candidates should be known for their seriousness, honesty, and self-discipline, especially with regard to alcohol and money. They should be committed to the faith transmitted to them, and they should be morally upright and good husbands and fathers (if in fact the person is already such; celibacy does not seem to be ruled out) (1 Tim 3:8–14).

Two of the early Christian writings that scholars sometimes refer to as borderline New Testament volumes—because they not only existed alongside the New Testament but also, in some places and by some late first-century and early second-century witnesses, were considered as scripture—are the *Didache* and *The Shepherd of Hermas.* The New Testament as we know it today was not completely formed into a canon until well into the fourth century, and so other writings were read alongside what came to be canonical writings. The *Didache,* written somewhere between AD 70 and 110, possibly in Syrian Antioch, speaks about the character of the man called to the diaconate in ways similar to 1 Timothy: These men must be of such good character because they "carry out the ministry of the prophets and teachers." In addition to and precisely

3. Kenan B. Osborne, OFM, *The Diaconate in the Christian Church: Its History and Theology* (Chicago: National Association of Diaconate Directors, 1996), 17.

because of this ministry, people are to treat them with honor, being as important to the community as the presbyters.[4] In *The Shepherd of Hermas,* written in Rome near the middle of the second century, the deacon is clearly mentioned as an integral part of ministry to be found in the city of Peter and Paul. Describing the church as a building, he writes, "The stones that are fair and white and fit their joints are the apostles and bishops and teachers and deacons who have walked according to the holiness of God and who have sincerely and reverently served the elect of God as bishops and teachers and deacons."[5] As we look closely at this passage, we note the need for good character, a description found elsewhere in *Hermas* and similar to the one in 1 Timothy. With the phrase "fit their joints," we note the intimately close ministerial relationship among the community's leadership, which is clearly an organic relationship. *Hermas* also describes one of the most important tasks of the deacon: his managing of the community's finances, especially for the purpose of caring for widows and orphans, who would have been among the poorest within the community.[6]

In addition to these two writings, the letters of Saint Ignatius of Antioch, who was martyred very early in the second century, give us one of the clearest examples of church order in the post-apostolic Christian community. Although the threefold ministry of bishop, presbyter, and deacon would take several more decades to develop throughout the church, such a ministry appears to have existed in Syrian Antioch at the time of Ignatius's tenure as bishop. He calls for respect for bishops, presbyters, and deacons, but only deacons are referred to as his own "fellow-servants" or "special friends." He compares deacons to Christ.[7] To the Trallians he writes in somewhat the same vein as 1 Timothy, but in more detail; for him the deacon must

---

4. *Didache,* ed. and trans. Aaron Milavec (Collegeville, MN: Liturgical Press, 2003), 35.

5. *The Shepherd of Hermas,* in *The Faith of the Early Fathers,* ed. William A. Jurgens, vol. 1 (Collegeville, MN: Liturgical Press, 1970), 34.

6. Ibid.

7. Ignatius of Antioch, *Letter to the Magnesians,* in *Ancient Christian Writers,* vol. 1 (Philadelphia: Westminster Press, 1953), 69.

always remain worthy of the calling given to him by God. Ignatius points to this need because he does not believe that deacons are limited to serving food but that they are "servants of the church of God." Again, he makes the point that deacons are to be respected as Jesus Christ should be respected.[8] All of Ignatius's seven letters are about the importance of the people maintaining unity with their bishop, clergy (presbyters), and deacons, who once again in the *Letter to the Philadelphians* are described as his "fellow-servants." In this same letter, Ignatius makes it clear that deacons preach the word, as helpers of the bishop. Likewise, they are the bishop's ambassadors, a task he considers to be an act of charity.[9] In the *Letter to the Church of Smyrna,* in the context of his theme of unity, Ignatius writes that the deacons are to receive "the same reverence that you would to a command from God."[10] This reverent obedience to the deacon is once again mentioned in his *Letter to Polycarp,* who himself calls for such obedience as if to Christ; he also calls for the deacon to be worthy of such obedience by the example he gives of an upright life.[11]

It is also during the second century, as the church was immersing itself more and more in the Greco-Roman culture of the time, that thinkers and teachers called "apologists" were present on the scene to defend Christian belief and practice. One of the most famous of the apologists was Justin from Rome, known commonly as Justin Martyr. We have in his *First Apology* the first explicit reference to the liturgical function of the deacon: he distributes communion to both those present at the celebration of the Eucharist and those who were unable for one reason or another to participate in the community's celebration of praise and thanksgiving.[12] Turning to another important source of our knowledge of the diaconate, Tertullian's *On Baptism* (written about 200), we have the work of a man who gave Western Christianity much of its theological vocabulary about God and Christ.

---

8. Ibid., *Letter to the Trallians,* in *Ancient Christian Writers,* vol. 1, 75–76.

9. Ibid., *Letter to the Philadelphians,* in *Ancient Christian Writers,* vol. 1, 86.

10. Ibid., *Letter to the Smyrneans,* in *Ancient Christian Writers,* vol. 1, 95.

11. Ibid., *Letter to Polycarp,* in *Ancient Christian Writers,* vol. 1, 98.

12. Justin Martyr, *First Apology,* in *Fathers of the Church,* vol. 6 (New York: Christian Heritage, 1948), 105, 107.

Tertullian took Christianity so rigorously, however, that he became a Montanist, a sect that thought most Christians were not living the gospel strictly enough. In his piece on baptism, Tertullian gives a hierarchy of ministers who can baptize, starting with the bishop as having top priority, all the way to the laymen who can baptize in an emergency. In between, the presbyter and then the deacon can baptize with the permission of the bishop.[13] He is also insistent, especially during his Montanist period, that all office holders, be they bishop, presbyter, or deacon, are to be married but once. Hippolytus was of the same mindset.

From the Third Century to the Fifth Century

Also called "The Teaching of the Twelve Holy Apostles and Disciples of Our Savior," a third-century document known as the *Didascalia Apostolorum* provides our history with some of the most explicit information on the diaconate to date. The author, apparently a bishop, outlines the relationship between a bishop and a deacon. Since both bishop and deacon are to be of one heart and mind in carrying out the one mission assigned to both—the carrying out of the gospel—the deacon (being subordinate to the bishop) must obey the bishop and execute his ministry in accord with the bishop's wishes, and he must do so to the best of his ability. The impression is that the tasks of deacon include a ministry of the word, but it is not clear if that means preaching or simply bearing an oral message from the bishop to a particular party. The *Didascalia* does hold that the deacon is "the bishop's ear, mouth, heart, and soul," so either interpretation is valid and both were probably taken up by the deacon. Spiritually, the author of the *Didascalia* likens the bishop to God the Father and the deacon to Jesus Christ. He also educates the bishop to "take to yourself workers for justice, helpers who will

---

13. Tertullian, *On Baptism,* in Jurgens, *Early Fathers,* vol. 1, 128.

cooperate with you in guiding others towards life." The men the bishop chooses to be deacons should be this type of worker, this type of helper. The deacon is, in fact, to be the chief administrator of all things assigned by the bishop. It is clear from this writing that at the time the deacon was of far greater importance than the presbyter; he was the bishop's right-hand man.[14]

Hippolytus's *Apostolic Tradition* is not only the earliest but also the best source for information about the sacramental rituals of the late second and early third centuries (redacted in the fourth century), particularly as practiced in Rome. The ordination rites for the threefold ministry are clearly and with great detail spelled out in this "manual." The distinction between the deacon and the presbyter is made very clear in the rubrics, these being supplied with reasons. Unlike the presbyter, the hands of the bishop are the only hands laid on the head of the candidate for diaconate, because "he is not ordained to the priesthood but to the service of the bishop, that he may do those things that are ordered by him." It is also pointed out that the deacon does not belong to the body of elders, to which only the presbyters belong, "but taking care of and indicating to the bishop what is necessary, not receiving the common spirit of the presbyterate…but that which is entrusted to him under the power of the bishop." The sense is that the deacon carries out administrative tasks for the bishop but also that the deacon keeps the bishop informed of what needs to be done for the betterment of the community. That God has chosen and the candidate freely responded to the call of God to be a deacon is exemplified in the prayer of ordination prayed by the bishop: "God, who created all things and ordered [them] by [your] word, Father of our Lord Jesus Christ, whom you sent to serve your will and manifest to us your desire, give the Holy Spirit of grace and caring and diligence to this your servant, whom you have chosen to serve for your church."[15] The ordination prayer continues by identifying the

---

14. *Didascalia Apostolorum,* in Edward P. Echlin, *The Deacon in the Church: Past and Present* (Staten Island, NY: Alba House, 1971), 47–51.

15. Hippolytus, *The Apostolic Tradition,* ed. Paul F. Bradshaw, Maxwell E. Johnson, and L. Edward Phillips (Minneapolis: Fortress Press, 2002), 60–61.

liturgical roles in which the deacon has been called to serve: "and to present in your holy of holies that which is offered to you by your anointed high priest [bishop] to the glory of your name." Further, the ordination prayer recalls to the deacon the true motive of his service, which is the praise and glory of God.[16]

With Cyprian, the great bishop of Carthage in the African province of the Roman Empire during the middle of the third century, the liturgical role of the deacon only suggested in *The Apostolic Tradition* is more clearly defined. In his theological contribution on the state of those who lapsed from the faith during the persecutions of Decius, *On the Lapsed,* Cyprian notes that the deacon distributes communion and, under the most dire of circumstances and confined to the immediate context, can hear confessions—when no bishop or presbyter is available—of those who had fallen away and wanted to return to the church. Since this ministry by a deacon was such an extraordinary one, it is important to hear from Cyprian at length:

> They who have received certificates from the martyrs, and may be assisted by their privilege with God, if they should be seized with any misfortune and peril of sickness, should, without waiting for my presence, before any presbyter who might be present, or if a presbyter should not be found and death becomes imminent, before even a deacon, be able to make confession of their sins, that, with the imposition of hands upon them for repentance, they should come to the Lord with the peace which the martyrs have desired, by their letter to us, be granted to them.[17]

Like other attestations we have tendered, Cyprian likewise mentions the nonliturgical works of the deacon, namely, acting as ambassador from the bishop to other bishops, and, as noted in the Acts of the Apostles, administering charity. While Cyprian himself was in exile, he allowed deacons to accompany the presbyters on

---

16. Ibid.

17. Cyprian, *Letter 12,* in *Fathers of the Church,* vol. 51 (Washington, DC: Catholic University of America Press, 1964), 34–36.

visitations, presumably to the sick, and therefore, deacons would administer viaticum.[18] In letters during this exile, he asks that deacons be the means by which he would receive communications on what was happening with the Christian community of Carthage; he could then communicate to the deacon what needed to be done for the service of his people. During this same period two bishops of Rome, Cornelius and Fabian, emphasized that deacons be "men of authority and responsibility."[19]

Reflecting his belief in the harmony between heaven and earth, Clement of Alexandria in the third century says in his *Stromata* that "according to my opinion the grades here in the church of bishop, presbyters, deacons are imitators of the angelic glory of the heavenly economy which, the scriptures say, awaits those who, following the footsteps of the apostles, have lived in perfection of righteousness according to the gospel."[20] Origen, another Alexandrian, was quite clear that deacons were to engage above all in preaching God's word.[21] A third Alexandrian, Denis, according to Eusebius, praises the clergy, including deacons, and the laity, for giving their lives to Christ while ministering to the sick during the most difficult of times.[22]

The record of the fourth-century Spanish nun Egeria's pilgrimage to Jerusalem has been one of the most important ways historians of the liturgy have come to know what exactly was transpiring in Jerusalem as far as worship is concerned. Her diary is detailed and includes mention of what appears to be another liturgical role of the deacon, the reciting of the general intercessions between an opening and closing prayer by the bishop.[23] Also,

---

18. Ibid., 38.

19. Owen F. Cummings, *Deacons and the Church* (Mahwah, NJ: Paulist Press, 2004), 48.

20. Clement of Alexandria, *Stromata,* in Jurgens, *Early Fathers,* vol. 1, 184.

21. Origen, *Homilies on Joshua,* in *Fathers of the Church,* vol. 105 (New York: Christian Heritage, 1960), 37–38.

22. Eusebius, *The History of the Church,* trans. G. A. Williamson, rev. and ed. Andrew Louth (New York: Penguin Books, 1989), 237.

23. Egeria, *Egeria's Travels to the Holy Land,* in *Ancient Christian Writers,* vol. 38, 65, 90–91, 216–17, n. 273.

Jerome, the father of biblical scholarship, is always a good source for information about the early church. In a letter contemporary with Egeria's pilgrimage to Jerusalem and noted especially for descriptions of the liturgical celebrations of the Triduum, Jerome mentions that deacons are better paid than presbyters; more important, Jerome notes that the deacon is responsible for the blessing of the paschal candle.[24] Egeria was probably aware of this, because she intimates that the deacon has other parts to play in the liturgy.

The councils of the ancient church are a vital source for uncovering the history of the diaconate as it moved from the implicit in the New Testament to the explicit in late antiquity. At the Council of Arles (what is today France) in AD 314, a prohibition of deacons presiding at the celebration of the Eucharist was put into place. Although not a widespread practice, nevertheless it should not have been the case at all.[25] In the same year, at a council held in Ancyra, Asia Minor, the same practice seems to have been forbidden as well.[26] Other local councils in the fourth century also legislated the activities of deacons, but the first general or ecumenical council held at Nicaea in AD 325—at which the future Patriarch of Alexandria, Athanasius (then the archdeacon), participated in an important way—legislated with strict abandon for all clergy when it came to celibacy[27] and the need to minister only in the church for which they had been ordained.[28] It is Canon 18 that deals with deacons by themselves:

> It has come to the attention of this holy and great synod that in some places and cities deacons give communion to presbyters, although neither canon nor custom allows this, namely that those who have no authority to offer should give the body of Christ to those who do offer. Moreover it has

---

24. Jerome, *Epistle 28,* in Cummings, *Deacons,* 49.

25. Council of Arles, in Echlin, *Deacon,* 54.

26. Council of Ancyra, in Echlin, *Deacon,* 55.

27. Council of Nicaea, Canon 3, in *Decrees of the Ecumenical Councils,* ed. Norman P. Tanner, SJ (London: Sheed & Ward; Washington, DC: Georgetown University Press, 1990), 7.

28. Ibid., Canon 16, in Tanner, *Decrees,* 13–14.

become known that some of the deacons now receive the eucharist even before the bishops. All these practices must be suppressed. Deacons must remain within their own limits, knowing that they are the ministers of the bishop and subordinate to the presbyters. Let them receive the eucharist according to their order after the presbyters from the hands of the bishop or the presbyter. Nor shall permission be given for the deacons to sit among the presbyters, for such an arrangement is contrary to the canon and to rank. If anyone refuses to comply even after these decrees, he is to be suspended from the diaconate.[29]

This canon is obviously referring to previously drafted canons and is not inconsistent with the warnings that can be found at local councils and in the writings of bishops with regard to the behavior of deacons. On the positive side, this canon does confirm the relationship of the deacon to the bishop and that the deacon does in fact have a liturgical role.

Increasingly, from the late third century into the fifth century and thereafter, the importance of an individual order called "deacon" became less and less important. There is, if you will, a reduction from a threefold ministry to a twofold ministry. In the first two to three centuries, Christianity was essentially located in the cities of the Roman Empire and, therefore, the bishop with the help of the deacon could handle the size of the congregations then existing. As Christianity increased in size and began to move out into the countryside, however, the bishop, who remained in the city, needed to provide for the celebration of the Eucharist; he therefore began to assign presbyters to take over the priestly role that once was solely his in the small city congregations. The deacon, by his very ordination, being assigned to the bishop, did not accompany the presbyters out into the countryside. Thus, eventually the diaconate ceased to be a distinct permanent ministry and became a step to the priesthood. Before this decline really gained momentum, however, there are other witnesses to the importance

---

29. Ibid., Canon 18, in Tanner, *Decrees,* 14–15.

of the diaconate in the fourth and fifth centuries. One of the most important of these was the *Apostolic Constitutions,* written in the fourth century for organizing church order either in Syria or Constantinople. This source makes abundantly clear what are and are not the proper roles for deacons, and it also deals with aberrant behavior by deacons. Positively speaking, the *Apostolic Constitutions* allows for the deacon to represent the bishop at synods when the bishop is unable to attend and, interestingly, to preside "with other ministers over solemn assemblies when quarrels among Christians were adjudicated."[30] Liturgically, the deacon assisted at baptism but did not baptize; proclaimed the gospel and read the intentions in the prayer of the faithful during the celebration of the Eucharist; was responsible for maintaining the proper order in the assembly and correcting behavior as well; stood guard against intrusions from outsiders; and took his place next to the bishop during the eucharistic prayer.[31] Negatively speaking, the *Apostolic Constitutions* issued numerous canons regarding deacons, but too many to detail here. Most of them deal with liturgical, residential, and behavioral matters that were common to much legislation with regard to ministry in late antiquity.

For Augustine in North Africa, one of the deacon's most important roles was catechesis,[32] and for Athanasius, now Patriarch of Alexandria, the deacon's role continued to include mediating between the bishop and his people and keeping the former apprised of community events and issues.[33] For Cyril of Alexandria, the deacon assisted at baptisms, but where no other usual minister was available, the deacon could do the baptism.[34] John Chrysostom, who was very insistent on the similarity of ordination between bishop and presbyter, was also very firm on the

---

30. *Apostolic Constitutions,* in Echlin, *Deacon,* 61–64.

31. Ibid.

32. Augustine, *The First Catechetical Instruction,* trans. and annot. Joseph P. Christopher (Chicago: Henry Regnery, 1966), 13.

33. Athanasius, *Against the Arians,* in Echlin, *Deacon,* 69.

34. Cyril of Jerusalem, *Catechetical Lectures,* in *Fathers of the Church,* vol. 61 (New York: Christian Heritage, 1952), 110.

subordination of the deacon to these other ministers.[35] Another fourth-century eastern bishop, Serapion, lays out in neat order in his *Euchologium* what he considers most important about the deacon: to assist at the celebration of the Eucharist, to be "pure in body and soul and with a clear conscience do their service and watch over the holy body and the holy blood," and in an ordination prayer to have God "give him [the deacon] the Spirit of knowledge and discernment, that he may be able to offer you pure and blameless service among your holy people, through your Son, Jesus Christ."[36] In a letter by Pseudo-Clement, the deacon is called the "eyes of the bishop," in that he is to continue the role of mediation between the bishop and his people, especially the sick.[37] Also, the deacon is understood as a minister of reconciliation "who exhorted sinners to return to Church."[38] Pope Saint Leo the Great (440–461) in many of his writings outlined the tasks of deacons, and these include the usual ones of mediator, ambassador, and, especially, representative at councils, including Chalcedon in 451.[39]

There are many other examples from the patristic period that witness to these same roles and tasks of the deacon.[40] Needless to say, as we move further along in late antiquity and into the early medieval period, with the sacerdotal role of the presbyter becoming increasingly more dominant, the need for a permanent deacon declines. More and more the diaconate became a step to the priesthood, even if the deacon continued to practice the works for which the earlier distinct order was well known, but these would now include service to the presbyter as well as to the bishop as he had in the past. This service of the presbyter was

---

35. John Chrysostom, *Homilies on Galatians, Ephesians, Philippians, Thessalonians, Timothy, Titus, and Philemon,* in Echlin, *Deacon,* 70–71.

36. Serapion, *Euchologium,* in Echlin, *Deacon,* 71–72.

37. Pseudo-Clement, *Letters,* in Echlin, *Deacon,* 73.

38. Ibid., *Homilies,* in Echlin, *Deacon,* 73.

39. Leo I, *Letters,* in *Fathers of the Church,* vol. 34 (New York: Christian Heritage, 1949), 248.

40. Pseudo-Dionysius, Philostorgius, *Testament of Our Lord,* Council of Vaison (442), *Statuta Ecclesiae, Antiqua* (c. 480), Gregory I, Venerable Bede, and the *Gelasian Sacramentary,* to name but a few sources.

thought of as comparable to the service of Christ, but it involved the more lowly forms of service, such as Christ washing the feet of the disciples at the Last Supper.

The Medieval Period

In the Middle Ages it was the liturgy that became increasingly the context for diaconal service. Many of the writers of this time made it a point to stress what the deacon was to do during the liturgy, as well as the relationship he was to have with the presiding presbyter. For example, Isidore of Seville in the seventh century wrote that the ministry of the deacon is so important liturgically that without it

> [a] priest has the name, [but] he does not have the office. The priest consecrates, the deacon dispenses the sacrament. The priest prays, the deacon recites the psalms. The priest sanctifies the oblations, the deacon dispenses what has been sanctified. It is not permitted for priests through their presumption to take the chalice from the table of the Lord unless it is handed to them by the deacon.[41]

An anonymous ninth-century German document relates the role of the deacon in language similar to Isidore:

> It behooves the deacon to minister at the altar and to baptize.... The minister is called levite or deacon because he ministers at the altar to the priest offering. He places the oblations on the altar; and he dispenses the sanctified oblations. A priest without a deacon has the name, he does not have the office.[42]

Peter Lombard in the twelfth century summarizes very neatly in his famous *Sentences* the role of deacon during the Middle Ages:

---

41. Isidore of Seville, *De Ecclesiasticis Officiis,* in Echlin, *Deacon,* 81–82.

42. Anonymous, in Echlin, *Deacon,* 83, citing Roger Reynolds, "A Florilegium on the Ecclesiastical Grades in CLM 19414," *Harvard Theological Review* 63, no. 2 (April 1970): 251.

These are called deacons in Greek, ministers in Latin because just as in the priest consecration, so also in the deacon dispensation of the mystery. It pertains to deacons to assist priests and to minister in all things which are done in the sacraments of Christ; that is, in baptism, in chrism, in the paten and chalice, to carry the oblations and place them on the altar, to take care of and decorate the table of the Lord; to carry the cross, and to read the epistle and gospel to the people. Just as lectors in the Old Testament, the deacons of the New are ministers of the word. To deacons also pertains the recitation of prayer and the reading of names of new catechumens. The deacon admonishes all to hear the Lord; he gives the peace and he announces....Deacons receive the texts of the gospel that they may know themselves to be preachers of the gospel of Christ.[43]

The medieval period can be concluded with what Saint Thomas Aquinas has to say about the deacon in the *Summa Theologiae:*

Deacons are called ministers because it does not pertain to deacons principally and *ex officio* to confect a sacrament but to minister to higher orders in the performance of sacraments....It pertains to the deacon to read the gospel in church and to preach catechetically....It does not pertain to a deacon as from his proper office to give the sacrament of baptism, but to assist in the administration of this sacrament and to minister to higher orders....Because baptism is a necessary sacrament deacons are permitted to baptize in urgent necessity when higher orders are not present.[44]

Thomas has a fascinating reason as to why deacons are not allowed to administer extreme unction even in emergency circumstances: It is because the diaconate itself is compared to the purgative way,

---

43. Peter Lombard, *Sentences,* in Echlin, *Deacon,* 84–85.

44. Thomas Aquinas, *Summa Theologiae Tertium Partem,* q.67 a.1 and ad.1–3 (Cambridge, UK: Blackfriars; New York: McGraw-Hill, 1964–). References to the diaconate in the *Summa* can be found in this edition as follows: q.57 a.57; q.59 a.109; q.39 a.251; q.57 a.55; q.83; q.47 a.47; q.56 a.103; q.59 a.157.

while "the dispensation of sacramental grace" is compared to the illuminative way.[45] The deacon, furthermore, like other ordained ministers, must be celibate, "so that they who are concerned with holy things may be clean."[46] He continues in the same place to distinguish between presbyters and deacons, even though both have the bishop's hands imposed on them, because only the priest is given the power to confect the Eucharist, and the deacon can only dispense the sacraments along with the priest. To conclude our look at Aquinas, a quote from him setting the deacon once again in the hierarchy of orders is apt:

> The power of the deacon is midway between the power of the priest and that of the subdeacon. The priest directly has power over the body of Christ; the subdeacon, however, over the vessels only, but the deacon over the body contained in the vessel. Therefore it is not for him to touch the body of Christ but to carry the body in the paten, and to dispense the blood with the chalice. And so his power for the principal action cannot be expressed through the bestowal of the vessel only nor through the bestowal of the matter. But his power for the secondary act is expressed in this that the book of the gospels is given to him; and in this power the other is understood. And so in the very giving of the book the character is impressed.[47]

---

45. Ibid., *Supplementum Tertiae partis,* q.30 a.1. The purgative way is a period of struggle against habitual sin and vice. The way of illumination takes hold of the believer when the struggle against sin is outweighed by the practice of virtue. In the illuminative way, the person begins to be intrigued by the spiritual and intellectual truths of following Christ. The believer sets out on a course of meditation on the word of God, attending to the word, and having the mind and affections formed by the word. One is given a new way of thinking. This kind of thinking works in such a way that charity founds and moves the person to obey the truth that conscience comes to recognize. The unitive way, finally, is the phase where we live out of the gifts of the Holy Spirit. The purgative, illuminative, and unitive ways are not strictly successive phases. One can possess virtue even while struggling with sin; in fact, it is necessary to have some virtue in order to enter the struggle (see Louis Bouyer, *Introduction to Spirituality* [Collegeville, MN: Liturgical Press, 1961], 243–85).

46. Ibid., q.37 a.3.

47. Ibid., ad.5.

Although there would be individual men, such as Saint Francis of Assisi, who would remain lifelong deacons, nevertheless the norm became that the deacon remained in his office for awhile and then moved on to ordination to the priesthood. This remained the case until Vatican II, despite the attempt during the Council of Trent to revive the diaconate order.

The Council of Trent

An Italian bishop at the Council of Trent put his desire for diaconal revival this way:

> I desire the function of the subdeacon and deacon, diligently collected from the writings of the fathers and decrees of the councils, to be restored and put to use, especially the functions of deacons. The Church has always used [the service of deacons]. Not only in ministering at the altar, but in baptism, in care of hospitals, of widows, and of suffering persons. Finally all the needs of the people are mediated to the bishop by deacons.[48]

Here we have a laying out of everything the deacon did during the early centuries, but although any number of Catholic reformers wanted such a restoration, the attacks upon the priesthood and the sacrificial view of the Mass by the Protestant reformers, among other reasons, prevented this once highly esteemed order from returning at the time. Credit must be given to the Council of Trent, however, for considering the following at the time of the final sessions in 1563:

> It is clear how many and necessary and sacred were the services committed to the order of deacons which is distinct from other orders and the next to the priesthood. They are the eyes of the bishops and special ministers of the church whose office of celebration of sacred mysteries and care of the church

---

48. *Concilium Tridentinum,* in Echlin, *Deacon,* 100; Cummings, *Deacons,* 50.

should never be lacking. And in holy sacrifice they offer at the altar the oblations received from the subdeacon. They care for the table of God. They announce the gospel to the people. They assist the consecrating priests. They admonish the people about the solemn rites to be observed in church. They ought to exhort that these raise their hearts and prepare their souls for prayer, and to warn those who intend to be present at the sacrifice to have no adversity among themselves, not hatred, not wrath or ill will, but mutual charity. The ministry of deacons should be diligent in governing the church. Their office is to guard the preaching bishop lest he be approached by vicious enemies or the divine word be reviled by insults and despised. When the bishop so directs it pertains to deacons to baptize and preach, also to reconcile to the church public penitents in case of necessity and in the absence of the bishop and priests, providing they reconcile with solemnity. Deacons should seek out and care for with zeal whatever pertains to the corporate assistance of widows, of students, of orphans, of incarcerated, of sick and all afflicted persons, and provide for the spiritual help of the faithful. They have loving concern for all the faithful in works of mercy, especially for those in whom they observe a greater need for their charity.[49]

Therefore this sacred synod considers all these things so necessary that bishops should take care that those things which have been done to this day should be holily and religiously continued. Let them restore with zeal those which were interrupted by negligence, so that the faithful, with the help of God, may more easily attain eternal beatitude.[50]

These paragraphs boldly summarize what the church of antiquity experienced so well as a distinct and permanent order, and yet these responsibilities were to be carried out by those ordained to the diaconate who would eventually step along to the priesthood.

---

49. Ibid., in Echlin, *Deacon*, 102–4.
50. Echlin, *Deacon*, 108–9; Cummings, *Deacons*, 51.

Rev. Edward J. Enright, OSA, STD

The Twentieth Century

It was nearly four hundred years later before two German priests who were imprisoned at Dachau, Frs. Otto Pies, SJ, and Wilhelm Schamoni, started the effort to restore the diaconate. Their ideas were published by Fr. Pies in the important German journal *Stimmen der Zeit;* by Fr. Schamoni in a book, *Married Men as Ordained Deacons;* and by a civilian government officer, Josef Hornef, in an article entitled "Restorating the Diaconate."[51] Germany, where so much of the larger liturgical revival took place in the early to mid-twentieth century, became the "testing site" for the renewal of the permanent diaconate. The idea caught on in other parts of the globe, furthering the momentum.

It was finally Vatican II that brought all of these ideas and practices to fruition. After much debate and even attempts to quell the discussion on this topic, the council's Dogmatic Constitution on the Church, *Lumen Gentium,* restored the permanent diaconate to the hierarchy of the church:

> At a lower level of the hierarchy are deacons, upon whom hands are imposed "not unto the priesthood, but unto a ministry of service." For strengthened by sacramental grace, in communion with the bishop and his group of priests, they serve the People of God in the ministry of the liturgy, of the word, and of charity. It is the duty of the deacon, to the extent that he has been authorized by competent authority, to administer baptism solemnly, to be custodian and dispenser of the Eucharist, to assist at and bless marriages in the name of the Church, to bring Viaticum to the dying, to read the sacred Scripture to the faithful, to instruct and exhort the people, to preside at the worship and prayer of the faithful, to administer sacramentals, and to officiate at funeral and

---

51. Otto Pies, "Block 26: Erfahrungen aus dem Priesterleben in Dachau," *Stimmen der Zeit* 141 (1947–48): 10–28; Wilhelm Schamoni, *Married Men as Ordained Deacons* (1955; London: Burns Oates and Co., 1962); Josef Hornef, "Restoring the Diaconate," *Concilium: International Journal for Theology* 8 (1968): 64–68. Chapter 2 of *The Deacon Reader* goes into greater detail about these contemporary beginnings.

burial services. Dedicated to duties of charity and of administration, let deacons be mindful of the admonition of Blessed Polycarp: "Be merciful, diligent, walking according to the truth of the Lord, who became the servant of all."[52]

Although other constitutions and decrees further detailed some aspects of what is found in this text, it is, nevertheless, the crown of modern attempts to restore the diaconate to its full and distinct place in the church.

In conclusion, it is clear that the order of deacon is necessary to the church and her mission. It evolved gradually from the implicit diaconal ministries in the apostolic church to its peak in late antiquity, and it saw its demise as one of the threefold hierarchical orders to a mere step to the priesthood. With the roles so familiar from earlier ages, however, it was restored to complete health in the twentieth century. Despite its ups in the ancient church and downs in the medieval church, Roman Catholicism has continually appreciated to one degree or another the importance of the diaconal order, and, due to the power of the Holy Spirit, who was working all along, the church is once again blessed with the ordained service of Jesus Christ himself.

---

52. Vatican Council II, *Lumen Gentium* (Dogmatic Constitution on the Church, 1964), no. 29, in Walter M. Abbott, SJ, *The Documents of Vatican II* (New York: America Press, 1966), 55–56.

CHAPTER 2

The Contemporary Renewal of the Diaconate

Dcn. William T. Ditewig, PhD

Introduction

The purpose of this essay is to outline the contemporary renewal of the diaconate up to and including the work of the Second Vatican Council. Long before the council took up the question of renewing the diaconate as a permanent state of ordained ministry, there had been growing interest in the subject by theologians, bishops, and others involved in pastoral ministry through the first half of the twentieth century. Appreciating the catalysts leading to the council's decision and Pope Paul VI's eventual implementation of that decision is a necessary first step in developing a contemporary theology of the diaconate.[1] Developing a theology for a newly renewed, ancient order of ministry that had not been exercised on a permanent basis (with a few notable exceptions) for well over a millennium would be challenging enough, but

> the challenge increases exponentially…when coupled with the two chronologically coincident realities of a veritable explosion in lay ecclesial ministries and a drastic drop in the number of presbyters. The confluence of these three realities—the

---

1. See, for example, K. Rahner and H. Vorgrimler, *Diakonia in Christo: Über Die Erneuerung des Diakonates* (Freiburg: Verlag Herder, 1962); O. Pies, "Diakonat, Stufe oder Amt," *Theologie und Glaube* 50 (1960): 17–193.

growth of lay ecclesial ministry and the sacramental diaconate with the decline in numbers of presbyters—has…only underscored the critical need for continuing scholarly and pastoral discourse on the sacramental identity of all who minister, and the relationships that ought to exist between them.[2]

Roots of Renewal

At least four streams of influence[3] converged at the council: (1) the German experience prior to the Second World War, (2) the Dachau experience and postwar developments centered in Germany and France, (3) pastoral developments related to the *missio ad gentes* and catechetics, and (4) significant papal teachings.

The German Experience Prior to World War II

Josef Hornef, in a classic text on the restoration of a permanent diaconate, traced the written record suggesting a renewal of the diaconate to an 1840 letter from a Frankfurt physician, J. K. Passavant, to a friend who would become the future Cardinal Archbishop of Breslau, Melchior van Diepenbrock. Passavant observed that the priesthood was too divorced from the daily life of people, and he proposed two possible solutions:

> The Church can either permit priests to marry in the manner in which the Greek Uniates are permitted to do, or she

---

2. William T. Ditewig, "The Once and Future Diaconate: Notes from the Past, Possibilities for the Future," *Church* 20, no. 2 (Summer 2004): 52.

3. The material in this section was originally presented in William T. Ditewig, "The Exercise of Governance by Deacons: A Theological and Canonical Study" (PhD diss., Catholic University of America, 2002), and in abridged form in William T. Ditewig, "The Deacon as a Voice of Lament and Link to Thanksgiving and Justice," *Liturgical Ministry* 13 (Winter 2004): 24–28, and William T. Ditewig, "From the Ashes of Dachau: The Contemporary Diaconate," *Seminary Journal* 10, no. 3 (Winter 2004): 10–14.

can expand the sphere of activity of deacons, so that these men, who would be allowed to be married, could carry out in part the teaching office and other ecclesiastical functions, while the priest (who would therefore have to be senior) would exclusively administer the sacraments, especially confession. If in the considered opinion of the bishops, then, several deacons (archdeacons) could be drawn from the best educated ranks of the so-called laity, then the Church would have excellent ministers at her disposal.[4]

The letter hints of the possibilities of a renewed diaconate as a sacramental sign of an expanded ministry. There is no indication that Passavant's suggestions were considered beyond this exchange of letters. While Hornef identifies similar suggestions outside Germany, it is generally acknowledged that the German experience was to be the most influential voice in the call for a renewed diaconate. One reason for this may be found in the growth of the idea within the context of the German *Caritas* movement.

The history of the *Deutscher Caritas Verband* began in 1897 when the Catholic bishops of Germany directed their establishment to carry out a ministry of charitable outreach to those in need.[5] Following the devastation of World War I, *Caritas* expanded its efforts into every German diocese. Training centers were established, and many of the country's leading churchmen supported its work. Articles appeared in the *Caritas* journal that proposed and developed the notion of a renewed diaconate, especially after Hitler's rise to power in 1933.

For example, in 1934 *Caritas* director G. von Mann wrote of a renewed diaconate of charity, which, rooted in the sacramental life of the parish community, would be charged with "the

---

4. Josef Hornef, "The Genesis and Growth of the Proposal," in National Conference of Catholic Bishops, Bishops' Committee on the Permanent Diaconate, *Foundations for the Renewal of the Diaconate,* trans. David Bourke et al. (Washington, DC: United States Catholic Conference, 1993), 6.

5. See Margret Morche, *Zur Erneuerung des Ständigen Diakonats* (Freiburg: Lambertus-Verlag, 1996), esp. 15–21.

stimulation of charitable activities by the parish community."[6] While he does not specifically propose an ordained diaconate as such, he stresses the importance of diaconal ministers operating as a kind of diaconal team. In 1936, Hans Schütz published "Diakonie der Liebe" in *Caritas*. Schütz reported on a September 1935 meeting of *Caritas* workers in Cologne in which von Mann's notion of a diaconal association developed even further. During the meeting, the participants discussed the possibility of a restored permanent diaconate with a threefold ministry "of liturgy, charity, and catechesis." There would need to be specific formation for this diaconate, and the ordination of such deacons would include a "missioning" by the bishop.

> The restoration of this office was at that time a necessity, if charitable service was to survive in both the deeds and consciousness [of the people], given the current maelstrom of national events (the "Third Reich" and the domination of the National-Socialist Peoples' Welfare Association).[7]

Four points may be noted from this early "German period." First is the realization that leadership in providing charitable service, sacramentally linked to the ministries of word and sacrament, is a constitutive element of the life of the church. Second is the understanding that this service, while in its various functions may be exercised by laypersons, is deserving of sacramental recognition and empowerment by the church. Third is the insight that this development was needed as part of an overall renewal of the church in a contemporary world in need of creative responses to extraordinary needs. Fourth is the emphasis on the fact that the deacon's authority is derived sacramentally through the deacon's ordination, which links him in a special way to the apostolic ministry of the bishop.

---

6. G. von Mann, "Der Caritasdiakonat und seine Erneurung," *Caritas* (July/August 1934), cited in Hornef, "Proposal," 7.

7. Hornef, "Proposal," 7–8.

The Dachau Experience and Postwar Developments

The journey toward a renewed diaconate took on added urgency during and after the Second World War. In 1933, Nazi Germany opened its first concentration camp at Dachau. A large number of clergy and religious were apprehended, and in accordance with Nazi policies, they were not given any preferential treatment in the camp. Incarcerated with the general prison population, they continued to minister secretly. Eventually, the Nazis relocated the clergy to Cell Block 26, which became known as *der Priesterblock*.

During discussions while incarcerated, especially later in the war, several prisoners raised a number of possibilities concerning the renewal of the church following the war. One of these possibilities was the restoration of the diaconate as a permanent state. Fr. Wilhelm Schamoni kept notes of these discussions while interned in the camp, and he was able to save these notes after the collapse of the Third Reich. After the war, Schamoni and another former prisoner, Fr. Otto Pies, wrote about their experiences and in particular about a renewed diaconal order.

Seriously ill after his incarceration in Dachau, it was not until 1947 that Pies was able to document his experiences. In October he published "Cell Block 26: Experiences of Priestly Life in Dachau."[8] He described discussions on the future of ministry after the war, suggesting that the Holy Spirit was calling new ministries into existence, including the diaconate. Wilhelm Schamoni, finally responding to pleas from Pies and others to publish his own reflections on the question, published *Married Men as Ordained Deacons* in 1953.[9]

Grounding his work in a historical study of the ancient diaconate, Schamoni drew parallels to the postwar world, with the

---

8. Otto Pies, "Block 26: Erfahrungen aus dem Priesterleben in Dachau," *Stimmen der Zeit* 141 (1947–48): 10–28.

9. Wilhelm Schamoni, *Familienväter als geweihte Diakone* (Paderborn: Schöningh, 1953). English translation: *Married Men as Ordained Deacons,* trans. Otto Eisner (London: Burns & Oates, 1955).

devastation of the war causing massive relocations of peoples, increased missionary activity, and the need for the traditional duties of deacons in administration, liturgy, and sacrament. He also cited the value of deacons in teaching, liturgy, sacrament, and Catholic Action. What is perhaps most significant about his work is that, while prescinding from a desire to counteract the growing shortage of priests due to the war, his suggestions were not merely to supply more ministers to "fill in" for priests; rather, his goal was to extend the church's ministry even further, including ministry to priests themselves. He moved beyond the traditional functions of deacons to suggest that they could even counter "the fact that the clerical state has become a profession, a fact that has been allowed to become a cause for resentment, of estrangement from the church and of anti-clericalism," and that deacons could serve as a sign of "assimilation to the practice of the Eastern Church that can be traced back to apostolic times."[10]

Responding to this call for a renewed ordained diaconate was a young forestry worker named Hannes Kramer, who had already been associated with *Caritas* and its ministry.[11] He dedicated himself to a diaconal ministry. In 1951 he formed the first *diakonatskreis* (diaconate circle) in Freiburg. In addition to providing direct charitable service, these would-be deacons dedicated themselves to exploring the possibility of a renewed, ordained diaconate. The question of the ordained diaconate began to spread outside Germany, largely through the work of the growing number of diaconate circles (Munich, Cologne, Trèves, Essen, and Lyons) and the contributions made by theologians considering the issue. Although the diaconate was envisioned in slightly different ways from country to country, one idea remained constant: "In each case liturgical involvement is necessary. Even for the deacon, liturgy should be the center of his life."[12]

Eventually the diaconate circles organized into an association known as the International Diaconate Circle and, eventually, the

---

10. Ibid., 7.
11. Morche, *Diakonats*, 36–39.
12. Hornef, "Proposal," 18.

International Diaconate Center. The deacon circles became so well versed in the question of the renewed diaconate that they opened an office in Rome during Vatican II to serve as a resource for council fathers interested in researching the matter. At about the same time, Karl Rahner and Herbert Vorgrimler edited a text containing a variety of articles on the history of the proposal, the general lines of theological inquiry that had already been pursued, and how the diaconate might be developed in a variety of different countries and cultures.[13] This now classic text was made available to the world's bishops in advance of the council.

Pastoral Developments in Mission and Catechetics

A clear sign that the idea of a renewed diaconate was reaching far beyond the borders of Western Europe took place in 1956 at the First International Congress on Pastoral Liturgy held September 18–22 in Assisi, Italy. Dutch Bishop Wilhelm van Bekkum, serving in Indonesia, suggested the restoration of a permanent diaconate for mission countries, pointing out that he was not speaking for himself alone but in the name "of countless colleagues" in the missions.[14] This event took on added significance because it was the first time a *bishop* had spoken publicly about the possibility and desirability of a restored diaconate. As Johannes Hofinger would write several years later:

> This is the first time that a missionary bishop had spoken out so clearly and urgently for the restoration of the diaconate, and at such a large and illustrious gathering. Bishop van Bekkum's words have special importance in view of the fact that he had been requested by the organizing committee not

---

13. Karl Rahner and Herbert Vorgrimler, ed., *Diakonia in Christo: Über die Erneuerung des Diakonates* (Freiburg: Herder, 1962).

14. Wilhelm van Bekkum, "The Liturgical Revival in the Service of the Missions," in *The Assisi Papers,* Proceedings of the First International Congress on Pastoral Liturgy (Assisi-Rome, September 18–22, 1956) (Collegeville, MN: Liturgical Press, 1957), 95–112.

so much to give his own personal wishes as an objective picture of the missions today and their needs.[15]

It was Hofinger himself who would next take up the cause of a restored diaconate. Among the duties deacons might perform in the absence of priests (bring communion and viaticum to the sick and dying, conduct worship services, and administer solemn baptism, marriages, and funerals), Hofinger highlighted the deacon's preaching role and service in administration.[16] The powerful combination of van Bekkum and Hofinger added to the growing chorus of voices rising from around the world for a restored diaconate.

Under Hofinger's leadership, a series of six International Catechetical Study Weeks on Mission and Liturgy was organized from 1959 to 1968. These Study Weeks have been referred to as "key moments in the evolution of catechetics,"[17] and they have proved critical in related fields as well, including the development of the proposal to restore the diaconate. During the 1959 Study Week, held September 12–19 in Nijmegen, Holland, Archbishop Eugene D'Souza of Nagpur, India, spoke on "Permanent Deacons in the Missions."[18] In his talk he asserted, "We respectfully submit that nothing short of the restoration of the permanent diaconate will be of any practical value and permanent advantage to us in the missions."[19] He also referred to the pope's 1957 comment that "the time was not yet ripe" for restoration and suggested that certain parts of the world may be more ready than others for the restoration, and he urged restoration in those places immediately.

Finally, mention must be made of the French movement toward a permanent diaconate. In 1957, Rev. Michel-Dominique

---

15. Johannes Hofinger, "The Case for Permanent Deacons," *Catholic Mind* 57 (1959): 116.

16. Ibid., 119.

17. Michael Warren, ed., *Source Book for Modern Catechetics* (Winona, MN: St. Mary's Press, 1983), 25.

18. Eugene D'Souza, "Permanent Deacons in the Missions," in *Liturgy and the Missions: The Nijmegen Papers,* ed. Johannes Hofinger (New York: P. J. Kenedy & Sons, 1960), 177–90.

19. Ibid., 188.

Epagneul published "On the Role of Deacons in the Church Today,"[20] in which he proposed the restoration of the diaconate as a permanent order primarily as an assistance to overworked priests. He suggested that since priests would now have qualified assistance in ministry, even greater numbers of men may be attracted to the priesthood. What is most significant about this article, however, is that Epagneul forwarded a copy of it to Pope Pius XII. The Holy Father acknowledged receipt of the article in April[21]; he remarked on the diaconate at the Second World Congress of the Apostolate of the Laity in October 1957 (discussed following).

Papal Statements

An important development in the contemporary renewal of the diaconate is the November 30, 1947, Apostolic Constitution *Sacramentum Ordinis* of Pius XII. The purpose of the document was to establish clearly the matter and form of the sacrament of holy orders. Among other concerns, the question persisted whether orders other than the presbyterate were sacramental. The pope resolved the matter by declaring that for ordinations to diaconate, presbyterate, and episcopate, the matter and form are the laying on of hands and the prayer of consecration. By including the diaconate in this document, the pope affirmed the sacramentality of the diaconate.[22]

Pope Pius XII provided another significant impetus to the renewal of the diaconate through an October 5, 1957, address to the Second World Congress of the Apostolate of the Laity in Rome, where he remarked:

> We know that there is thought these days to introduce the order of the diaconate conceived as an ecclesiastical function

---

20. Michel-Dominique Epagneul, "Du role des diacres dans l'Église d'aujourd'hui," *Nouvelle Revue Théologique* 79 (1957): 153–68.

21. See Paul Winninger, *Vers un renouveau du diaconat* (Paris: Desclée de Brouwer, 1958), 13.

22. See Bruno Kleinheyer, "Le diaconat a la lumière du rituel d'ordination selon le Pontifical Romain," trans. Joseph Breitenstein, in *Le Diacre dans L'Église et le Monde d'Aujourd'hui,* ed. Paul Winninger and Yves Congar, *Unam Sanctam,* no. 59 (Paris: Éditions du Cerf, 1966), 109.

independent from the priesthood. The idea, at least today, is not yet ripe. If one day it becomes such, nothing of what we have said would change, except that this diaconate would take its place with the priesthood in the distinctions which we have indicated.[23]

Following the pope's remarks, theological and pastoral activity concerning the diaconate rose dramatically.[24]

These four streams of influence—the early German experience, the Dachau experience, the growth of the proposal in mission and catechetical fields, and the interventions of Pius XII—all converged on January 25, 1959, when Pope John XXIII declared his intention to convene the Second Vatican Council.

Vatican II and the Diaconate

While *Lumen Gentium* paragraph 29 is the principal conciliar text on the diaconate, the renewal of the order was also strongly encouraged for those Eastern churches in which "it has fallen into disuse."[25] The diaconate is referred to as well in *Ad Gentes, Sacrosanctum Concilium,* and *Dei Verbum.*[26]

In this section three conciliar sources are surveyed: (1) the *Antepraeparatoria series,* which contains the tabulation of topics submitted by the world's bishops for discussion during the council,[27]

---

23. Pius XII, "Quelques aspects fondamentaux de l'apostolat des laïcs: Hiérarchie et Apostolat," *AAS* 49 (1957): 925.

24. See Piercarlo Beltrando, *Diaconi per la Chiesa* (Milan: Instituto Propaganda, 1977), for a detailed discussion of the various theological contributions made.

25. Vatican Council II, *Orientalium Ecclesiarum* (Decree on Eastern Catholic Churches, 1964), no. 17, in Walter M. Abbott, SJ, *The Documents of Vatican II* (New York: America Press, 1966).

26. Vatican Council II, *Ad Gentes* (Decree on the Church's Missionary Activity, 1965), no. 16; *Sacrosanctum Concilium* (Constitution on the Sacred Liturgy, 1963), no. 35; and *Dei Verbum* (Dogmatic Constitution on Divine Revelation, 1965), no. 25, respectively; in Abbott, *Documents of Vatican II.*

27. *Acta et documenta Concilio oecuminco Vaticano II apparando; Series prima (antepraeparatoria)* ([Civitas Vaticana]: Typis Polyglottis Vaticanis, 1960–61).

(2) the *Praeparatoria series,* which traces the formulation of the initial drafts of the council documents[28] and (3) the *Acta* of the council itself, which contain the actual debate surrounding the proposal to restore the diaconate.[29]

The Antepreparatory Stage

One hundred and one specific proposals were made concerning the restoration of the diaconate during the initial consultations for the council; of these, only eleven were against the restoration. The proposals fall into four categories: Category I includes thirty-seven proposals on the restoration in general[30]; Category II contains another thirty-seven proposals on the requirement for celibacy[31]; Category III lists sixteen proposals on the requirements and functions of deacons[32]; and Category IV contains the eleven proposals against restoration.[33] Table 1 (on the next page) summarizes these categories, showing the number of proposals within each category and the number of bishops supporting each category.[34]

---

28. *Acta et documenta Concilio oecuminco Vaticano II apparando; Series secunda (praeparatoria)* ([Civitas Vaticana]: Typis Polyglottis Vaticanis, 1969).

29. *Acta Synodalia Sacrasancti Concilii Vaticani II* ([Civitas Vaticana]: Typis Polyglottis Vaticanis, 1970–).

30. *Acta et documenta, Series prima,* II/II, 115–21.

31. Ibid., 122–28.

32. Ibid., 128–31.

33. Ibid., 131–32.

34. Only eight U.S. bishops listed the diaconate as a topic for discussion, and none recommended against it. Foery of Syracuse, O'Connor of Madison, and Primeau of Manchester supported a proposal to discuss the diaconate in general. The bishops of Stanford, Dubuque, Dallas-Ft. Worth, Rockford, and Sacramento supported a different proposal that specified that married men should be admitted to the diaconate (ibid., 125).

Table 1. *Antepreparatory Proposals on the Diaconate*[35]

Category Number	Title	Number of Proposals	Number of Supporting Sees
I	*On Restoring the Order of the Diaconate*	37	283
II	*On the Diaconate without the Obligation of Celibacy*	37	138
III	*On the Prerequisites and Functions of Deacons*	16	71
IV	*On the Inadvisability of Restoring of the Diaconate*	11	21

Category I: On the Restoration of the Order of Deacon

Of the thirty-seven proposals[36] in this list, by far the most strongly supported was the second; namely, that deacons should be restored to the offices and in the form of previous ages *(ad officia et in forma priorum saeculorum).* While the majority of proposals related to the diaconate were suggested by only one or two bishops, this one lists more than 135 individual bishops as well as all 51 bishops from the Congo and Rwanda (voting as a bloc), for a total of 186. This constitutes nearly two-thirds (65 percent) of all the proposals in this category alone, and more than one-third (36 percent) of all the proposals received across all four categories.

Of particular interest is the great geographical distribution of these proposals. A common perception maintains that the impetus behind the diaconate's restoration came from the bishops of the so-called third world or mission countries. Many of the proposals came from the bishops of Latin America and Africa (well over one hundred of the total number were from these two areas). A significant number of proposals, however, was received

---

35. *Acta et documenta, Series prima, Appendix, II / II* ([Civitas Vaticanis]: Typis Polyglottis Vaticanis, 1961).

36. *Acta et documenta, Series prima,* II / II, 115–21.

from bishops from Europe (especially Spain, Germany, France, the Netherlands, and countries of Eastern Europe) and Asia (especially Micronesia, Indonesia, India, and Pakistan). In light of the historical development of the proposal to restore the permanent diaconate that originated in Germany and France and spread outside Europe in the 1950s, these numbers indicate that by the time of the council, the proposal had significant support from bishops around the world.

Category III: On the Requirements and Functions of Deacons

The sixteen proposals[37] in this category, while they reflect the thoughts of only seventy-one of the bishops, offer some insight into the areas of ministry deacons might be assigned. Table 2 outlines the proposals contained in Category III; while many of the functions listed reflect the practices of the early diaconate, two of the bishops even recommend that deacons might anoint the sick, a function not previously assigned to deacons.

Table 2. Antepreparatory Proposals, Functions in Category III

Proposal Number	Text	Number of Supporting Sees
1	Deacons should be forty years old and their doctrine and morals investigated	2
2	Deacons should be forty years old and exemplary catechists.	1
3	The following offices are the deacons': preaching; administration of baptism, even solemnly; distribution of holy communion; exposition of the blessed sacrament and eucharistic blessing; and taking of viaticum to the sick.	3

37. Ibid., 128–31.

Proposal Number	Text	Number of Supporting Sees
4	Deacons may be installed, especially in mission areas and where there is a shortage of priests, for the following offices: solemn administration of baptism; valid assistance of matrimony; to administer the Holy Eucharist, even as viaticum; to preach the word of God in the church; and to administer the goods of the church.	2
5	Deacons should be of mature age; of evident Christian spirit; of sufficient knowledge of dogmatics, morals, scriptures, and liturgy. Their offices may be: to be devoted to catechesis, to assist the parish priest in the Eucharist, and to distribute holy communion to the faithful, upon the prudent judgment of the parish priest.	25
6	They are bound by the law of residency, under the supervision of the parish priest, sustained by the faithful or by the curia.	1
7	Deacons may assist at marriages.	5
8	The faculty to preside at solemn benediction with the blessed sacrament may be granted to deacons.	3
9	The administration of the temporal goods of the church may be transferred by the parish priest to the deacon so that the parish priests may focus on spiritual care.	1
10	Deacons attend to the administration of goods.	1

Proposal Number	Text	Number of Supporting Sees
11	In accordance with canon 938, the deacon may be the extraordinary minister of extreme unction when there are not enough priests or in urgent necessity.	1
12	Deacons may confer extreme unction in the absence of priests.	1
13	Deacons may bring solace to the faithful in extreme situations.	21
14	Deacons may conduct burials.	2
15	The order of the diaconate may be conferred on catechists and assisting laity.	1
16	Deacons may be named as professors of religion.	1

The Preparatory Stage

A total of 8,972 proposals were received in Rome from the world's bishops, including the 101 described previously. "From this mass of very diversified interests the themes were chosen which seemed to be of the greatest importance, and put before various commissions for a preliminary investigation."[38] The overall topic of the possible renewal of the diaconate was assigned to the commission *De disciplina Sacramentorum* under the leadership of Cardinal Masella. Two other commissions also drafted materials on the diaconate: the Commission for the Oriental Churches and the Commission for the Missions.

On Wednesday, January 17, 1962, Cardinal Masella presented the draft *De Sacramento Ordinis*[39] to the third meeting of the Central

---

38. Gerard Philips, "History of the Constitution," in *Commentary on the Documents of Vatican II*, vol. 1, ed. Herbert Vorgrimler (New York: Herder & Herder, 1967), 106.
39. *Acta et documenta, Series secunda*, II/II, 138–50.

Preparatory Commission, at which time the first general debate *De diaconatu permanente seu stabili instaurando* took place.[40] Masella began the discussion by reviewing the four questions considered by the commission: (1) Should the minor orders and the diaconate be restored? (2) In what way should they be restored? (3) At what ages should the major orders be conferred? and (4) What should the intervals be between the various orders?

The question that caused the greatest debate, according to Masella, was whether the diaconate should be restored in the Latin church. He referred to the 1957 allocution by Pius XII, which emphasized the ordained character of the diaconate (as opposed to a so-called lay diaconate), and he encouraged continued study on the subject of restoration. Masella pointed out that the question had now been examined from every aspect: theological, juridical, pastoral, and social. Last, Masella reported that his commission had prepared the schema from the analysis of the many desires of bishops from around the world during the antepreparatory stage.

Masella offered the following points for discussion: (1) that the permanent diaconate, according to ancient practice, should be restored immediately in the Latin church, especially in those dioceses and regions with a shortage of priests; (2) that this restoration may not take place without the approval of the Holy See; (3) that permanent deacons are ordained into the clerical state; and (4) that permanent deacons should also be restored in various religious communities, with the approval of the superiors and the Holy See.

Masella concluded his remarks by addressing the issue of admitting married men. He pointed out that there was considerable support for the proposal, driven in large part by the great shortage of priests in mission territories. Nonetheless, he also pointed out that, while the majority of the commission's members approved the ordination of married men to the diaconate in certain areas with the approval of the Holy See, the commission also unanimously emphasized that this in no way suggested that the law of celibacy for priests be altered.

---

40. Ibid., 150–53.

In the discussion that followed, ten bishops presented their views on the proposal.[41] Six cited serious problems with ordaining married men to the diaconate, most frequently because of the effects they saw this having on the law of priestly celibacy as well as the possible impact this could have on the number of vocations to the priesthood. As Archbishop Lefebvre put it, "There is the certain danger of a lessening of vocations to the priesthood in favor of a married diaconate."[42]

Cardinals Frings and Jullien were concerned over the impact a restored diaconate might have on the lay apostolate, although Frings supported the notion of a restored celibate diaconate as long as the deacon had no desire to ascend to the priesthood.[43] There was an appreciation that many of the functions formerly assigned to deacons were already being performed by laypersons, and that this renewed lay apostolate should not be thwarted by the restoration of another hierarchical order.

Fifty-six fathers on the commission voted on the draft *De Sacramento Ordinis.* Thirty-one voted *non placet* (literally, "it does not please"), most objecting to the proposal to restore the diaconate in general or objecting to the possibility of ordaining married men (ironically, Cardinal Montini was among this number; as Pope Paul VI he would ultimately implement the renewal). Eight more fathers voted *placet* ("it pleases") on the overall schema while specifically rejecting the diaconate proposal. One father abstained, leaving only sixteen who voted *placet* without reservation. At the end of this meeting, the commission began the task of redrafting the document to reflect the observations of the Central Commission.

Two days after Cardinal Masella's presentation to the Central Commission, on January 19, 1962, Cardinal Amleto Cicognani presented the draft "De Ecclesiae Sacramentis," prepared by the Commission for the Oriental Churches. The draft affirmed the ancient roots of the diaconate and, citing the shortage of priests,

---

41. Ibid., 154–68.
42. Ibid., 167.
43. Ibid., 154, 159–61.

called for the revitalization of the office.[44] Cicognani reminded the Central Commission that while the diaconate continued to exist in some Eastern churches, it had ceased in others. Since there were many favorable reasons to restore the order, and since the *Code of Canons of the Eastern Churches* already provided for a permanent diaconate, the council should mention the diaconate's value in a general way for the East.[45]

On March 28, 1962, Cardinal Gregorio Agagianian presented the Commission for the Missions' draft to the Central Commission. Among the functions that might be assigned to deacons were that they could preach the gospel, have a liturgical ministry, and be responsible for charitable works.[46] The presbyteral and diaconal vocations are distinct, and many who could not or would not become priests, for whatever reason, could become deacons.[47] Deacons could be married, and this marriage would not detract from priestly celibacy.[48] The schema proposed further that the church not grant diaconal functions to those who do not seek ordination, since the diaconate has its own proper functions that should not be performed by the laity. In a point later stressed by Cardinal Suenens during the conciliar debate, ordination gives a special grace with a sacramental character.[49] Finally, the commission proposed that episcopal conferences be given the authority to allow local bishops to confer the permanent diaconate upon those who may even be married.[50]

Lumen Gentium (1963)

Lumen Gentium[51] was presented at the Thirty-Seventh General Assembly on Monday, September 30, 1963. The council focused

---

44. Ibid., II/VI, 262.
45. Ibid., 265.
46. Ibid., II/III, 211.
47. Ibid., 212.
48. Ibid.
49. Ibid.
50. Ibid., 213.
51. The schema *De Ecclesia* (1962), which was to become *Lumen Gentium*, consisted of eleven chapters and an appendix on Mary. Chapter III was a mere two

largely on this document for the next month. The organization of the schema was completely revised. The eleven dogmatic essays were replaced by four chapters, with the hierarchy (now including the diaconate) included in chapter II: *De Constitutione Hierarchica Ecclesiae et in specie: De Episcopatu.* Even more significant were the changes in style and content. The chapter on the hierarchy, for example, opens with a pastoral statement on the people of God and the nature of ministry as something good given to nurture the entire body. The fathers accepted this draft for discussion on October 1, 1963, by a vote of 2,231 to 43.[52]

This draft describes deacons as "in a lower level of the ministerial hierarchy." Deacons assist the bishop and priests—by serving in celebrations of sacrifice, as extraordinary ministers of baptism and holy communion, and by performing various public works of charity, proclamation, and administration as assigned by competent authority. The draft continues by noting that today the diaconate is primarily a step toward the priesthood, but that in the future, in places where the church discerns the pastoral necessity, it will be possible to establish the diaconate as a proper and permanent level of the hierarchy. It is up to the church to decide whether such deacons ought to be bound by the law of celibacy.[53]

Reports and Speeches

Cardinal Browne, vice-president of the commission *De Doctrina Fidei et Morum,* provided an overview of the revised draft to the assembly, focusing on three significant issues. First, he stated that a major objective of the text was to complete the work of

---

paragraphs of some thirty-one lines, with no mention of the diaconate (*Acta Synodalia,* I/IV, 23–24). There were, however, far greater problems with the document. Various speakers cited a lack of cohesion between the chapters, which reflected a much deeper issue; namely, the document presented no coherent vision of the church. Many fathers were troubled by the highly juridical and legalistic tone of the schema, well exemplified by the title of the first chapter, *De Ecclesia Militantis Natura.* Given these foundational concerns, the schema was sent back to committee for rewriting prior to the 1963 session.

52. See Vorgrimler, *Commentary,* 111.

53. *Acta Synodalia,* II/I, 235.

Vatican I, which had declared and affirmed the pope as the successor of Peter, by declaring Catholic doctrine on the bishops as successors to the other apostles. Second, this objective was met through nine paragraphs, one of which was "On the divinely instituted assistants of the bishops, i.e., on presbyters and deacons."[54] This is significant since the text itself did not specify the divinely instituted nature of the diaconate in those terms. Also, all of these nine paragraphs were considered part of the first objective, which was to talk about the bishops; as noted previously, the presbyterate and diaconate are defined in terms of their relationship to the episcopate, and Browne emphasized this. Third, he asserted that the text, after dealing specifically with hierarchical ministry, moved into other forms of ministry, with specific paragraphs on the threefold *munus* of the church: *munus docendi, munus sanctificandi,* and *munus regendi.*[55]

Finally, Cardinal Frings and Bishop Gargitter recommended that the chapters be reordered, with the second chapter becoming *De Populo Dei* and the third chapter becoming *De Hierarchica.*[56] With the acceptance of these recommendations, the structure of *Lumen Gentium* was close to its final form.

The *Acta* of the Council: The Conciliar Debate

The principal conciliar debate on the subject of restoring the permanent diaconate in the Latin church occurred during the 41st to the 49th general assemblies (October 4–16, 1963). In reviewing the interventions, the climax of the debate occurred on October 8, with the intervention of Cardinal Suenens.

Cardinal Spellman of New York opened the debate on the diaconate on October 4.[57] He objected to the proposal on three grounds.

---

54. Ibid., 340.

55. Meaning "teaching office" (prophet), "sanctifying office" (priest), and "ruling office" (king), respectively. Cf. Ray R. Noll, "The Sacramental Ministry of the Deacon in Parish Life," chapter 11 of this volume.

56. *Acta Synodalia* II/I, 345 and 360.

57. Ibid., II/II, 82–87.

First, while acknowledging that the diaconate had once flourished in the West, he urged further study into the reasons it became obsolete, since these reasons might indicate the difficulties inherent in its restoration. Second, he cited the difficulties with regard to training deacons, since seminaries (for candidates for the priesthood) were already hard enough to maintain, and distinct houses of formation would need to be established for deacons, since he believed it would be improper to train married men in the same institution as celibate men. Third, he stated that a reason the diaconate had faded in the West was that deacons were unable to provide the necessary sacred ministries for the care of the faithful. Spellman concluded by asking whether it would not be better to encourage vocations to the priesthood. He felt that the diaconate would result in fewer vocations to the priesthood, leading him to pose the question: Is it better to have fewer priests along with permanent deacons, or to have no deacons but more priests?[58]

Cardinal Spellman's objections were echoed by Cardinal Bacci and Bishop de Mello, both of whom thought the diaconate, especially if opened to married men, was not necessary and was perhaps even dangerous to priestly celibacy and priestly vocations. Cardinal Bacci went so far as to indicate that any young man would prefer to enter a ministry that allows them a much easier way to serve the church (without celibacy), and that therefore vocations to the priesthood would fall drastically. He strongly urged the council to delete the notion of a married diaconate. Bishop de Mello, in a written animadversion, observed that in his opinion, the restoration of the diaconate in any manner, in any place, was extremely dangerous. He claimed that in today's world, it was not possible to find "men of good repute, filled with the Holy Spirit

---

58. In the recently published journal of Yves Congar, the French theologian's entry for 4 October 1963 reads that Spellman did not think the topic of the diaconate belonged in a dogmatic Constitution. "Il est contre un diaconat permanent. Il ne comprend rien. Pour lui, ce serait archéologisme condamné par Pie XII" ("He is against a permanent diaconate. He does not understand anything. For him, this would be the archeologism condemned by Pius XII."), Yves Congar, *Mon Journal du Concile,* 2 vols. (Paris: Les Éditions du Cerf, 2002), 1:433.

and wisdom" as Peter called for in Acts 6:1–6. Bishop de Mello asserted, "There are no people like this today, not even among Catholics" *("Non sunt, nec inter catholicos").*[59]

The first speaker in favor of restoration was Cardinal Doepfner.[60] He strongly urged acceptance of the draft, and he addressed the concerns already raised. He supported the inclusion of the diaconate in a dogmatic document because the issue of the hierarchical orders of the church is a dogmatic issue, a part of the divine law and therefore an essential part of the nature of the church. He pointed out that the diaconate, ever since Trent, had been seen as part of the sacramental priesthood. Looking to the present situation in many parts of the world, Doepfner pointed to the fact that there are many persons, many of them married, who are serving the church in diaconal roles. He asked, "Why should these people be denied the grace of the sacrament?"[61] The law of celibacy is sacred, but it should not become an obstacle for the evolution of beneficial ways to serve that may be necessary in our times.

Cardinal Landazuri Ricketts, speaking for himself and ninety-five other Latin American fathers, spoke to the benefits of a renewed diaconate.[62] While many functions (which he does not articulate) of the diaconate were already performed by laypersons, there were still others that the deacon could carry out as an ordained member of the hierarchy. The restoration of the diaconate was not to lessen the role of the laity but to increase it; and the lay apostolate, while most important, is not an end in itself.

It was at this point that Cardinal Suenens presented what is arguably the strongest and most coherent argument for the diaconate evident in the documents.[63] Before considering his intervention, however, one should first examine his original recommendation in support of a renewed permanent diaconate. During the antepreparatory phase, Suenens indicated his support

---

59. *Acta Synodalia,* II/II, 120.
60. Ibid., 227–30.
61. Ibid., 229.
62. Ibid., 314–17.
63. Ibid., 317–19.

in his letter of November 10, 1959. First alluding to the 1957 address by Pius XII, in which the pope had observed that the question of restoring the diaconate was "not yet ripe" but was worthy of continued attention, Suenens wrote that the council would provide a most appropriate opportunity to highlight this question. He wrote that a diaconate distinct and separate from the priesthood, a state in which married men might also be admitted, would be part of a movement of overall renewal in the church. The diaconate was one of several ministries consistently and traditionally recognized in the life of the church. Suenens wrote that the church has a command from the Lord to proclaim the gospel to all peoples and to baptize all nations. Such a task is impossible without the coming together of all the faithful, especially those whose lives are devoted to the mission of evangelization. The deacon is presented as a minister of this evangelization who can be assigned to serve in different ways depending upon the pastoral needs of the area in which he serves, including the proclamation of the gospel, catechesis, and other areas for the work of redemption. Cardinal Suenens would write later, "Undoubtedly, this decision [to renew the permanent diaconate] was made for pastoral reasons, but these were not the only factors operative. The restoration of a Permanent Diaconate finds its fundamental clarification and justification in the sacramental character of the diaconate itself."[64] During the conciliar debate, it will be Suenens himself who attempts to articulate this "sacramental character of the diaconate."

In his intervention, Cardinal Suenens began by outlining the theological principles upon which the diaconate is based. Citing the authority of scripture, the apostolic fathers, constant tradition, and the liturgical books of East and West, he spoke of the many charisms evident throughout the church, distinct from the priesthood, that were set up to provide direct assistance to the bishop in the care of the poor and the nurturing of the community. To say

---

64. Leo Cardinal Suenens, "The Coresponsibility of Deacons," in National Conference of Catholic Bishops, Bishops' Committee on the Permanent Diaconate, *Diaconal Reader: Selected Articles from the "Diaconal Quarterly"* (Washington, DC: NCCB, 1985), 47.

that these tasks can be given to laypersons does not mean that the diaconate is not needed. These tasks should only be given to persons (whether ordained or not) who have the necessary graces. The church has the right to the benefit of all the graces given to it by God, including the graces of the diaconate.

Suenens then turned to the situation in the contemporary world. He urged the fathers *not* to make a universal decision for or against the diaconate. Rather, they should decide whether there was any area or situation that might benefit from it, and then phrase its decision in such a way as to enable it to take effect in those regions in which the bishops decided it was appropriate. In other words, the council should not close off universally any means by which the grace of God may flow into the church. Therefore (quoting from the draft), "where episcopal conferences judge the restoration of a permanent diaconate opportune, they should be free to introduce it."[65]

In reviewing the debate from this point on, the arguments in favor of the restoration take on a much more positive note, with fewer objections being raised. Suenens's intervention signaled a milestone in the debate, for his articulation of a theology of the diaconate helped focus for the fathers the essential elements of the issue, and not just on the functional dimension of the diaconate. Furthermore, he added an important tactical element previously lacking in the argumentation: namely, that the council was not being asked to dictate a universal course of action for the church. Rather, their duty was to look for ways in which bishops (and conferences of bishops) could be enabled to use whatever means necessary and available to provide pastoral care for their people. One such means is the diaconate. Finally, this was a way of supporting the developing discussions the bishops were having concerning the nature and role of the episcopate itself. With the bishop seen as responsible for the ordering of ministry in his own diocese, in collaboration and discussion with fellow bishops in the region, the

---

65. *Acta Synodalia,* II/II, 319.

concepts of episcopal collegiality, subsidiarity, and collaboration were highlighted.

Following Cardinal Suenens's address the discussion continued, but all interventions show the influence of his thought. Cardinal Richaud spoke strongly in favor of the restoration (although he had originally opposed the proposal during the preparatory phase), especially with the option given to the conferences of bishops to decide whether or not to request its implementation.[66] Bishop Šeper favored the restoration because of the nature of the diaconate itself and for ecumenical (between the Eastern and Western churches) and pastoral reasons.[67] He disagreed with those who feared that ordaining married men to the diaconate would weaken the celibacy of priests. On the contrary, he stated that the service of married deacons would strengthen the church. He concluded by saying (like Suenens) that the council was not to say "Amen" to the status quo but to provide for the future needs of the church.[68]

Bishop Franič rejected the proposal but for many of the same reasons cited previously: (1) It would be dangerous for vocations to the priesthood; (2) it would be dangerous for the law of celibacy; (3) it would be dangerous to have a married diaconate in many parts of the world; (4) a permanent, married diaconate was unnecessary; (5) it would be easier to install laymen into various ministries than to restore the diaconate; and (6) it would be imprudent for economic reasons.

From this point on, the speakers emphasized points previously made, either for or against restoration. Vorgrimler reports that a total of forty-five bishops, speaking on behalf of 795 fathers, spoke in favor of restoration. Twenty-five speakers, representing only eighty-two fathers, rejected the idea. Because the debate on the diaconate was part of the much larger debate on the episcopacy, however, and particularly on the notion of episcopal collegiality, a

---

66. Ibid., 346–48.
67. Ibid., 358–60.
68. Ibid.

document consisting of five questions was drafted that sought "to learn the mind of the assembly as exactly as possible."[69] The first four questions concerned the sacramental nature of the episcopate and the relationship between papal primacy and episcopal collegiality. The fifth question pertained to the diaconate: "Whether it pleases the Fathers to have the schema consider the opportuneness of restoring the diaconate as a distinct and permanent level of the sacred ministry, as necessary for the Church in various regions."[70]

Since the debate on the diaconate was so heated concerning the possibility of a married diaconate, the subject of the restoration of the permanent diaconate in theory (that is, with no mention of celibacy or any other particular questions of ecclesiastical discipline) was added to the list of questions on the episcopate. The vote, taken on October 30, 1963, shows that of 2,120 votes cast, 1,588 were in favor of restoration and 525 were against it (seven were invalid).[71]

Armed with the opinions expressed during the debate and the vote of October 30, the text was revised one final time.

The Final Draft: Lumen Gentium (1964)

The third draft of *Lumen Gentium* was distributed at the 80th General Assembly on September 15, 1964. The text on the diaconate was now paragraph 29 of chapter III.[72] The text was in two parts and greatly expanded over the previous draft. The first part deals with the office of deacon in general and some of the functions of the deacon in particular. The second part deals with the rationale and procedures for the diaconate's restoration as a permanent order, one which is open to married men.

Part One: The diaconate is still described as in a "lower order of the hierarchy," an order in which he is installed through the imposition of hands. The diaconate is clearly a part of the sacrament of

---

69. Vorgrimler, *Commentary,* 115.
70. *Acta Synodalia,* II/III, 573–75.
71. Ibid.
72. Ibid., III/I, 227–29.

orders according to the text, since deacons are "strengthened by sacramental grace." The ancient threefold ministry of the deacon is stressed more strongly than in the second draft. Instead of the rather limited list of functions of the former draft, this one describes the deacon's ministry as "a service of liturgy, word and charity to the People of God," which he exercises in communion with the bishop and his presbyterate: one ministry, with the responsibilities shared among the three orders. The bishop has ultimate authority and responsibility, but his priests and deacons, who share in his ministry, assist him.

The ten functions listed are clearly illustrative and not meant to be exhaustive. They expand on the theme of *diaconia* in liturgy, the word, and charity. Deacons administer baptism solemnly (as *ordinary* ministers, a change from the second draft); they care for and distribute the Eucharist; they assist at and bless marriages in the name of the church (not listed in the second draft); and they bring viaticum to the dying (not listed in the second draft). They proclaim sacred scripture to the faithful, instruct and exhort the people, preside at the worship and prayer of the faithful, minister sacramentals, and preside at funerals and burials. These and additional functions are summarized by saying that deacons are dedicated to works of charity and administration.

Part Two: Having outlined the *munera* of the diaconate, the draft declared them to be of the highest importance to the life of the church *("ad vitam Ecclesiae summopere necessaria")*. The current discipline of the Latin church made it difficult for them to be provided in many areas, however. Therefore, in the future, the diaconate can be restored as a permanent level of the hierarchy. Regional conferences of bishops, with the approval of the pope, can decide whether these deacons should be appointed *pro cura animarum* and where. Finally, it would be reserved to the pope to decide whether the diaconate could be conferred on married men of mature age or on qualified young celibate or married men. A *nota explicativa* informed the fathers that this section would be handled by separate votes to allow a precise counting on the critical question of celibacy and the diaconate. The commission already knew, from the results of the voting on October 30, that the council wanted to restore the diaconate. It was still the sticky question of celibacy that was troublesome.

The Voting on Celibacy[73]: *Lumen Gentium* was divided into thirty-nine sections for voting, with a final vote on the entire document taken on October 30, 1964. Five of these sections related directly to the diaconate. Specifically, paragraph 29 (on the diaconate) was divided into five sections (35–39), each with its own vote. On October 28, votes were taken on sections 35 and 36. These were fairly certain, since they pertained to the office of deacon in particular and the desirability to restore it as a permanent rank. The section on the *munus diaconi* (section 35) passed with a vote of 2,055 to 94; the voting on restoration (section 36) was 1,903 pro and 242 contra.

On October 29, the tougher questions were faced. Section 37 included the text that the conferences of bishops needed the consent of the pope to restore the diaconate in their regions. This was passed by 1,523 to 702. The diaconate could be conferred on mature married men (1,598 pro; 629 contra), but the clause allowing diaconate to be conferred on younger men without the law of celibacy was rejected by a vote of 1,364 to 839. (It is interesting to note, however, that more than 800 bishops had no objection to ordaining younger men deacons without the obligation of celibacy.[74])

The Final Text: With the voting complete, the only change to the text that was necessary was the final sentence, which now read, "With the consent of the Roman pontiff it will be possible to confer this diaconate on married men of more mature age, and also on suitable young men for whom, however, the law of celibacy must remain in force."[75]

---

73. Ibid., III/VIII, 53.
74. See Vorgrimler, *Commentary*, 227.
75. *Acta Synodalia*, III/VIII, 811.

Conclusion

Many reasons led to the decision of the Second Vatican Council to renew the diaconate. For many of the bishops, the sacramental diaconate became a way to recognize the lessons learned so tragically at Dachau: that the church herself was Christ's servant in and for the world, and that there was a need for a sacramental expression of that diaconal nature. At the very end of the council, Pope Paul VI reflected on the work of the council and what it meant to the church:

> We stress that the teaching of the Council is channeled in one direction, the service of humankind, of every condition, in every weakness and need. The Church has declared herself a servant of humanity at the very time when her teaching role and her pastoral government have, by reason of this Church solemnity, assumed greater splendor and vigor. However, the idea of service has been central.[76]

This vision of the church-as-servant finds a concrete sacramental expression within the renewed diaconate. Over the past forty years, much has been done and learned about the diaconate throughout the world. Nonetheless, we have only begun to scratch the surface. Keeping the radical roots of diaconate renewal in mind will be a constant inspiration and challenge as this renewed ordained ministry continues its response to the needs of the contemporary church.

---

76. Paul VI, *Hodie Concilium* (December 7, 1965), *AAS* 58 (1966): 57–64.

CHAPTER 3

The Deacon and
Gaudium et Spes

Rev. Paul McPartlan, DPhil

If we would really understand the diaconate, we must set it back within the totality of the teaching of the Second Vatican Council that restored this ministry to the Catholic Church.[1] Strictly speaking, as the International Theological Commission (ITC) notes, what the council reestablished was *"the principle of the permanent exercise of the*

---

1. In recent years, the Catholic Church has been trying to clarify the diaconate, which Vatican II restored as "a proper and permanent rank of the hierarchy" (Vatican Council II, *Lumen Gentium* [Dogmatic Constitution on the Church, 1964], no. 29). Quotations from Vatican II documents are from Walter M. Abbott, SJ, *The Documents of Vatican II* (New York: America Press, 1966). The *Ratio Fundamentalis* and *Directorium* that were issued by two curial congregations in the Vatican in 1998 were expressly said to be "a response to a widely felt need to clarify and regulate the diversity of approaches adopted in experiments conducted up to now." There is a need, it was said, "for a certain unity of direction and clarification of concepts, as well as for practical encouragement and more clearly defined pastoral objectives," in line with "the desire and intention of the Second Vatican Council" (*Joint Declaration,* prefixing Congregation for Catholic Education, *Ratio fundamentalis institutionis diaconorum permanentium [Basic Norms for the Formation of Permanent Deacons],* and Congregation for the Clergy, *Directorium pro ministerio et vita diaconorum permanentium [Directory for the Ministry and Life of Permanent Deacons]* [jointly published February 22, 1998]). Then, in 2002, the International Theological Commission that is attached to the Congregation for the Doctrine of the Faith also produced a major study of the diaconate (International Theological Commission [ITC], *Le diaconat: Évolution et perspectives* [2002]. I quote from the unofficial English translation of the French original [London: Catholic Truth Society, 2003; Chicago: Hillenbrand Books, 2004], which unfortunately gives to the whole text what is simply the title of the first chapter, *From the Diakonia of Christ to the Diakonia of the Apostles*).

diaconate, and not one particular form which the diaconate had taken in the past." Indeed, Vatican II "seemed open to the kind of form it might take in the future, in function of pastoral needs and ecclesial practice, but always in fidelity to tradition."[2] We must try, therefore, to relate the diaconate, which historically has been a very flexible and multifaceted ministry, to some of the major principles of Vatican II's teaching. We must try to get into the mind of the council, or, perhaps better, into the *heart* of the council, because one of the overriding features of Vatican II was that it tempered the more cerebral, intellectual, and scholastic approach to the Catholic faith that was characteristic of the second millennium by returning to the wisdom of the fathers from the first millennium and especially from the early centuries. In a sense, Saint Augustine speaks for them all with his famous words: "You have made us for yourself, [Lord,] and our heart is restless until it rests in you."[3] There we see a focus on the heart rather than on the head, and the pope who called the council was known and loved throughout the world for his big heart. Blessed Pope John XXIII can certainly take us to the heart of the council.

Pope John announced the calling of a council on January 25, 1959, at the end of the Week of Prayer for Christian Unity. Just five days later he told the clergy of Rome that one of his main aims was church unity, but viewed in a new way. He said, "We do not intend to set up a tribunal to judge the past. We do not want to prove who was right and who was wrong. Responsibility was divided. All we want to say is: 'Let us come together. Let us make an end of our divisions.'" In the same week, he foreshadowed the great examination of conscience that Pope John Paul II led the church to perform at the millennium, admitting previous faults and apologizing for

---

2. *From the Diakonia of Christ,* 62 (italics in original). We may note that although the ITC text has a detailed chapter on the restoration of the diaconate at Vatican II, which notes six conciliar documents that touch upon the diaconate (59), very surprisingly it makes no reference at any point to *Gaudium et Spes* (Pastoral Constitution on the Church in the Modern World, 1965). Admittedly, *Gaudium et Spes* makes no specific reference to the diaconate, but it is my suggestion here that it provides the basic frame of reference for understanding diaconal ministry.

3. Augustine, *Confessions,* 1,1,1 (*Patrologia Latina* 32, 661).

them. Pope John said this, with regard to previous Catholic attitudes to our Christian brothers and sisters in other churches:

> The faults from which we Catholics are not, alas, free, lie in our not having prayed enough to God to smooth the ways that converge on Christ's Church; in not having felt charity to the full; in not having always practised it toward our separated brethren, preferring the rigour of learned, logical, incontrovertible arguments to forbearing and patient love, which has its own compelling power of persuasion; in having preferred the philosophical rigidity of the lecture room to the friendly serenity of the *Controversies* of St. Francis de Sales.[4]

It is very clear that Pope John thought that Catholics had argued with their fellow Christians rather too much and loved them rather too little. He wanted to reinstate the primacy of love in the Christian life: Win people over with love! Let the Catholic Church be known for having the fullness of love! Forbearing and patient love, he said, has "its own compelling power of persuasion." Love for our fellow Christians was to be reinstated in ecumenism, and love for the world as a whole was to be reflected time and again in the council's major documents.

Dei Verbum opened by saying that the council wanted to "set forth authentic teaching about divine revelation and about how it is handed on, *so that by hearing the message of salvation the whole world may believe; by believing, it may hope; and by hoping, it may love.*"[5] We should note again the desire to help the world find love. *Lumen Gentium* starts by saying that Christ is the light of humanity, *he* is the *"Lumen Gentium,"* and that "this most sacred Synod...eagerly desires to shed on all men that radiance of His which brightens the countenance of the Church. This it will do by proclaiming the gospel to every creature."[6] The church is newly described as a great sacrament

---

4. Bernard Leeming, *The Vatican Council and Christian Unity* (New York: Harper & Row, 1966), 19 and 258, respectively.

5. Vatican Council II, *Dei Verbum* (Dogmatic Constitution on Divine Revelation, 1965), no. 1 (my emphasis).

6. Vatican Council II, *Lumen Gentium,* no. 1.

of salvation, a "fellowship of life, charity, and truth" that Christ has established in order to use it "for the redemption of all."[7] So much did the council want to emphasize its new spirit of solidarity with the world that it set about producing a document specifically on "the Church in the Modern World." When many bishops wanted this document to just have the rather lower status of a "declaration" or even a "letter," Archbishop Karol Wojtyla was one of those who insisted that this text was so utterly important and indicative of a whole new attitude toward the world that it should be put into the top rank of documents and be designated as a "constitution."[8] *Gaudium et Spes* duly became one of the four key constitutions of Vatican II, alongside *Dei Verbum, Lumen Gentium,* and *Sacrosanctum Concilium.*[9]

The Basic Context: *Gaudium et Spes*

The pontificate of the late John Paul II was in many ways the lived implementation of *Gaudium et Spes.*[10] That text, on which he personally worked with other bishops and theologians in drafting committees at the council, is really the key to so much of what he did as pope. The outreach he showed in his frequent apostolic journeys was rooted here, as was his desire to defend the rights of every human being whatever their religion or circumstance. His heart reached out to all that God has made, and he showed in that way the authentic spirit of *catholicism,* in accordance with the vision of the great French Jesuit, Henri de Lubac (1896–1991), who strongly influenced him and who also worked on *Gaudium et Spes.* De Lubac said in 1938 that the Catholic Church wishes "to gather

---

7. Ibid., no. 9.

8. Cf. Xavier Rynne, *Vatican Council II* (Maryknoll, NY: Orbis, 1999), 550.

9. Vatican Council II, *Gaudium et Spes; Sacrosanctum Concilium* (Constitution on the Sacred Liturgy, 1963).

10. Cf. Paul McPartlan, "The Legacy of Vatican II in the Pontificate of John Paul II," in *New Catholic Encyclopedia,* Jubilee Volume, *The Wojtyla Years* (Washington, DC: Catholic University of America, 2001), 63–70.

in everything for its salvation and sanctification" and that "nothing authentically human, whatever its origin, can be alien to her."[11]

Let us recall some of Pope John Paul II's words to religious leaders in Assisi in 2002:

> With daily-renewed wonder, we note the *variety of manifestations of human life,* from the complementarity of male and female, to a multiplicity of distinct gifts belonging to the different cultures and traditions that form a multifaceted and versatile linguistic, cultural and artistic cosmos. *This multiplicity is called to form a cohesive whole,* in the contact and dialogue that will enrich and bring joy to all....
>
> Now is the time to overcome decisively those temptations to hostility which have not been lacking in the religious history of humanity. In fact, when these temptations appeal to religion, they show a profoundly immature face of religion. True religious feeling leads rather to a perception in one way or another of the mystery of God, the source of goodness, and that is a wellspring of respect and harmony between peoples: indeed religion is the chief antidote to violence and conflict.[12]

These words convey a profound sense of the ultimate unity of all true religious striving in the one mystery of God. The church is placed in the midst of a world that is united by its orientation to a single fulfilment. Privileged to know of that single fulfilment, she exists to help all to find that one fulfilling destiny. Everything she does is for the salvation of the world, of which she is thoroughly part.

It was not always so. In truth, we are here at the nub of the teaching of *Gaudium et Spes,* where effectively a battle that had been fought in Catholic doctrine for decades and even for centuries was

---

11. Henri de Lubac, *Catholicism* (1938; San Francisco: Ignatius, 1988), 297–98. Cf. Paul McPartlan, *Sacrament of Salvation: An Introduction to Eucharistic Ecclesiology* (1995; Edinburgh: T & T Clark, 2003), chapter 4 on de Lubac.

12. Extract from the "Address of His Holiness Pope John Paul II to the Representatives of the World Religions," Assisi, January 24, 2002. Available at www.vatican.va/holy_father/john_paul_ii/speeches/2002/january/index.htm.

declared to have been won by the big-hearted. It is said that when Pope John was asked one day what the new council would do, he went and opened a window and said, "*That* is what it will do." The church had been a fortress defended *against* the world for a long time, and Pope John wanted to open the windows and doors, to let down the drawbridge and make contact once again with the world, recognizing that it is in fact *God's* world.

In his book, *Crossing the Threshold of Hope,* Pope John Paul II recalled the intense and exciting work that went on in the drafting of *Gaudium et Spes,* particularly early in 1965 when the work of the council was reaching a final crescendo. He says, "I am particularly indebted to Fr. Yves Congar and Fr. Henri De Lubac," both of whom, great pioneers of the council, he subsequently made cardinals. He goes further and says, "From that moment on, I enjoyed a special friendship with Fr. De Lubac."[13]

For thirty years before the council, amid mounting opposition, de Lubac had patiently championed that ancient saying of Saint Augustine: "You have made us for yourself, [Lord,] and our heart is restless until it rests in you."[14] Every human heart has the same restlessness in it, all are called to the same divine destiny, and the church must therefore reach out to all. More specifically, he had championed Saint Thomas Aquinas's version of the same principle, namely that every human being has a natural desire for the vision of God,[15] which amounts to the same thing. I say "championed" because the neoscholastic establishment, the professed disciples of Aquinas, denied that very teaching, because they thought that it somehow inhibited God's freedom. They preferred to say that there is a purely natural destiny that human beings naturally desire, and it is only an extraordinary, special, and extra call of God

---

13. John Paul II, *Crossing the Threshold of Hope* (London: Jonathan Cape, 1994), 159. Cf. also John Paul II, *Rise, Let Us Be on Our Way* (London: Jonathan Cape, 2004), 165.

14. Augustine, *Confessions* 1, 1, 1 (*Patrologia Latina* 32, 659–61), as cited in *Catechism of the Catholic Church* (2000), no. 3.

15. Cf. Paul McPartlan, *The Eucharist Makes the Church: Henri de Lubac and John Zizioulas in Dialogue* (Edinburgh: T & T Clark, 1993), 30–34.

that lifts us above that and draws us to see God face to face. It is a very short step from there to seeing the world divided into those who are destined for the vision of God, the members of the church, and those who have not been called, the world *out there;* and de Lubac thought that the church of the 1930s and '40s had actually taken that step and started just to look after itself. Church and world had parted company and, in his view, the church had thereby lost its missionary identity and engagement. He was highly critical of what was being taught in the theological schools of his day and showed in learned studies how they were in fact betraying their supposed masters, Augustine and especially Aquinas. He made himself very unpopular![16]

De Lubac was silenced for the whole of the 1950s. In 1960, however, Pope John appointed him as one of the theological advisors for the new council and thereby endorsed what de Lubac had been saying and harnessed de Lubac's research to further his dream of a church newly in touch with the world of today, and, we must also say, newly in touch with its own authentic tradition reflected in Augustine, Aquinas, and so many others.

Also appointed after a period of repression was Yves Congar, the other theologian mentioned by Pope John Paul II in his memoir. Congar himself complained of the church's isolation from society at large. In 1965, at the end of the council, he gave a telling summary of what had been happening over the previous two hundred years or so as the church had progressively drawn in on itself: "Confronted by religion without a world, men formulated the idea of a world without religion." He added, however, "We are now emerging from this wretched situation; the People of God is rediscovering once again that it possesses a messianic character and that it bears the hope of a fulfilment of the world in Jesus Christ."[17]

We might well say, against this background, that *Gaudium et Spes* was the crowning achievement of Vatican II. It is sometimes

---

16. For more detail on this issue, see McPartlan, *Sacrament of Salvation,* 47–53; also Joseph Komonchak, "Theology and Culture at Mid-Century: The Example of Henri de Lubac," *Theological Studies* 51 (1990): 579–602.

17. Yves Congar, "The Church: The People of God," *Concilium* 1, no. 1 (1965): 10.

said to be a dated text, but in a very real sense *Gaudium et Spes* can never date, because it challenges the church in every age to read "the signs of the times" and respond to them.[18] That challenge will be fresh in every generation. Admittedly, *Gaudium et Spes* itself tries to grapple with that challenge for the mid-1960s, but it does so in its second part, and of course that part now looks a bit dated, but that is only Part Two. Part One, which expounds the basic principles of the church's relationship with the world, will never fade and is worth reading and rereading in order to absorb its perspectives.

Why should the church read the signs of the times? Should it not just look after its own, the spiritual chosen few? No, because the resounding message of *Gaudium et Spes* is that the Spirit is at work *everywhere*.

> The People of God believes that it is led by the Spirit of the Lord, who fills the earth. Motivated by this faith, it labors to decipher authentic signs of God's presence and purpose in the happenings, needs, and desires in which this People has a part along with other men of our age.[19]

It follows that the church does not just give something *to* the world, it also learns *from* the world. *Gaudium et Spes* acknowledges:

> The Church herself knows how richly she has profited by the history and development of humanity....
>
> With the help of the Holy Spirit, it is the task of the entire People of God, especially pastors and theologians, to hear, distinguish, and interpret the many voices of our age, and to judge them in the light of the divine Word. In this way, revealed truth can always be more deeply penetrated, better understood, and set forth to greater advantage.[20]

The council teaches that we will penetrate more deeply the revealed truth that has been entrusted to us by listening to the

---

18. Vatican Council II, *Gaudium et Spes,* no. 4.
19. Ibid., no. 11.
20. Ibid., no. 44.

voices and needs of the world of today. This is for a rather complex, twofold reason: First, Christ has told us that he is to be found in the needy. "Just as you did it to one of the least of these..., you did it to me" (Matt 25:40). Second, Christ is also the Savior of the world of today, and where it is hurting is where he is healing or wanting to heal. The more that we understand the nuances of human need, guided by the Holy Spirit, the better we will understand the nuances of the gospel. Saint Jerome once said, "Ignorance of the Scriptures is ignorance of Christ."[21] *Gaudium et Spes* shows that there is also a profound sense in which ignorance of today's world is ignorance of Christ.

> While helping the world and receiving many benefits from it, the Church has a single intention: that God's kingdom may come, and that the salvation of the whole human race may come to pass....
>
> The Lord is the goal of human history, the focal point of the longings of history and of civilization, the center of the human race, the joy of every heart, and the answer to all its yearnings.[22]

These words occur at the climax of the first part of *Gaudium et Spes*. What is probably the decisive passage in the whole text occurs halfway through it, in paragraph 22. It certainly seems that this paragraph had an extraordinary impact upon Pope John Paul II. He quoted one sentence from it in virtually every major text that he wrote: "The truth is that only in the mystery of the incarnate Word does the mystery of man take on light."[23] The basic idea, indeed the basic motif of *Gaudium et Spes,* is that every human life is a riddle until Christ comes and unlocks the mystery; every human heart is waiting for him, knowingly or unknowingly; every heart is restless for him. It is no surprise to discover that those enduring words of Augustine have just been quoted at the end of

---

21. Jerome, as quoted in Vatican Council II, *Dei Verbum,* no. 25.
22. Vatican Council II, *Gaudium et Spes,* no. 45.
23. Ibid., no. 22.

paragraph 21: "'Thou hast made us for Thyself,' O Lord, 'and our hearts are restless till they rest in Thee.'" Those words pave the way for paragraph 22, which builds up to the following decisive argument: "Since Christ died for all men, and since the ultimate vocation of man is in fact one, and divine, we ought to believe that the Holy Spirit in a manner known only to God offers to every man the possibility of being associated with this paschal mystery."[24]

So, there are not *two* destinies, one for human beings left to their natural devices and one for the chosen few; no, *all* are called to one and the same destiny, which is *divine,* the vision of God face to face. De Lubac's victory was won! Furthermore, God in his mercy ensures that *every* human being is given the chance to embrace the one way to that fulfilment, which is by entering into the paschal mystery of Christ. That encounter happens explicitly in the preaching and sacraments of the church, but it happens implicitly at some point in the life of every human being, in a way that escapes our understanding but is known to God. It must be so, for only Christ fulfills our human longing, and God wants everyone to be fulfilled. So, the church exists in a graced world; it goes out into a world already touched by the Spirit, in order to identify clear signs of the life of Christ having already been embraced by good and holy people of all faiths and no faith, to tend those shoots wherever possible, knowing them for what they are, and to help bring in the harvest.

Deacons and the New Ecclesial Embrace of the World

All in all, there is a *seamlessness* between the church and the world in the teaching of Vatican II—no gulf, no divide. The church exists everywhere in the world, seasoning it for salvation, speaking of the one loving embrace that holds all things in being. As we have seen, this was very much a new stance, or a newly restored stance,

---

24. Ibid.

and we can understand the council wanting to consolidate this new stance in every way possible. One of the principal ways by which the council made provision for living out this newly restored stance of the church vis-à-vis the world was by the newly restored ministry of the diaconate. The ancient model of the deacon from the early centuries, those centuries that were the pattern for so much of the council's reforms, perfectly exemplifies the new stance. The early church shows deacons who had a ministry at the heart of the life of the church, standing at the very altar itself, and a ministry also at the heart of the world's affairs, standing often in the midst of the poor and needy with charge of the church's charitable funds and outreach.[25] In their own persons, they expressed the seamlessness between church and world, moving smoothly from one to the other. That is why I would like to say, "Deacons, S.O.S.!" and suggest that deacons are signs of seamlessness, signs of solidarity.

The 1998 Vatican documents on the diaconate *(Ratio Fundamentalis [Basic Norms]* and *Directorium [Directory for the Ministry and Life of Permanent Deacons])* recall something very significant that Pope John Paul II said in 1993: "A particularly felt need behind the decision to restore the permanent diaconate was that of a greater and more direct presence of sacred ministers in areas such as the family, work, schools, etc., as well as in various ecclesial structures."[26] It is worth remembering the Worker Priest movement in France and Belgium after the Second World War. More than a hundred priests joined the workforce to be alongside working people in the world at large and particularly to evangelize lapsed Catholics in the workplace. The movement was steadily suppressed by Rome from the mid-1950s, because that sort of engagement with the world was regarded as inappropriate for priests. By the time of

---

25. See, for example, Edward P. Echlin, *The Deacon in the Church: Past and Future* (New York: Alba House, 1971), 27–58; James Monroe Barnett, *The Diaconate: A Full and Equal Order,* rev. ed. (1981; Valley Forge, PA: Trinity Press International, 1995), 43–87.

26. John Paul II, General Audience of October 6, 1993; quoted in Introduction to the *Joint Declaration* (see note 2 of this chapter), n. 29. This valuable audience address, entitled "Deacons Serve the Kingdom of God," is available at www.vatican.va/holy_father/john_paul_ii/audiences/alpha/data/aud19931006en.html.

Vatican II, the movement was almost finished. The council's *Presbyterorum Ordinis* did pay tribute to those priests who engage in "manual labor [and] share in the lot of the workers themselves—if there seems to be need for this and competent authority approves,"[27] but that approval had by then been largely withdrawn. We may perhaps speculate that, having concluded from experience that the priesthood does not sit well with that sort of worldly engagement, the bishops discovered at Vatican II the ordained ministry that *does* sit well with it, namely the diaconate. Furthermore, we may suggest that wanting precisely to secure, as Pope John Paul II says, the presence of ordained ministers in the workplace and elsewhere, they duly restored the permanent diaconate.

Lumen Gentium maps out the portfolio of tasks that characterizes the deacon. With reference to early church sources, it says that the deacon has various liturgical tasks, but he is also "dedicated to duties of charity and of administration."[28] The deacon stands at the altar and prepares the gifts with clean hands, but he stands also where the practical need is greatest, getting his hands very dirty. Those whom the church traditionally regards as the first deacons were commissioned to take charge of an unruly food distribution (Acts 6:1–6). By being visibly at home *in both places,* the deacon embodies the great message of Vatican II, namely that the whole world is taken up in what happens at the altar and that the sacrifice of the altar is celebrated for the sanctification of the whole world.

We should also note what the council says about the restoration of the diaconate in *Ad Gentes.* There, too, the diaconal bond between charitable work and the altar is emphasized, though the accent is slightly different in that this text starts by recognizing that there are laymen who already carry out the preaching, governing, and charitable ministry of a deacon. These men, it says, could be helped and strengthened by ordination as deacons. "It will be helpful to strengthen them by that imposition of hands which has come down from the apostles, and to bind them more closely to the altar.

---

27. Vatican Council II, *Presbyterorum Ordinis* (Decree on the Ministry and Life of Priests, 1965), no. 8.

28. Vatican Council II, *Lumen Gentium,* no. 29.

Thus they can carry out their ministry more effectively because of the sacramental grace of the diaconate."[29]

The 1998 Vatican documents plug the deacon firmly into the agenda of *Gaudium et Spes* by asserting that the deacon "should be conversant with contemporary cultures and with the aspirations and problems of his times....In this context, indeed, he is called to be a living sign of Christ the Servant and to assume the Church's responsibility of 'reading the signs of the time and of interpreting them in the light of the Gospel.'"[30] Through his engagement with "family, work, schools, etc.," to recall the pope's profile of a deacon, he is indeed particularly conversant with the aspirations and problems of his times. He sees the signs of the times close up every day, but, as an ordained minister of the gospel, he is particularly called to *read* the signs and to interpret them in the light of the gospel, so as to lead his Christian brothers and sisters, who are all charged with the same responsibility. Properly understood and lived, the diaconate should surely, therefore, be a leaven for the apostolate of the laity.

Signs of Seamlessness

The seamlessness of church and world is there already. Deacons do not create it; that is how God has willed it to be. They do, however, show it forth and embody it as a clear and constant reminder to all of us in the church—and to everyone in the world, for that matter—that that *is* how God has willed it to be. History shows that the church certainly needs that visible reminder in its

---

29. Vatican Council II, *Ad Gentes* (Decree on the Church's Missionary Activity, 1965), no. 16. The ITC suggests that "there was a shift in the Council's intentions" regarding the restoration of the diaconate from *Lumen Gentium* (1964) to *Ad Gentes* (1965). For the former, the diaconate seemed primarily to be a means of supplying important liturgical functions in a situation of priestly shortage, whereas for the latter it was "a confirmation, a reinforcement and a more complete incorporation into the ministry of the Church of those who were already *de facto* exercising the ministry of deacons" (*From the Diakonia of Christ,* 59).

30. Congregation for the Clergy, *Directory,* no. 43.

midst in order to prevent it from pulling up the drawbridge against the world.

Pope John Paul II said that, at the time of its restoration, "Some saw the permanent diaconate as a bridge between pastors and the faithful."[31] We might also say that it is the link between the church and the world, between liturgy and life, and so on. That terminology has great attractions and is still often used. The term *bridge,* however, also has some problems, which are important to identify.[32] The deacon is spoken of as a bridge precisely to stress the connectedness of church and world, liturgy and life, pastors and faithful, as I have been emphasizing here. The danger, however, is that the very image itself suggests a gap that needs to be bridged (and, moreover, that is not bridged unless there is a deacon)—that is not our basic view of things. Yes, there *was* a gap between the church and the world prior to Vatican II, but there should *not* have been; and if we call the deacon a bridge as a matter of course, we are in danger of implying that there is *of course* a gap between the church and the world, between the pastors and the faithful, and so on. As the ITC says, the idea of the diaconate as *medius ordo* (that is, bridge) "might end up by sanctioning and deepening, through that very function, the gap which it was supposed to fill."[33] I would suggest that it is truer to the vision of Vatican II, particularly as set forth in *Gaudium et Spes,* to speak of the *seamlessness* or *solidarity* between the church and the world, and to speak of the deacon as a splendid and very special sign of that seamlessness or solidarity.

In so many ways, the implementation of *Gaudium et Spes* still lies ahead of us, and part of the struggle to implement this magnificent text is surely the struggle to gain clarity about the ministry and life of deacons, because, as I have maintained here, the program that *Gaudium et Spes* maps out is the very charter of the diaconate. Our struggle for clarity with regard to the diaconate is actually part of a bigger struggle to implement the teaching of

---

31. John Paul II, "Deacons Serve the Kingdom of God."
32. See the interesting discussion of the idea of bridging or mediating in the ITC text, *From the Diakonia of Christ,* 92–93.
33. Ibid., 93.

Vatican II, which Pope John Paul II identified as *"the great grace bestowed on the Church in the twentieth century."*[34] This is a grace, he strongly implied, still awaiting its full reception, so that the church may really be, in this new century, what *Gaudium et Spes* so emphatically called it, "the universal sacrament of salvation," at once manifesting and actualizing the mystery of God's love for humanity.[35]

The Wider Context

A remarkable ecumenical consensus has been steadily forming with regard to the diaconate.

> In recent ecumenical reflection on the diaconate,...the ministry of deacons has been seen as that of a go-between, a bridge, an envoy, whose special ministry is to take the message, meaning and values of the liturgy, as a key expression of the gospel, into the heart of the world and, by the same token, to bring the needs and cares of the world into the heart of the Church's worship and fellowship. Deacons have been seen as those who, grounded in the teaching and worship of the Body of Christ, carry the good news, in word and sacrament, and through compassionate service, to those whom Christ came to seek and to save.[36]

This splendid description makes us realize that deacons are, in fact, *signs* to the church of what *all* in the church should be doing. It is mistaken to describe and evaluate the diaconate purely in functional

---

34. John Paul II, Apostolic Letter, *Novo Millennio Ineunte* (2001), no. 57.

35. Vatican Council II, *Gaudium et Spes,* no. 45.

36. Report to the General Synod of the Church of England of a Working Party of the House of Bishops, *For Such a Time as This: A Renewed Diaconate in the Church of England* (London: Church House Publishing, 2001), 21–22. There is a very substantial account of the growing ecumenical consensus on the diaconate by Sven-Erik Brodd, "An Escalating Phenomenon: The Diaconate from an Ecumenical Perspective," in Gunnel Borgegard and Christine Hall, *The Ministry of the Deacon* (Uppsala: Nordic Ecumenical Council, 1999), 11–50.

terms. The 1998 Vatican documents on the diaconate *(Basic Norms* and *Directory for the Ministry and Life of Permanent Deacons)* richly express the sign value of the diaconate by referring to the deacon as "a living icon of Christ the servant within the Church."[37] At the deacon's ordination, the bishop prays to God the Father that the new deacon may be "the image of your Son who did not come to be served but to serve."[38] Particularly since the Second Vatican Council, we have understood that the whole church is called to a "spirituality of service," because it exists in the world to serve the salvation of the world, as we have seen. Vatican II restored the diaconate as a stable and lifelong ministry in the Catholic Church because this ministry acts as a lasting, living reminder to us all of our collective calling to serve. The 1998 documents go right to the point when they say, "So that the whole Church may better live out this spirituality of service, the Lord gives her a living and personal sign of his very being as servant."[39] It is important always to retain that ecclesial context for the diaconate.

For many centuries, however, Catholics regarded the diaconate simply as a step on the way to priestly ordination, rather than as a distinct ministry in its own right. That view actually originated in the fifth and sixth centuries, when the permanent diaconate became virtually extinct. Before that time, for the fathers of the early church, the ministry of deacons was a vibrant and distinctive one. Pope Paul VI said, "The writers of the first centuries…give many examples of the manifold important tasks entrusted to them, and clearly show how much authority they held in the Christian communities and how great was their contribution to the apostolate."[40] The fathers of the early centuries who so influenced the teaching of Vatican II faced the challenge of preaching the gospel to a largely pagan world. In this third millennium, we ourselves face the challenge of a new evangelization, and the Second

---

37. Congregation for Catholic Education, *Basic Norms,* no. 11.
38. Congregation for the Clergy, *Directory,* no. 38; cf. Matt 20:28.
39. Congregation for Catholic Education, *Basic Norms,* no. 11.
40. Paul VI, Apostolic Letter, *Ad Pascendum* (Norms for the Order of Diaconate, 1972).

Vatican Council, enriched by their teaching, has equipped us for that task. The restoration of the permanent diaconate should surely also be seen in that light, as an integral part of the council's work of preparing the whole church for a renewed apostolate in today's world. Deacons are "pioneers of a new 'civilisation of love.'"[41]

Pope John Paul II acknowledged that one of the main reasons for the council's decision to restore the diaconate was "to provide for the scarcity of priests, as well as to assist them in many responsibilities not directly connected to their pastoral ministry." He very importantly noted, however, that those immediate, rather pragmatic reasons for restoring the permanent diaconate should not restrict our vision of this ministry today. In other words, now that we have deacons again, let us really try to understand this ministry and benefit from it to the full. He wrote, "The Holy Spirit, who has the leading role in the Church's life, was mysteriously working through these reasons connected with historical circumstances and pastoral perspectives" in order to restore in the church the "complete picture" of the ordained ministry, which is "traditionally composed of bishops, priests and deacons." "Thus a revitalization of Christian communities was fostered, making them more like those founded by the apostles which flourished in the early centuries, always under the impulse of the Paraclete, as the Acts of the Apostles attest."[42]

These words rather suggest that the threefold ministry of bishops, presbyters, and deacons was a kind of engine that hummed at the heart of vibrant communities of Christians in the early church. Doing without a third of that group for many centuries has made the church's engine underpowered, and the pope looked forward to what might happen when full power was restored. It is notable that the centuries when the diaconate was effectively absent have also been centuries when the laity became increasingly passive in the liturgy and increasingly neglected in terms of a formal apostolate.

---

41. Walter Kasper, *Leadership in the Church* (New York: Herder & Herder, 2003), 44.

42. John Paul II, "Deacons Serve the Kingdom of God."

There is at least a hint here again that a flourishing diaconate and a flourishing laity actually go together.

As I emphasized at the start, it is important to see the restoration of the permanent diaconate within the overall context of Vatican II, in order to understand it properly. In fact, four particular reference points stand out. First, as we have just seen, deacons are animators of service so as to help form a servant-church. Vatican II taught that the church is "the universal sacrament of salvation,"[43] outward looking and at the service of the salvation of the world. Deacons, particularly dedicated as they are to service, play a vital role of anchoring that self-understanding in the community life of the church as a whole. In 1982, the Faith and Order Commission of the World Council of Churches expressed this point very clearly: "Deacons represent to the Church its calling as servant in the world."[44] Conversely, the more we live as a servant-church, the more likely we are to understand the diaconate and to discern diaconal vocations.

Second, drawing upon the letters of Ignatius of Antioch (about AD 100), the *Apostolic Tradition* (third century), and other ancient sources, Vatican II taught that the bishop has "the fullness of the sacrament of orders" and that he is the primary celebrant of the Eucharist among his people.[45] "The Church reveals herself most clearly when a full complement of God's holy people, united in prayer and in a common liturgical service (especially the Eucharist), exercise a thorough and active participation at the very altar where the bishop presides in the company of his priests and other assistants" (that is, the deacons).[46] Episcopal collegiality follows from the renewed recognition of all the bishops as high priests, living icons, we might aptly say, of Christ the High Priest

---

43. Vatican Council II, *Lumen Gentium,* no. 48.

44. Faith and Order Commission, World Council of Churches, *Baptism, Eucharist and Ministry (Lima Report),* Faith and Order Paper, no. 111 (Geneva: World Council of Churches, 1982), "Ministry," no. 31.

45. Vatican Council II, *Lumen Gentium,* nos. 21, 26.

46. Vatican Council II, *Sacrosanctum Concilium,* no. 41.

(Heb 7:26, 9:11) within the church, presiding in different places over the one eucharistic mystery that unites the church.[47]

When the bishops at the council returned to these ancient sources to clarify what sort of bishop the early church had, they could hardly fail to notice the (permanent) deacon, who was regularly at the bishop's side in the early church. Vatican II's teaching on the permanent diaconate must be seen within its overall ordering of the church around the Eucharist, "the fount and apex of the whole Christian life,"[48] and of the celebration of the Eucharist around the bishop. In his service of the church, the deacon is fundamentally linked both to the Eucharist and to the bishop.

Third, the council taught that the liturgy is "the summit toward which the activity of the Church is directed" and also "the fountain from which all her power flows."[49] The whole church, therefore, has a double movement in its life, a regular rhythm of gathering for liturgy and then going back out into the world to proclaim and live the gospel. Good liturgy animates the apostolate. The Catholic Church had always tended to focus on just the priest in the liturgy: as long as you had a priest, you could have the Mass. Vatican II put the bishop back at the heart of the liturgy, returned the laity to an active participation in the liturgy,[50] and restored the diaconate to its proper place there, too. The liturgy suddenly became a crowded place, and rightly so. As we all engage in our respective roles there, we are all confirmed in our complementary ministries in the church and animated for our complementary apostolates in the world.[51] Pope Benedict XVI (then Cardinal Ratzinger) neatly summarized the teaching of Vatican II in this area when he said that the church's "worship is its constitution, since of

---

47. Cf. McPartlan, *Sacrament of Salvation,* 42, 67–68; regarding "episcopal collegiality" see Vatican Council II, *Lumen Gentium,* no. 22, and regarding bishops as high priests see Vatican Council II, *Sacrosanctum Concilium,* no. 41.

48. Vatican Council II, *Lumen Gentium,* no. 11.

49. Vatican Council II, *Sacrosanctum Concilium,* no. 10.

50. Ibid., nos. 14, 28; *Lumen Gentium,* no. 10.

51. Cf. Paul McPartlan, "Liturgy, Church, and Society," *Studia Liturgica* 34 (2004): 147–64.

its nature it is itself the service of God and thus of men and women, the service of transforming the world."[52]

Since, under the guidance of the Holy Spirit, the same council both restored the permanent diaconate and gave great prominence to the apostolate of the laity,[53] it really cannot be the case that the diaconate, properly understood and lived, in any way inhibits the true apostolate of the laity—rather the opposite, as I have suggested. One of the practical challenges we certainly face in implementing the restoration of the permanent diaconate, however, is to discover how it can indeed enhance and promote the apostolate of the laity, as it should.

Last and by no means least, we must recall the profound linkage between the diaconate and the vision and program of *Gaudium et Spes* with which I began. The deacon particularly demonstrates the solidarity between the church and the world that is asserted in the opening sentence of *Gaudium et Spes,* a solidarity that needs to be shown forth, strengthened, and protected, because history shows how easily it can break down. It is important to have walking, talking signs of seamlessness, signs of solidarity in our midst as a church, to anchor that understanding in us all. Because they have a sacred ministry, publicly expressed in the liturgy, and also, more often than not, a secular profession and a wife and family, deacons remind us all that church and world *do* belong together. This point, too, was well expressed by the Faith and Order Commission of the World Council of Churches in 1982: "By struggling in Christ's name with the myriad needs of societies and persons, deacons exemplify the interdependence of worship and service in the Church's life."[54]

So far, only one ecumenically agreed statement specifically on the subject of the diaconate has been produced, namely the so-called Hanover Report of the Anglican-Lutheran International Commission, entitled *The Diaconate as Ecumenical Opportunity.* This

---

52. Joseph Ratzinger, *Church, Ecumenism and Politics* (Slough, UK: St. Paul Publications, 1988), 8.

53. Cf. also the council's *Apostolicam Actuositatem* (Decree on the Apostolate of the Laity, 1965).

54. *Lima Report,* "Ministry," no. 31.

valuable text reinforces the point just made: "The integration of worship and service remains a concern for the various diaconal ministries of the Church."

> Diaconal ministry typically seeks not only to mediate the service of the church to specific needs, but also to interpret those needs to the church. The "go-between" role of diaconal ministry thus operates in both directions: from church to the needs, hopes and concerns of persons in and beyond the church; and from those needs, hopes, and concerns to the church.

Moreover, in a remarkable sentence rather like that of the former Cardinal Ratzinger quoted earlier, it affirms, "The celebration of the eucharist is a paradigm for the interrelationship of various ministries in the church. It is, among other things, a kind of 'dress rehearsal' for life."[55]

It follows that what deacons do in the liturgy and how they relate there to the church's other ministries will be symbolic of their activity and relationships in the world at large. By proclaiming the gospel, then taking the people's gifts and preparing them for the presider to offer, then taking the consecrated gifts back to the people in communion, deacons symbolize the proclamation of the good news and practical service of their brothers and sisters to which they are committed at every moment in the world at large.

The 1998 Vatican documents on the diaconate assert that the deacon participates in "the mystery of Christ the Servant,"[56] who gave his life as "a ransom for many" (Matt 20:28), and that the deacon is to be "a driving force for service."[57] It should be repeated, finally, that the deacon has no monopoly of service; it is the calling of every disciple of Christ. Precisely because it is the calling of all, however, it is very helpful for all to have in their midst those who

---

55. The Hanover Report of the Anglican-Lutheran International Commission, *The Diaconate as Ecumenical Opportunity* (London: Anglican Communion Publications, 1996), nos. 28, 51, 22, respectively; available at www.anglicancommunion.org/documents/lutheran/hanover.html.

56. Congregation for the Clergy, *Directory*, no. 57.

57. Congregation for Catholic Education, *Basic Norms*, no. 5.

are specifically pledged to an intense, selfless configuration to Christ the Servant, persons who can stand as examples and reminders to all of what we are really about. It is very heartening to discover that though they are divided on so many other things—for example, whether to have bishops, whether the minister is a "priest"—nevertheless all of the main Christian traditions *do* have deacons. At that basic level of ministry and service we are at one.

Fundamentally, as we have seen, the church exists to love the world and to serve its salvation. We must look outward to a needy world. The 1998 documents tell us never to forget that "the object of Christ's diaconia is mankind."[58] The church continues to be "the sign and instrument" of Christ's *diakonia* in history,[59] and the deacon is the sign and instrument of that *diakonia* in the church.

---

58. Congregation for the Clergy, *Directory,* no. 49.
59. Ibid.

CHAPTER 4

The Diaconate as *Medius Ordo:* Service in Promotion of Lay Participation

Rev. William S. McKnight, STD

Introduction

The restoration of the permanent diaconate by the Second Vatican Council forty years ago left many questions unresolved about the identity and role of the deacon among the people of God. A vague and sometimes disputed understanding of the diaconate continues to hamper the effectiveness of diaconal ministry in our day. A scientific study of the diaconate in the United States of America shows that many deacons experience anxiety in the performance of their ministry, even though they express satisfaction with their decision to serve the church as a deacon.[1] Role conflict is to blame, which results from differing expectations between clergy and laity over the diaconate's place in the organizational structure of the church.[2] In many dioceses deacons are asked to help meet the demands of the dwindling number of parish priests. Consequently,

---

1. National Conference of Catholic Bishops, Bishops' Committee on the Permanent Diaconate, *A National Study on the Permanent Diaconate of the Catholic Church in the United States, 1994–1995* (Washington, DC: United States Catholic Conference, 1996).

2. F. DeRego and J. Davidson, "Catholic Deacons: A Lesson in Role Conflict and Ambiguity," in *Religion in a Changing World: Comparative Studies in Sociology,* ed. M. Cousineau (Westport, CT: Praeger, 1998), 94.

diaconal ministry today often centers on the fulfillment of sacramental and other liturgical needs of the parish, where they perform baptisms, weddings, funerals, and preach at Sunday masses. This emphasis upon the deacon's liturgical functions, however, comes at a cost to the diaconate itself. The use of deacons as supply ministers in the absence of parish priests prevents the diaconate from developing its own unique identity and purpose as a legitimate and beneficial sacramental order among the people of God.

Another perspective of the diaconate emphasizes the ministerial role of the deacon as a humble servant and agent of charity. The Second Vatican Council taught that deacons are dedicated to works of charity and administration,[3] and that the sacramental grace of the diaconate would help those who already perform the ministry of the deacon by "presiding over scattered Christian communities in the name of the pastor and the bishop, or by practicing charity in social or relief work."[4] This particular emphasis of the diaconate is also reflected in the document from the Congregation for Catholic Education on the formation of permanent deacons, which states that the ministry most characteristic of the deacon is the service of charity.[5]

This perspective of the diaconate, however, is not completely satisfactory either. To say that the deacon is a minister of charity says nothing unique about the deacon. How is the deacon's ministry of charity different from that of bishops and priests, or even the laity? Are not bishops and priests, and in fact all the baptized, charged with the responsibility of charitable service? There exists, then, the objective need to define more precisely the place of the

---

3. Vatican Council II, *Lumen Gentium* (Dogmatic Constitution on the Church, 1964), no. 29. All conciliar decrees, including English translations, are from Walter M. Abbott, SJ, *The Documents of Vatican II* (New York: America Press, 1966).

4. Vatican Council II, *Ad Gentes* (Decree on the Church's Missionary Activity, 1965), no. 16.

5. Congregation for Catholic Education, *Basic Norms for the Formation of Permanent Deacons* (Washington, DC: United States Catholic Conference, 1998), no. 9, p. 27: "Finally the *munus regendi* is exercised in devotion to works of charity and assistance in motivating communities or sectors of ecclesial life, especially in what has to do with charity. This is the ministry which is most characteristic of the deacon."

deacon in the organizational structure of the church today and, accordingly, his unique role in supporting the mission of the church. If the diaconate is to be successful, it must have a specialized ministry of some sort that it can truly call its own. Moreover, if the diaconate is to be truly beneficial to the mission of the church in the modern world, the deacon's ministry must be integrally related to the renewal begun by the Second Vatican Council.

As the previous chapters have explored, the renewal of the diaconate as a permanent state occurred at the same time that the council called for greater participation of the laity. In the Dogmatic Constitution *Lumen Gentium,* the council elucidated the universal call to holiness. As a result, the life and mission of the church are no longer understood to be the exclusive domain of the clergy and religious alone. Distancing itself from the medieval notion of ministry, *Lumen Gentium* harkens back to the liturgy and theology of the first centuries of the church. By embracing a concept of ministry sourced in baptism and holy orders, the council liberated itself from the restricted understanding of medieval times, which had centered ministry on the power of consecration vested in the priest.[6] *Lumen Gentium* thus espouses a communion of a variety of ministries within the one church. It is not, therefore, merely coincidental that the council's doctrinal foundations for the ordained ministry are set out in the very same constitution that calls for the active participation of the laity in the life and mission of the church.

This renewed understanding of ministry colors the restoration of the diaconate as a permanent sacramental ministry. In referencing the biblical understanding of *diakonia,*[7] the ordination liturgies of the

---

6. See Thomas Aquinas, *Supplementum Tertia Partis,* q.37, a.4, in *Summa Theologica: First Complete American Edition in Three Volumes,* trans. Fathers of the English Dominican Province (New York: Benziger Brothers, 1947), 2692: "In this sense there are only three sacred Orders, namely the priesthood and the diaconate, which exercise an act about the consecrated body and blood of Christ, and the subdiaconate, which exercises an act about the consecrated vessels."

7. In Vatican Council II, *Lumen Gentium,* no. 24, the fathers of the council described the office of the bishop as "a true service, and in sacred literature is significantly called 'diakonia' or ministry." In *Lumen Gentium,* no. 29, the council used the language of *"in diaconia liturgiae, verbi et caritatis"* to give a general description of the deacon's service to the

early church, and the theology of the patristic era, the council distanced itself from models of the diaconate that were more in keeping with the medieval era. This approach allowed the council to clarify, to a certain extent, the relationship of the deacon to the bishop, priests, and laity within the context of the church as the people of God. The restoration of the diaconate as a permanent state did not simply arise from a new awareness of early theological sources, however. The pastoral sense of the bishops for the needs of the church in the modern world also influenced their call for a renewed diaconate.

The Teaching of Paul VI

Following the conclusion of the Second Vatican Council, Pope Paul VI issued several documents implementing the permanent diaconate as outlined by the council.[8] The final document, the apostolic letter *Ad Pascendum,* further specified the role of the diaconate as a *medius ordo:*

> Finally, Vatican Council II approved the wishes and requests that, where it would lead to the good of souls, the permanent

---

people of God. John N. Collins's revolutionary word study of *diakonia* in the New Testament, however, fundamentally alters the heretofore common understanding of *diakonia* as humble service of those in need. Collins's research shows that *diakonia* actually connotes the fulfillment of a charge or mandate received from a higher authority and does not carry in itself the meaning of humble service. A *diakonos* in the New Testament is therefore an individual with a noble charge received from Christ, the church, or the *episkopos.* See J. N. Collins, *Diakonia: Re-interpreting the Ancient Sources* (New York: Oxford University Press, 1990) and *Deacons and the Church: Making Connections between Old and New* (Harrisburg, PA: Gracewing, 2002).

8. The apostolic letter *Sacrum Diaconatus Ordinem, AAS* 59 (1967): 697–704, implemented the recommendations of the Second Vatican Council by determining general norms governing the restoration of the permanent diaconate in the Latin church; the apostolic constitution *Pontificalis Romani Recognitio, AAS* 60 (1968): 369–73, approved the new rite of conferring the episcopacy, presbyterate, and diaconate; the apostolic letter *Ministeria Quaedam, AAS* 64 (1972): 529–34, suppressed the minor orders and declared that entry into the clerical state is joined with the diaconate—lectors and acolytes are no longer "ordained" but "installed"; and finally, the apostolic letter *Ad Pascendum, AAS* 64 (1971): 534–40, clarified the conditions for admission and ordination of candidates, as well as the purpose of the diaconate.

> Diaconate should be restored as an intermediate order
> [*medius ordo*] between the higher grades of the ecclesiastical
> hierarchy and the rest of the people of God, being as it were
> a mediator [*interpres*] of the needs and desires of the Christian
> communities, an animator of the service of *diaconia* of the
> Church among the local Christian communities, and a sign or
> sacrament of Christ the Lord himself, who *came not to be
> served, but to serve.*[9]

The idea of the diaconate as an intermediate order is not entirely
original to Paul VI. The recent document on the diaconate from the
International Theological Commission points out that interventions
made at the council, and the notes of the Conciliar Commission itself,
had already attributed to the permanent diaconate a mediating or
bridging function between the higher clergy and the people.[10] What
does it mean for the deacon to be a mediator?

Some have interpreted the "intermediate" character of the
diaconate as a step in a linear hierarchy separating the bishop further from the laity,[11] but it is more likely here to have a different
meaning. The ecclesiology of the Second Vatican Council envisions
the ordained ministries within the context of *communio* (communion) rather than the *cursus honorum* (literally "course of honors").
Instead of the conception of the ordained ministry as a series of
steps through which a candidate for the priesthood must travel, all
three orders are directly oriented to the service of the people of

---

9. Paul VI, *Ad Pascendum*, p. 536, my translation.

10. International Theological Commission, *From the Diakonia of Christ to the
Diakonia of the Apostles* (Chicago: Hillenbrand Books, 2004), 103.

11. Ibid., 103–4: "It would be a theological error to identify the diaconate as
'medius ordo' with a kind of intermediate (sacramental?) reality between the baptized
and the ordained faithful. The fact that the diaconate belongs to the sacrament of Holy
Orders is sure doctrine. Theologically, the deacon is not a 'layperson'" (104). It is worth
noting that the scholastic perspective of the ordained ministry as necessarily some form
of participation in the priesthood of Christ is evident in this passage. In fact, however,
the council taught that the deacon truly shares in the sacrament of holy orders and, at
the same time, that he does not have a share in the ministerial priesthood. See Vatican
Council II, *Lumen Gentium*, no. 29: "At a lower level of the hierarchy are deacons, upon
whom hands are imposed 'not unto the priesthood, but unto a ministry of service.'"

God. The exercise of presbyteral and diaconal charisms, nonetheless, falls under the oversight of the bishop, who is the principle of unity and is responsible for the harmonious coordination of the diverse charisms among the people of God. Paul VI's concept of the intermediary character of the diaconate should not, therefore, be understood as an additional barrier between the higher clergy and the laity. Instead, the diaconate as proposed by Paul VI is more like a bridge that binds the members of the local church more closely together in an ever greater communion.

This understanding of the deacon as mediator is apparent when Paul VI goes on to specify the diaconate as a structure to express the needs and desires of the Christian faithful, to animate the membership of the church to fulfill her obligation of charity, and to serve as a symbol of Christ the servant to all. If the diaconate were truly to serve the church in these ways, then the deacon would not merely be an additional rank-figure in the structure of power and authority between the bishop and priests on the one hand and the laity on the other. To the contrary, the notion of the diaconate as a *medius ordo* opens a new door for the articulation of the uniqueness of diaconal ministry among all others and how it could be a benefit to the church.

Paul VI's vision of the diaconate as a *medius ordo* finds acceptance in the recent document on the permanent diaconate from the Congregation for Catholic Education. Drawing on Paul VI's *Ad Pascendum,* the document *Basic Norms* gives a brief theological outline of the deacon's ministry:

> As a participation in the one ecclesiastical ministry, he is a specific sacramental sign, in the Church, of Christ the servant. His role is to "express the needs and desires of the Christian communities" and to be "a driving force for service, or *diakonia*", which is an essential part of the mission of the Church.[12]

The deacon's ministry flows from his being a sacramental symbol among the people of God. As a "specific" symbol of Christ the

---

12. Congregation for Catholic Education, *Basic Norms,* no. 5, pp. 24–25.

servant, the deacon's fundamental ministry is the support of the laity's participation in the apostolic mission of the church. This mission necessarily entails the corporal and spiritual works of mercy. As such, the deacon is expected to support and carry out in some manner the various charitable works of the church and thereby fulfill his role as a true servant of charity. Notice, however, that the deacon does not fulfill his obligations by simply doing these works himself; rather, he is to facilitate the participation of the people in this important enterprise of the church.

Furthermore, it is the deacon's task to "express the needs and desires of the Christian communities." What are the needs and desires that are to be expressed, and to whom are these needs and desires communicated? The answers to these questions lie in the conception of the diaconate as a structure for social mediation within the church.

Intermediate Social Structures

Sociologists tell us that intermediate institutions, which stand between the individual in his or her private life and the larger, more powerful institutions of public life, are necessary to bridge the gap between the individual and his or her social group. Power (as the *ability* to act) and authority (as the accepted *right* to exercise power) are spread throughout every social body—but not equally. Differences in power and authority engender the need for mediating structures, structures that help to "spread power around a bit more" and reduce social tensions.[13] Individuals bridge the division

---

13. P. Berger and R. Neuhaus, *To Empower People: The Role of Mediating Structures in Public Policy* (Washington, DC: American Enterprise Institute, 1977). Republished in *To Empower People: From State to Civil Society*, ed. M. Novak, 2nd ed. (Washington, DC: AEI Press, 1996), 164: "The theme is *empowerment*. One of the most debilitating results of modernization is a feeling of powerlessness in the face of institutions controlled by those whom we do not know and whose values we often do not share....The mediating structures under discussion here are the principal expressions of the real values and the real needs of people in our society....The paradigm of mediating structures aims at empowering poor people to do the things that the more affluent can already do, aims at spreading the power around a bit more."

between the two spheres of public and private successfully only when they have access to institutions mediating between the two spheres.[14] These mediating institutions help to bring the individual into the social world and the social world into the individual.

The usefulness of the diaconate as an intermediate structure within the church is magnified by our cultural context. Individualistic ideologies confront contemporary Americans with false and destructive opinions in almost every arena of their lives. The socialization of children into a competitive race for success raises them to seek out superficial relationships, to merely "get along with others" rather than form deep and enduring social ties. It is no wonder that a society dominated by utilitarian individualism will have trouble with traditional institutions, like marriage, that require sacrifice for the good of others.[15] The support of healthy institutions is needed to combat these strong societal forces that reinforce a tendency toward individualism. The exercise of responsibility for others is something we exercise as individuals, but only within and on behalf of institutions.[16]

Intermediate Structures in the Church

My reflection on the deacon as an intermediary figure should not be considered simply as a concession to sociological needs but as an instrument of the Spirit for the growth of the church in service to the gospel. The Second Vatican Council expressed its understanding of the relationship between the social structure of the church and her divine nature in the following manner:

---

14. Ibid., 159: "For the individual in modern society, life is an ongoing migration between these two spheres, public and private."

15. R. Bellah et al., *The Good Society* (New York: Vintage Books, 1991), 43: "Socialization in the middle-class family reinforces this pattern through its emphasis on doing well in school, being competitive (in sports as well as studies), and getting along with others. In family, leisure, school, and work the fine calculation of the relation of means to ends is emphasized, and this gives rise to the pattern 'of utilitarian individualism."

16. Ibid., 13.

Christ, the one Mediator, established and ceaselessly sustains here on earth His holy Church, the community of faith, hope, and charity, as a visible structure. Through her He communicates truth and grace to all. But the society furnished with hierarchical agencies and the Mystical Body of Christ are not to be considered as two realities, nor are the visible assembly and the spiritual community, nor the earthly Church and the Church enriched with heavenly things. Rather they form one interlocked reality which is comprised of a divine and a human element. For this reason, by an excellent analogy, this reality is compared to the mystery of the incarnate Word. Just as the assumed nature inseparably united to the divine Word serves Him as a living instrument of salvation, so, in a similar way, does the communal structure of the Church serve Christ's Spirit, who vivifies it by way of building up the body (cf. Eph. 4:16).[17]

In the complex reality of the church, priority is given to the supernatural dimension of the church. Her human dimension is in service to the divine. The thrust of this passage, however, does not emphasize a difference between the divine and human elements, but their unity. Instrumentally related to the Spirit, social structures are part of the very constitution of the church.

Furthermore, power within the church is different from that found in the civic order. Civic power has been defined as the ability to dominate or force others to act despite their resistance.[18] The philosopher Hannah Arendt, however, made the distinction between power and violence (force used against another) in the following way:

> *Power* corresponds to the human ability not just to act but to act in concert. Power is never the property of an individual; it belongs to a group and remains in existence only so long as

---

17. Vatican Council II, *Lumen Gentium*, no. 8.

18. See M. Weber, *The Theory of Social and Economic Organisation* (New York: Oxford University Press, 1947), and R. Adams, *Energy and Structure: A Theory of Social Power* (Austin: University of Texas Press, 1975).

the group keeps together. When we say of somebody that he is "in power" we actually refer to his being empowered by a certain number of people to act in their name.[19]

"Acting in concert" is the key element of Arendt's definition of power, connecting the harmonious activity of the community with the exercise of true power. In contrast to the sociological schools, which see the core of the phenomenon of power in making one's own will prevail even against opposition, Arendt rejects the notion that force or violence is the culmination of true power. In her perspective the origin of true power lies in the decision to act jointly. Thus the community, and not the individual, figures prominently in her conception of power.

The importance Arendt gives to the community in her definition has a certain affinity with the theology of power in the Gospel of John. In this Gospel, authority is not so much power over others but freedom from coercion. For example, Jesus' authority is revealed in his freedom to lay down his own life. The mission of Jesus is described in John as the work of a shepherd (John 10:11–18). Qualifying the image of the shepherd-ruler from the Old Testament, Jesus presented himself as the Good Shepherd, who lays down his life for his sheep: "For this reason the Father loves me, because I lay down my life in order to take it up again. No one takes it from me, but I lay it down of my own accord. I have power to lay it down, and I have power to take it up again. I have received this command from my Father" (John 10:17–18). Having the power and authority to lay down his life for his sheep implies his freedom to love his sheep. Power and authority in the Johannine concept are never separate from the service of love.

Although the Gospel of John never mentions Jesus commissioning others with power and authority over evil spirits (as in the Synoptic Gospels), the epilogue (chapter 21) includes a passage where Jesus invites Peter to become the shepherd of his flock. In the dialogue between Peter and the resurrected Jesus, we read of

---

19. H. Arendt, *On Violence* (New York: Harcourt, Brace & World, 1970), 44.

Peter's reparation for the threefold denial at Annas's house. Jesus is about to leave his sheep, so he entrusts his flock to Peter. He "first insists on the Johannine criterion of love, and then makes Peter a shepherd—but the sheep remain Jesus'."[20] The authority of Peter is therefore rooted in love. As a matter of fact, Peter is to manifest the love of the Good Shepherd by laying down his own life for Jesus' sheep. From the Johannine conception we can consider power as the intrinsic ability to love, and authority as the freedom to exercise that love. Pastoral authority, as in the image of Peter in the epilogue, has its basis in the pastoral authority of the Good Shepherd. Sharing in the authority of Jesus ultimately means sharing in his salvific love for others.

Authority and power in the New Testament therefore presuppose their responsible use: Authority is to be at the service of love in the Christian community. Those who hold pastoral authority can use it for either their personal benefit or for the good of the church. Domination is one way to exercise authority, but love is the Christian way. Saint Paul had this concern in mind when he wrote to the Christians of Rome and Corinth about the charisms they had received from the Holy Spirit.[21] As we turn our attention to the consideration of power and authority vested in the bishop and the laity, it is important that we keep before our eyes the ultimate objective—charity.

Echoes of the New Testament understanding of power and authority are found in the teachings of the Second Vatican Council. If power concerns the capacity to influence the thinking and behavior of a human community, then power in the church concerns the ability to bring about, influence, and sustain her life and mission.[22] Charisms from the Holy Spirit are what make everyone, from the newly baptized to the bishop, capable of actions that pertain to the spread of the gospel. Thus charisms are, in a very real sense, power.

---

20. Raymond Brown, *The Gospel and Epistles of John: A Concise Commentary* (Collegeville, MN: Liturgical Press, 1988), 103.

21. See 1 Corinthians 12 and Romans 12.

22. D. N. Power, "The Basis for Official Ministry in the Church," *Jurist* 41 (1981): 329.

The relationship between the ordained ministers and the laity is expressed in the link between baptism and Eucharist. Although the laity do not fulfill an ecclesiastical office by virtue of ordination, they nonetheless have their own place in the eucharistic assembly by virtue of their baptism. Relying heavily on the New Testament, the Second Vatican Council declared the following in *Apostolicam Actuositatem:*

> The Holy Spirit who sanctifies the People of God through the ministry and the sacraments gives to the faithful special gifts as well (see 1 Cor. 12:7), "allotting to everyone according as he will" (1 Cor. 12:11)....From the reception of these charisms or gifts, including those which are less dramatic, there arise for each believer the right and duty to use them in the Church and in the world for the good of mankind and for the upbuilding of the Church. In so doing, believers need to enjoy the freedom of the Holy Spirit who "breathes where he wills" (Jn. 3:8). At the same time, they must act in communion with their brothers in Christ, especially with their pastors. The latter must make a judgment about the true nature and proper use of these gifts, not in order to extinguish the Spirit, but to test all things and hold fast to what is good (cf. 1 Th. 5:12, 19, 21).[23]

Charisms are not limited to a select few in the church. Everyone has their own particular gift of power to be used for the benefit of the church's life and mission. This power includes the skills, talents, expertise, or whatever may allow someone to contribute to the single purpose for which the church exists—the communion of all humanity with God and one another. The laity are empowered by baptism to take their place in the eucharistic assembly, and the clergy are empowered by ordination to fulfill the offices given them. With these charisms comes authority, that is, the right to utilize them. The sacramental distribution of power and authority throughout the people of God gives every member the right to

---

23. Vatican Council II, *Apostolicam Actuositatem* (Decree on the Apostolate of the Laity, 1965), no. 3.

participate in the life and mission of the church according to their own charism.

The origin of these powers is the Spirit, who "blows where he wills." The bishop, however, has the power and authority, charism and office, to judge their nature and to order their use for their harmonious exercise. The ecclesiastical ministry of the bishop is directed to assist the fulfillment of roles that pertain to the laity. The bishop is not the channel through whom the various charisms are given to the people of God, but he is their principle of unity. In coordinating all other ministries and services, the bishop exercises decision-making power for their harmonious and fruitful exercise.

It is the *whole* church, in *all* its members, that continues and extends the mission of Jesus Christ, not just the ecclesiastical ministers. Consequently, Vatican II has given a prominent place to the themes of coresponsibility, cooperation, and participation by the people of God in the life and mission of the church. The inter-relationship between the ecclesiastical orders and the laity flows from the ecclesiology sanctioned by Vatican II: the church as the people of God.

With priests and deacons as their helpers, bishops receive the charge of the community, "presiding in place of God over the flock whose shepherds they are, as teachers of doctrine, priests of sacred worship, and officers of good order."[24] Bishops are to exhort and instruct their people "to know and live the paschal mystery more deeply through the Eucharist."[25] By counsel, persuasion, example, authority, and sacred power, the bishop governs the local church.[26] "Bishops are the principal dispensers of the mysteries of God, just as they are the governors, promoters, and guardians of the entire liturgical life in the church committed to them."[27] Thus, the authority and power of the episcopacy is ordered to the active participation of all the people of God in spreading the gospel of salvation.

---

24. Vatican Council II, *Lumen Gentium,* no. 20.

25. Vatican Council II, *Christus Dominus* (Decree on the Bishops' Pastoral Office in the Church, 1965), no. 15.

26. Vatican Council II, *Lumen Gentium,* no. 27.

27. Vatican Council II, *Christus Dominus,* no. 16.

The ministry of the bishop, however, is not a matter of giving orders down a chain of command. Though the council desired to firmly establish the dignity, power, and authority of the episcopacy, it equally emphasized the promotion of the laity in the life and mission of the church. Thus we read the council's call to bishops to be among their flock as "a good shepherd who knows his sheep and whose sheep know him."[28] Bishops, the council states, are to

> strive to become duly acquainted with their [the laity's] needs in the social circumstances in which they live. Hence, he ought to employ suitable methods, especially social research. He should manifest his concern for all, no matter what their age, condition, or nationality, be they natives, strangers, or foreigners. In exercising this pastoral care he should preserve for his faithful the share proper to them in Church affairs; he should also recognize their duty and right to collaborate actively in the building up of the Mystical Body of Christ.[29]

In order to fulfill their ministry well, bishops must acquire knowledge of the people whom they serve. Since knowledge is socially distributed throughout the social body,[30] it is appropriate for the bishop to utilize institutions that mediate knowledge of the various sectors of the church. These mediating structures are also necessary to stabilize the individual's personal connection to the larger church. Here we see a function for the diaconate as an intermediate structure between the bishop and the laity, if we assume that the deacon's role-specific knowledge concerns the needs and desires of the laity.

Bishops are not only to *be* concerned about the needs of the laity; they are also charged to "manifest [their] concern for all." The bishop is not simply an administrator: he is to be a shepherd. In his service to the communion of the church, the bishop is a concrete

---

28. Ibid.

29. Ibid.

30. Berger and Luckmann, *To Empower People: From State to Civil Society* (Washington, DC: AEI Press, 1996), 134: "No individual internalizes the totality of what is objectivated as reality in his society."

expression of the love of Christ for his sheep. The bishop is to be concerned for the people he serves, not simply for the sociological motive of legitimating his own authority, but to fulfill his task as a *diakonos* or ambassador of Christ. The intermediary role of the deacon could, therefore, include representing the bishop's care and concern to the people of God. This intermediary function of the deacon is different from other intermediate structures that exist in the church between the bishop and the laity, such as councils and synods. As a unique representative of the bishop, the deacon could mediate the bishop's care and concern for the individual members of his flock in a personal manner.

Intermediate structures are also necessary for the laity to participate in decisions that concern the life and mission of the church. The Second Vatican Council, following this line of thought, encouraged the use of institutions set up by the church for the laity to freely make their opinions known to the pastors, especially in matters in which the laity are competent.

> Every layman should openly reveal to them [their pastors] his needs and desires with that freedom and confidence which befits a son of God and a brother in Christ. An individual layman, by reason of the knowledge, competence, or outstanding ability which he may enjoy, is permitted and sometimes even obliged to express his opinion on things which concern the good of the Church. When occasions arise, let this be done through the agencies set up by the Church for this purpose. Let it always be done in truth, in courage, and in prudence, with reverence and charity toward those who by reason of their sacred office represent the person of Christ....
>
> Let them [bishops] willingly make use of his [the layman's] prudent advice....
>
> Attentively in Christ, let them consider with fatherly love the projects, suggestions, and desires proposed by the laity.[31]

The image of the church presented here is not that of a linear hierarchy but a family. As brothers and sisters in Christ, the laity

---

31. Vatican Council II, *Lumen Gentium,* no. 37.

are encouraged to speak up to their brothers who are bishops on matters that concern the good of the church. It is more than a right; it is an *obligation* for the laity to be actively engaged in the affairs of the church.

What is sought here for the laity is not the right to make a choice, but shared responsibility in decision making.

> The making of a choice is only one element in decision-making, and not always the most important element or the most influential. Decision-making, whether undertaken by an individual acting alone or by small groups or large communities, is a complex process; it involves several stages, only one of which is the making of a choice, and all of which entail the exercise of influence and power. To participate in the making of a choice is one way to share responsibility. It is a way that should, perhaps, be available to more people in the church than just those who hold ecclesiastical office.[32]

The various degrees of power operative in the church come together in the way decisions are made. It is not an issue of having an equal amount of power, but in having as many as possible productively contribute to decisions made for the good of the church and her mission.

In order to realize this objective, the relevant information necessary for participation must be shared with the laity. With the social distribution of knowledge, power is also, to a certain extent, shared.

> How could someone take part in an action with generosity and imagination if the relative facts escape him? How could the information be spread if the person possessing it did not agree to share his knowledge, that is, share too the responsibility of intervention which knowledge permits? Anyone who has knowledge can give his authoritative opinion and put forward

---

32. R. Kennedy, "Shared Responsibility in Ecclesial Decision-Making," *Studia Canonica* 14 (1980): 9.

an appropriate solution; by the very act of doing so, he shares to a certain extent in power.[33]

While participation in the decision-making process does not necessarily involve the right to make the final choice, it does nonetheless entail a real influence on how a decision is made, and influence is real power. As noted previously, Hannah Arendt described power as the ability of the community to act in concert. The exercise of power and authority, understood as communal and not simply possessed by individuals, necessitates intermediate structures to distribute the requisite knowledge for participation. A dialogical style of communication can do much to alleviate crises of the legitimation of authority within the church by increasing the number of channels through which a greater number of individuals would be involved in the decision-making process.

The council fathers of Vatican II envisioned an ideal situation where the bishop and laity formed a "familiar relationship" through shared responsibility. The benefits of such a relationship they described as follows:

> A great many benefits are to be hoped for from this familiar dialogue between the laity and their pastors: in the laity, a strengthened sense of personal responsibility, a renewed enthusiasm, and a more ready application of their talents to the projects of their pastors. The latter, for their part, aided by the experience of the laity, can more clearly and more suitably come to decisions regarding spiritual and temporal matters. In this way, the whole Church, strengthened by each one of its members, can more effectively fulfill its mission for the life of the world.[34]

By binding the bishop and the laity closer together in communion, structures that enhance the bishop's familiarity with the people are

---

33. G. Wackenheim, "Ecclesiology and Sociology," in *The Church as Institution,* Concilium 91, ed. G. Baum and A. Greeley (New York: Herder & Herder, 1974), 39.
34. Vatican Council II, *Lumen Gentium,* no. 37.

a benefit to the church as a whole. The laity, for their part, would be more personally engaged in the life of the church. The bishop, on his part, would receive assistance in making better decisions through the consultation of the expertise and wisdom of the laity. As a result, the church as a whole would be more effective in proclaiming the gospel to the world.

Conclusions

Pope Paul VI's conception of the diaconate as a *medius ordo* provides the local church with the ability to craft a suitable place within the organizational structure of the church that deacons can call their own. Being a sacrament of Christ, the deacon is empowered with special gifts of the Holy Spirit to strengthen the communion of the church by facilitating the relationship between the higher clergy and the laity, and by animating the laity to fulfill the command of Christ to "love one another." What, however, is the relationship of the diaconate to other institutions of social mediation within the church?

The necessity of social mediation has produced many other structures in the church apart from the diaconate, such as councils, synods, and undoubtedly many other offices that can and should be fulfilled by the laity. The deacon, however, is unique among them. The deacon functions both in a personal and symbolic manner. As a personal agent and promoter of charity among the people of God, the deacon performs his ministry in a stable, day-to-day manner. In this he is distinct from other periodic forms of mediation. Furthermore, in distinction to the laity, who can be empowered by the church to fulfill tasks akin to social mediation, only the deacon is a sacramentally configured icon of Christ.

The unique sacramental character of the deacon distinguishes him among the laity and the members of the other clerical orders. In the process of ordination, candidates for the order of deacon receive special charisms to be industrious imitators of our Lord.[35] With the reception of these gifts comes the obligation, on the part

---

35. See the Prayer for the Ordination of a Deacon: "Send forth upon him, Lord, we pray, the Holy Spirit, that he may be strengthened by the gift of your sevenfold

of deacons, to fulfill the ministry for which they are given and received. In ordaining candidates to the order of deacon, the local church obliges herself to utilize these gifts well.

Deacons are to be concrete manifestations of Christ among us, bearing the presence of Christ to those they meet in the everyday affairs of their ministry. Additionally, the deacons represent the diaconal dimension of the church as a whole. There is a need for this special sacramental presence among us. As the presence of bishops and priests reminds the assembly of its dependence upon Christ the Head, the presence of deacons reminds us of our dependence on Christ the Servant. Only by allowing Christ to serve us can we respond to his command to be self-emptying servants of one another.

The diaconate as *medius ordo,* however, presents several challenges to the diaconate in its current shape. First, the emphasis upon the deacon's liturgical roles in the context of a lack of priests requires a fundamental readjustment in how deacons are normally utilized by the church. If deacons continue primarily to fulfill liturgical functions in the parish, then their identity in the minds of clergy and laity alike will continue to be in reference to preeminent cultic figures, the priests. This does not necessarily mean that deacons need to give up their current liturgical functions in order to secure their own identity; it does mean, however, that deacons need to do *more* than serve as sacramental functionaries. Their liturgical service should be a reflection of what they do among the people of God outside of the liturgy. The success of the diaconate in our day depends upon the ability of deacons to fulfill roles of mediation in the everyday governance of the church by bishops and parish priests, as well as in the promotion of works of charity by the laity. The bishop, in consultation with the clergy and laity of his diocese, could discern particular tasks that the local church would

---

grace for the faithful carrying out of the work of the ministry. May there abound in him every Gospel virtue: unfeigned love, concern for the sick and poor, unassuming authority, the purity of innocence, and the observance of spiritual discipline," from *Rites of Ordination of a Bishop, Priests, and of Deacons,* 2nd typical ed. (Washington, DC: United States Conference of Catholic Bishops, 2003), 160–61.

deliberately reserve for the ministry of deacons as recognized mediators. This particularization of their ministry would allow the deacons over time to develop requisite skills and knowledge to become recognized experts in their field of specialty.

After discerning what is desired from diaconal ministry, the local church must turn its attention to the selection and formation of candidates. The author of the First Letter to Timothy desires that the "deacons" of his time be good role models, who were "dignified, not deceitful, not addicted to drink, not greedy for sordid gain," and "faithful" (1 Tim 3:8). These basic human qualities should apply to anyone holding an official position within the church, but especially to the those who are ordained. *Basic Norms* also highlights certain qualities for the deacon candidate that pertain more precisely to the function of social mediation. The capacity for dialogue and for communication are essential qualities for a social mediator. According to *Basic Norms,* candidates are to have the following qualities: "psychological maturity, capacity for dialogue and communication, sense of responsibility, industriousness, equilibrium and prudence,…capacity for obedience and fraternal communion, apostolic zeal, openness to service, charity towards brothers and sisters."[36] Men who are individualistic in their motivation and orientation do not make good candidates for the diaconate. As *Basic Norms* states, "A candidate who was excessively closed in on himself, cantankerous and incapable of establishing meaningful and serene relationships with others must undergo a profound conversion before setting off with conviction on the path of ministerial service."[37] The candidate should have an understanding of the church as organic and collegial, and lack sentiments of clericalism. Above all, candidates must have a clear understanding of the diaconate as an institution in service to the promotion of lay participation.

Similarly, the formation of candidates should be influenced by the character of service they will provide as deacons. Specialized training must supplement the basic training common to all candidates

---

36. Congregation for Catholic Education, *Basic Norms,* no. 32, p. 42.
37. Ibid., no. 67, p. 59.

for the diaconate. A candidate designated to serve in a hospital or prison, for example, will need training that differs from the training needed for a candidate to serve in an office of the chancery. In every diaconal ministry, however, the underlying character of the deacon's ministry requires that he be able to articulate the faith, be an effective communicator, and be a patient listener. Through the acquisition and development of skills necessary for diaconal ministry, the candidate will have internalized his new identity as a mediator among the people of God.

The deacon has symbolized, more or less, the servant nature of the church in every period of her history. Perhaps now more than ever, however, the church can use a sacramental manifestation of its corporate obligation of charity. With the impetus of the Second Vatican Council, the church has made a decisive turn toward the active participation of the laity. She could therefore use the service of a ministry that works to ensure the proper distribution of power, authority, love, and concern throughout the body of Christ. In an age where participation in the decision-making process is perceived as a basic right in society, and distrust of authority figures is only growing, the pastoral authority of the church could benefit from the service of a sacramental ministry specially designed to communicate the needs and desires of the Christian faithful. In the end, the church needs a diaconate appropriately structured to respond to the many cultural challenges that face the people of God today.

CHAPTER 5

The Deacon: Icon of the Sign of Hope

Dcn. Michael Ross, PhD

Introduction

Ever since the Second Vatican Council addressed the permanent diaconate, it has become well established in the literature that
deacons are called to service.[1] In distinguishing deacons from
priests, *Lumen Gentium* says they are ordained *non ad sacerdotum, sed*

---

1. Vatican Council II, *Lumen Gentium* (Dogmatic Constitution on the Church,
1964), no. 29, in Walter J. Abbott, SJ, ed., *The Documents of Vatican II* (New York: America
Press, 1966). In 1967 Paul VI issued his *Motu Proprio, Sacrum Diaconatus Ordinem,* which
clarified the council's call in *Lumen Gentium,* no. 29, for the restoration of the permanent
diaconate. In authorizing national episcopacies to proceed, and while setting down
norms for this restoration, the first indication the Holy Father gave of the vocation of
this discipline occurs in section II, no. 8, where he says that only young men should be
admitted to training "who have shown a natural inclination of the spirit to *service* of the
sacred hierarchy and of the Christian community" *(qui naturalem animi inclinationem ad
sacrae Hierarchiae et christianae communitatis ministerium ostenderunt).* This endorsement of
service is repeated in Paul VI, Apostolic Letter *Ad Pascendum* (August 15, 1972), *AAS* 64
(1972): 534, where Paul shows approvingly that it was the central dimension of the
ancient church's understanding of the diaconate. A series of works followed that promoted the idea of service. Among those were Robert Nowell, *The Ministry of Service:
Deacons in the Contemporary Church* (New York: Herder & Herder, 1968); Norman
Brockman, *Ordained to Service: A Theology of the Permanent Diaconate* (Hicksville, NY:
Exposition Press, 1976); Patrick McCaslin and Michael G. Lawlor, *Sacrament of Service: A
Vision of the Permanent Diaconate Today* (New York: Paulist Press, 1986); Timothy Shugrue,
Service Ministry of the Deacon (Washington, DC: Bishops' Committee on the Permanent
Diaconate, National Conference of Catholic Bishops, 1988).

99

ad ministerium ("not unto the priesthood, but unto a ministry of service").[2] The ecclesiastical meanings of *ministerium* include ministry, service, office, and duty. Given the language of *Lumen Gentium,* these various definitions have raised several questions about the roles that might be considered proper to the diaconate. Clearly, deacons are in ministry to the church, which is dedicated to the mission of Jesus Christ, but are they ordained to it, and if so, in what sense do they differ from priests, who are also ordained in the ministry of Christ, who is the servant of God? By virtue of their ordination they have duties, but what are they, and how do these duties differ from and agree with those of the priests? Christ is the definer, the first holder of the office of priest, prophet, and king, and as well its very being. Priests are ordained into this office in the church, *in persona Christi Capiti in Ecclesia* ("in the person of Christ, the head of the church"), but are deacons also ordained to this office in the church? Clearly, as *Lumen Gentium* paragraph 29 implies, (*non. . .sed*) their grade *(gradus)* of ordination is not the same as that of priests.[3] As canons 1008 and 1009 imply, through the sacrament of orders they are "constituted sacred ministers" but not in the same way or according to the same *gradus.*[4] The two orders, however, share a pri-

---

2. Vatican II, *Lumen Gentium,* no. 29. In 1998, the Congregation for Catholic Education and the Congregation for the Clergy jointly issued *Basic Norms for the Formation of Permanent Deacons* and *Directory for the Ministry and Life of Permanent Deacons* (Washington, DC: United States Catholic Conference). *The Joint Declaration* (p. 13), which precedes *Basic Norms* and *Directory,* locates the service of the deacon in the sacrament of orders along with that of the rest of the hierarchy, while *Basic Norms,* no. 5, citing Paul VI, *Ad Pascendum,* says the deacon's role is to be a "driving force for service." Meanwhile *Directory,* no. 22, says that the permanent deacon serves the hierarchy and the community of the faithful. The most recent and certainly the most important expression of this idea is the International Theological Commission (ITC), *From the Diakonia of Christ to the Diakonia of the Apostles* (Chicago: Hillenbrand Books, 2004), 3–6, 108–10.

3. See ITC, *From the Diakonia of Christ,* 109, which speculates that the permanent deacon might be called the *icona vivens Christi servi in Ecclesia* ("living icon of Christ, the servant in the Church"). I will return to this idea.

4. The Canon Law Society of Great Britain and Ireland, *The Code of Canon Law* (Grand Rapids, MI: Eerdmans, 1983), canons 1008, 1009. Canon 1008 says that "marked with an indelible character" they are "consecrated and deputed so that, *each according to his own grade,* they *fulfill in the person of Christ* the Head, the offices of teach-

mary calling to the same *sacrificial* service in the way of Jesus Christ. Making matters more complex, there is also the relationship of deacons to the laity, who along with the ordained hierarchy share in ministry, service, and office and who also have duties. How do deacons and the laity both differ and yet agree in the ways in which they advance the mission of Christ in his church?

There are two vexing problems here. On the one hand, there is the problem of identifying just *how* deacons share in the sacramentally ordained status of priests and are ordained into a different order though still configured to Christ and his mission. On the other, there is the question of how deacons differ from the laity by virtue of this ordination and yet can share with them the marital state and their vocations to the temporal world. Theologically speaking, deacons are located in an ordained order that relocates their being in the ministry of Christ and in their worldly vocations. They have a dual existence; one located in the church's sacrament of orders and the other in the demands, duties, and offices of the worldly domain. In this sense, as noted in Fr. McKnight's chapter (chapter 4), they are an ontological bridge—an intermediary—joining the two orders. In the contemporary stance of the church, this bridge is a "seamless" joining of the transcendence and immanence of God, who comes toward us. As Paul McPartlan says, the deacon is a "sign of [this] seamlessness."[5]

The Deacon and Service: The Traditional View

These conceptual problems, which have remained unresolved since the council, lead to the question that interests me in this essay. If deacons are the bridge that links the service of the priestly

---

ing, sanctifying and ruling, and so they nourish the people" (my italics). Canon 1009 makes clear that deacons, like priests, receive the sacrament by the imposition of hands, but that the prayer that consecrates their ordained status differs from that of priests and is specific to their grade.

5. Paul McPartlan, "The Permanent Diaconate and *Gaudium et Spes,*" *Briefing* 32 (April 2002): 3.

and lay states of being, is there a specific service unique to their state, and if so, what is it? Much of the literature that identifies the deacon with service specifies three realms. These are (1) service to the church, especially to bishops and their priests in liturgical and administrative functions; (2) service to the laypeople of God; and (3) service to the world. The theology of the latter two kinds of service has been conceived primarily as the service of charity, but service to the world, which is consistent with charity in the church, has received much less emphasis.[6] This theology of the ministerial service of the diaconate emphasizes that by working in these three realms, the deacon is a sign of the communion that joins all in the church to each other and the church to the world.[7]

Is the language that has dominated the theology of the diaconate since the Second Vatican Council, however, an adequate account of the theologically specific ways and degrees in which deacons witness to service? In my view it is not, and for several reasons. Taken together, these reasons demonstrate the absence of a coherent account of the deacon's service. Such an account requires the

---

6. A number of works stress this aspect of the service or ministry of the permanent deacon. See especially *Lumen Gentium,* no. 29; Vatican Council II, *Ad Gentes* (Decree on the Church's Missionary Activity, 1965), no. 16; and *Directory,* nos. 37, 38, which talk about the "*diaconia* of charit," as does Congregation for Catholic Education, *Basic Norms,* no. 7. William S. McKnight, "The Latin Rite Deacon: Symbol of Communitas and Social Intermediary among the People of God" (STD diss., Pontificium Athenaeum S. Anselmi, 2001), 74, 79, 81, emphasizes the intermediary roles of the permanent deacon between the bishop and the presbyterate and between the bishop and the community, roles that are intended to further the goals of unity and charity.

7. McKnight, "Latin Rite Deacon," 132–34, 226–30, 290–92, 347–55; Walter Kasper, "The Deacon Offers an Ecclesiological View of the Present Day Challenges in the Church and Society," a paper presented at the International Diaconate Center Study-Conference (Brixen, Italy, October 1997; available at www.deacons.net/Articles/Kasper_1997.htm), 9–10 from the 17-page online printout; Owen F. Cummings, *Deacons and the Church* (New York/Mahwah, NJ: Paulist Press, 2004), 14–21. See also from the collected papers of the 2004 conference of the National Association of Diaconate Directors, a paper delivered by Cummings, "Theology of the Diaconate: State of the Question" (St. Benedict, OR: Mt. Angel Seminary, 2004), 21, and in the book of that same title, *Theology of the Diaconate: The State of the Question* by Owen Cummings, William T. Ditewig, and Richard R. Gaillardetz (New York/Mahwah, NJ: Paulist Press, 2005).

deacon's service to be grounded in his own unique relationship to Christ as first servant of God.

In the older view, there is a tendency to assimilate the service of the clergy, including deacons, to the vocation of service all baptized persons share, but there is a problem with this understanding. The service to which the Holy Father, bishops, ordinary priests, and deacons are called is one and the same, insofar as it is ordered to the work of Christ in the world. The service of each of these, however, has its distinct *vocation*. To clarify what this means, Pope John Paul II described his vocation to the papal office as the servant of Christ, who is the servant of God. According to his model, therefore, the vocation of bishop is to be the servant of the servant of the servant of God, while priests are in service to bishops—and deacons to both. The pope's metaphor clarifies the point that while the ordained orders are called into service, their vocations to it are hierarchically arranged and assigned different service tasks.

These are degrees of service to Christ in three senses. First, they imply that each degree of servant is *subordinate* to the servant above him, that is, each is under *(sub)* the order or authority *(ordinis)* of the one above. Second, the sign of this status of being above or below is the degree of sacrifice each makes for God. *Degree* here does not mean amount of sacrifice. It means instead that the sacrifice of each is *ordered* to the one above. Christ is the servant of God directly in that he is sent on a mission by the Father for the redemption of all and serves this mission in perfect sacrifice to the wisdom and will of the Father. Pope, bishop, priest, and deacon are each indirectly subordinate to Christ and thus to the Father: the deacon through the priest, the priest through his bishop, and the bishop through the Holy Father. Even with this clarification, however, which distinguishes properly between service and the hierarchic order of vocations in the church, we still do not have a conceptual model of what is unique about the deacon's vocation of service.

Second, we need further theological clarification and development so as to distinguish better between diaconal liturgical and administrative service, coherently incorporating both. Since the Second Vatican Council, both kinds of service have become favorite

assignments of deacons and priests alike. Diaconal liturgical service contributes in its subordinate way to the eschatological coming
forward of the Christ into the temporality of his communion with
the people of God in the Mass, and in the sacraments of baptism
and marriage, over which deacons may preside. In the liturgy of the
Eucharist, however, deacons assist bishops and priests as they stand
in persona Christi doing what Christ instituted *them* to do in the
liturgies of the word and Eucharist. While it is certainly true to say,
as *Lumen Gentium* notes, that priests are the assistants of their
bishop in his office of sanctifier, it is also true that deacons are assistants of these assistants, and their vocation falls outside the ontol-
ogy of those who stand *in persona Christi*.[8]

Administrative service is located more clearly in the temporal domain and has the role of mediating the social interactions of
the people of God with the temporal dimension of the church's
mission to do the will of God through the Christ.[9] Though administrative functions performed by deacons directly for bishops
and/or for parish priests may from the human perspective carry
less prestige than liturgical ones, they fall even more so outside the
sacerdotum. In the traditional view of diaconal liturgical and administrative service, distinctions between the roles proper to deacons
and priests have been blurred too frequently.

The understanding of the service rendered to the laity of the
church is the third area that needs further theological reflection.
Service to the laity is complex because it bridges the subordinate and
sacrificial aspects given to bishops and priests and the common service of all three with leadership service to the laity. The diaconal form
of ministry is self-effacing as well as sacrificial. These two fit well
when rendered to Christ through the other ordained orders, but
there is a tension in the deacon's ministry when he serves the laity.
Service to the laity is widely promoted in the traditional view, but
without an adequate theology. In service to the laity, the deacon's
witness is self-effacing and sacrificial, and at the behest of bishops

---

8. Vatican Council II, *Lumen Gentium*, no. 21.
9. See McKnight, "Latin Rite Deacon," 201–57, 294–310, for a discussion of this
role of the permanent deacon.

and parish priests. He must also, however, lead the people of God in the ways of the Christ, who comes into the world to lead it out of its fallenness. Here, the deacon is called to *witness* sacrificial service directly as the leader Christ was. This leadership is delegated by the *sacerdotum,* but it operates with a certain independence in the secular arena. Thus the call to service creates a tension between secular leadership models, which rely so much on the acquisition and exercise of power and authority, and the eschatological model of the church, which says that leadership is exercised as witness, self-effacement, and living without the trappings of power and authority. The traditional view often seems unaware of these tensions, which may be the cause of role confusions that have appeared in parishes where deacons work closely with the laity.

These tensions are intensified because the deacon owes so much to the world and is drawn almost inexorably against his will to live for its sake rather than for the kingdom. The temptations of the principalities and powers (Rom 8:38) for whom he may well work pull the deacon between his civil duties, which are often defined without reference to the needs of the kingdom, and his duties in the church, which though not the kingdom itself are the herald and harbinger of it. The deacon draws most of his well-being from the world through his family (if he has one), his source of income, and his circle of friendships and associates. His primary reference groups are likely to be living a more thoroughly secular existence than are those of bishops and priests. The social, spiritual, and even familial referents of bishops and priests are, and are supposed to be, other bishops and priests. Thus, unlike the other ordained orders, whose well-being centers on and draws its sustenance from the benefits given in and by the church, the deacon lives more so in the world, while also in the church, and draws his well-being from both. Despite this fact, however, he is called to be no more *of* the world than his fellow clerics.

Thus, liturgically and administratively, the deacon serves the Christ in subordination to bishops and priests, but he also serves the lay people of God through his sacrificial and self-effacing witness as a leader of their efforts to witness as well. In the liturgy, the deacon is not the sign of the being of Christ *(in persona Christi)* but the *icon* of the sacrificial servant of all in the church who come to the altar of God to receive the sustenance of temporal and eternal life. As an administrator of the church's temporal goods, the deacon is called to exercise skills that have been very likely honed in the circumstances of worldly power and authority, but to use them for the sake of the kingdom and especially for the sake of the laity. This account clarifies the traditional view, but it still leaves diaconal service without a comprehensive conceptual basis.

A fourth area calling for more profound research and reflection emerges when one considers the vocation of charity. This service is in the first instance something the deacon is expected to offer to the laity of the church. It too should be offered in self-effacement and sacrifice, and it is expressed in a great variety of specific activities, especially in pastoral care for the sick, the dying, and the imprisoned. The service of charity is also supposed to include traditional ministries of social justice, such as promoting the peaceful resolution of international disagreements, feeding the poor, and working for humane housing and employment opportunities for all. Often overlooked in this catalog of social ministries, but equally if not more important, are ministries that seek to protect the innocent lives of the unborn, young children, and the elderly, whose vulnerability is endangered by the indifference of modern culture.

All of these forms of service are certainly opportunities for the grace of Christ to purify the church in its worldly journey, but what, theologically speaking, does the deacon bring to these efforts besides his worldly skills? Bishops and their presbyters are called to work for the same charity in the church,[10] and the laity are uniquely called to it even more so.[11] Can we, however, say that this ministry is limited to the charity needed by the people of God alone? Does the servant of God come into the world to heal only those who know him in faith and thus to offer redemption to them

---

10. See Vatican Council II, *Presbyterorum Ordinis* (Decree on the Ministry and Life of Priests, 1965), no. 9.

11. See Vatican Council II, *Lumen Gentium,* nos. 13, 14, 32; Vatican Council II, *Apostolicam Actuositatem* (Decree on the Apostolate of the Laity, 1965), nos. 3, 8.

alone, or is this love of God, expressed in Christ's sacrificial service, offered to all in this life? Here too, then, there is need for a theological clarification of diaconal service.

Service and Hope: An Alternate View

The resolution of these as yet fully developed trajectories can only be found in a clarification of where the deacon stands, through his sacramental ordination, in the life of Christ. If it is the case, as *Lumen Gentium* paragraph 29 states, that the deacon is ordained *non ad sacerdotum, sed ad ministerium,* he certainly shares with priests an ordination into the life and meaning of Christ. As *From the Diakonia of Christ* says, the deacon is ordained *ad ministerium* but in the special sense that he is *icona vivens Christi servi in Ecclesia.*[12] Along with the priest, the deacon shares in the life of Christ as well as his service, albeit through his subordination to the other orders; but, uniquely he is the living icon of that service.

Christ is the sacrament of God given to the world so that through, with, and in him we might be brought into the life of God and in turn bring that life to the world. As this sacrament, Christ is the sign of God's love and the offer of hope to a tired and broken world. He is God's sacramental sign of hope because his fully human face *(res sacramentum)* leads us into the life of God and begins to bring into being that life *(ex opere operatum)* in this life wherever faith in him is present. This hope is first of all a share in the coming glory of God (Rom 5:2) initiated in the advent of the salvation of Christ (Rom 8:20). Hope in Christ is also the hope that all of "creation itself will be set free from its bondage to decay and will obtain the freedom of the glory of the children of God" (Rom 8:21). The realization of this hope and the freedom it brings begins in every earthly *now* where Christ's way is revered and imitated. This now is always the *not yet* of earthly being, which is driven through faith in Christ to look toward fulfillment, not passively,

---

12. ITC, *From the Diakonia of Christ,* 109.

but through grace-inspired action. This imitation is an enactment that anticipates the fulfillment of all hope in the eternal then.[13]

The sacred priesthood, first in the Holy Father and in the bishops of the world, and second in the diocesan and religious order priests, is through the actions of the episcopal order consecrated by Christ, who is the sacrament of that consecration. The priesthood of Christ is a sign of Christ's service given as his mission by the Father for the sake of the world. This service or *diakonia* is really a *doulou* (Phil 2:7), a free slavery to the wisdom and will of the Father. In this sense, God gifts himself as a *donum gratia* ("free gift") in slavery through his Son, who is the messenger of the gift, the gift itself, and the giver of the gift.

What is this gift? It is many transcendent and eschatological graces, but it is always, as Saint Paul says, the virtues of faith, hope, and charity (1 Cor 13:13). All three are borne by the Christ through the episcopacy and the presbytery. Saint Paul insists that charity is the greatest of these gifts of God. We might, however, say that the virtue of hope is the special gift borne by the diaconate in its mission of service, whether this service is liturgical or administrative, subordinate to bishops or priests, given in charity to the laity of the church for the sake of the kingdom, or offered to the whole world. Expanding the language of the International Theological Commission, we can say that the deacon is ordained in and acts as *icona vivens Christi servi qui est signum spei in Ecclesia ad mundoque* ("living icon of Christ the servant, who is the sign of hope in the Church and to the world").[14]

The religious connotations of the word *icon* help to elucidate the theology of diaconal service. An icon is an image painted or

---

13. See Josef Pieper, *Faith, Hope, Love* (San Francisco: Ignatius Press, 1997), 89–138, for the most important reflections on hope in the postconciliar period. Pieper emphasizes that Christ is the foundation of hope (105–6). He also stresses the nexus of the orientation toward fulfillment, the anticipation of it and fulfillment itself (93). For a discussion of the impact of Pieper's reflections, see Bernard Schumacher, *A Philosophy of Hope: Josef Pieper and the Contemporary Debate on Hope*, trans. D. C. Schindler (New York: Fordham University Press, 2003).

14. ITC, *From the Diakonia of Christ*, 109.

formed as a mosaic on wood. This image is usually a sacred figure, such as a saint, or a scene from scripture, and it is rendered stylistically, rather than in a realistic way, to emphasize its symbolic meaning. The artist who makes an icon is usually anonymous so that a viewer's religious attention is drawn into its symbolic meaning and is not diverted to the person or reputation of the artist. The reverence given to icons, which are widely used in Eastern Orthodox churches,[15] is to the symbolic meaning of the images, not the images themselves. It is as if the worshipper's religious attention and action, prompted by the icon, pass through the image itself into the noumenal world that is represented by it. Thus, an icon is a bridge that connects the worldliness of the believer with the transcendent focus of the believer's attention and action.

The anonymity of the icon's creator is expressed by the self-effacement of the deacon. As he lives the sacrificial service of Christ, he deflects attention away from himself toward the mission of service to which he and the laity are called. The meaning of the icon is expressed in the active witness that the deacon gives, which symbolizes to the laity Christ's actions. The reverence and action prompted by the icon are displayed in the sacrificial devotion to service that the deacon witnesses. The laity who follow the lead of the deacon are devoted not to him but to the mission of Christ, which he represents through his actions. It is here that the hope that is Christ, which he offers in his self-offering, is communicated. The deacon's actions connect those who follow his witness *not to him but through him* into the transcendent hope that they symbolize. By his servant actions in the world he connects the laity, among whom he lives, with the hope that Christ offers. He bridges this hope so that it is expressed and enacted in the world but in anticipation of its noumenal fulfillment. As Josef Pieper notes, there is a

---

15. It is interesting to note that in Greek Orthodox churches, an *iconostasis* is a screen or wall covered with icons that separates the sanctuary from the nave. The *iconostasis* has three doors: one is located in the center and is for the main celebrant, a second is on the left and connects the sanctuary with the chamber where the gifts are prepared, and the third is on the right and is called the *diakonikon,* which connects the sanctuary with the sacristy where the deacons vest.

positive, concrete side that anticipates this fulfillment. It is based in our orientation to the noumenal and is revealed in our ability to initiate by our own effort, presuming always unmerited grace "the possibility of meritorious action, which has the character of genuine 'progress.'"[16] Also, as the bridge between the church and the world, he does not suffocate the service to which all the laity are called[17]—far from it. Because he is the icon of the Christ's hope, an icon that is never revered itself, but is instead the channel through which reverence is offered, he opens up new possibilities for the laity to offer themselves in the loving service to the neighbor that Christ initiates.

The deacon's service is expressed in his liturgical and administrative actions but even more so in his ministry of charity. The various ministries of charity that have developed in recent years have not been adequately located in a theological tradition that gives them coherence and unites them under the banner of the hope that Christ brings to the world. This hope is first of all the possibility of intimate union with God obtained after the *parousia* in the beatific vision. This relationality to God is shrouded in the mystery of salvation and offers to the faithful a possibility of fulfillment that escapes the suffering and finitude of earthly life. Christ's hope is also, however, realized in the gradual maturing of the kingdom as his will for human flourishing is accomplished through human actions that conform to it.

Christ's hope is the salve that eases the suffering that can be overcome, but of course not all suffering is invincible. Biomedical death certainly cannot be defeated, though it is vincible through faith in Christ's triumph over mortality. There is much about dying,

---

16. Pieper, *Faith, Hope, Love,* 93–94. Pieper (105) notes that "hope, as a virtue, is something wholly supernatural," and that "man's innate capability plays a role in the gaining of that for which he hopes." This is an *ipse habitus spei* ("very habit of hope"), and as a supernatural virtue it is infused "solely from grace." In this sense, transcendent hope is the incentive for the acquired virtues, like courage and justice that implements hope in the earthly context, Pieper suggests.

17. Paul McPartlan, "The Permanent Diaconate: Catholic and Ecumenical Perspectives," *Briefing* 32 (April 2002): 14–15.

however, as there is about disease and neglect, that is vincible.[18] There is also much worldly suffering, in addition to the reality of death and dying, for which transcendent hope is an antidote. This hope energizes suffering humanity and intensifies the will to prevail. When it is implemented in human actions that mimic what Christ did in his personal sacrifice for others, it can conquer redeemable suffering. Suffering caused by the natural conditions of a fallen world, and the suffering created by some for others, is vincible by human wisdom and the actions it can support. The role of social knowledge and worldly skills as instruments for the alleviation of defeasible suffering cannot be underestimated. The deacon, ordained into the service of Christ, who is the sign of hope, has these resources and countless others that come from his experience as a man of the world. When harnessed to the hope that Christ brings, the deacon becomes an icon of that hope. It is precisely in this role of a living icon of Christ the servant, who is the sign of hope in the church and to the world, that the deacon's service emerges.

Hope, Service, and the Church's Social Teaching

The theology of the church's witness to the service that offers the hope that vincible suffering will be conquered is contained most extensively in the modern tradition of Catholic social teaching, begun by Pope Leo XIII in *Rerum Novarum* (1891), which for more than one hundred years has addressed in a complex and nuanced way this active service in the church and to the world. This tradition, which by now includes nine encyclical letters, the results of multiple synods of bishops, and the countless documents issued by national episcopal conferences, provides a rich tapestry

---

18. Physical pain associated with the diseases of natural dying, and even more so the suffering and pain of the diseases caused by human beings to themselves and others, is all defeasible. The church fully embraces the merciful alleviation of such pain and suffering just as much as it supports the defeat of the natural and the human causes themselves of human affliction.

of theological ideas and active vocations into which the service of hope can be located.[19]

The documents that advance the modern social teachings of the church contain numerous themes that fit well with the deacon's service of hope.[20] Among these I call attention especially to the defense and promotion of freedom, to justice and the common good, to solidarity, and finally to subsidiarity. That these themes in the mosaic of Catholic social thought are integrally related to the vocation of hope is evident. Freedom is hope realized, justice is the comfort that hope seeks, the common good is the wish of hope that all share in its benefits, solidarity is hope standing by others in their striving for its benefits, and subsidiarity is the locus of hope when it enters deeply into the lives of the people of God living in the world. The deacon's location in the church among the ordained, and yet living deeply in the world with the laity, equips him especially to be the iconic bridge of these themes.

Freedom in this Catholic mosaic cannot be solely identified with modern constitutional liberty or with the secular freedoms or rights they have spawned in contemporary social life, though it does not exclude them. This narrow concept of freedom is about having the right to personally develop and make choices between options within a system of laws that protects everyone so entitled. This *freedom to,* also called *autonomy,* cannot be the whole of freedom because it fails to locate the choices one makes in ends of human flourishing that exist apart from the particular choices one might or might not make.[21] As it has come to prevail in the contemporary world, human flourishing consists just in the option to choose and in the choices one makes.

---

19. See E. Christian Brugger, "Introduction to Catholic Social Teaching," *Josephinum Journal of Theology* 11, no. 2 (Summer/Fall 2004): 182–215, for a recent attempt to distill the essential themes in this tradition. Brugger identifies twelve such themes.

20. All references to these documents come from David J. O'Brien and Thomas A. Shannon, ed., *Catholic Social Thought: The Documentary Heritage* (Maryknoll, NY: Orbis, 1998).

21. See John Paul II, *Veritatis Splendor* (The Splendor of the Truth) (Boston: St Paul, 1999), nos. 38–41, for a discussion of freedom as autonomy.

In the Catholic view, however, this choice making only contributes to flourishing if the ends chosen *originate* in the divine will
for the human person and have their *terminus* in it. The deception
of freedom *to* is that it believes only in itself, which is why it fools
itself into believing that the opportunity to make choices and the
choices it makes are goods in themselves. In a sense, an exclusive
emphasis by contemporary life on freedom to make oneself what
one wants to be is an immature belief that life somehow is an
escape from discipline. Discipline in this world view is seen as an
impediment to fulfillment, but the origin of the idea is in the
Greek word *askēsis,* from which the idea of asceticism originates.
Originally, the word meant the exercises, practices, and training
required for a person to fulfill a mode of life, profession, or art.
The point is that the freedom to choose is never free of a mode of
life, however much one might deceive oneself. In fact, freedom to
choose is only realizable within a pattern of exercises that are
external to it and determine its ends. All who dedicate themselves
to some end by making a free choice to pursue it know that they
must fit into a larger structure or discipline. By itself, however, the
freedom *to* can never realize human hope.

When freedom *to* is integrated into freedom *of, for,* and *from,*
however, it becomes a vital ingredient in the realization of hope.
Freedom *of* refers to such opportunities in civil society as speech,
association, action, and worship (or nonworship), which make all
other freedom possible. These freedoms are guaranteed in modern
constitutions because they are the instrumental opportunities that
push forward the possibility that hope can be realized in the life
spans of human beings. Christians welcome this form of freedom
because it allows the acquisition of the virtues of human action that
are necessary for the anticipation of the kingdom of hope.
Meanwhile, freedom *for* is freedom for the sake of others. It has the
opposite trajectory of freedom *to* because it looks outward toward
otherness. It seeks the good that is external to ourselves and that is
given to us. It can serve the well-being of the self as well as that of
others, because it is at the same time heteronomous. If one locates
the ends of autonomous freedom in the otherness of the divine

image for all persons—an image that reflects God's absolute and ordered freedom—then those ends will serve both oneself as well as others. Autonomous freedom only has value for human flourishing when it is located within the kind of freedom that John Paul II called the "participated theonomy."[22]

Freedom *from* is freedom from the causes of despair, which is *hope-lessness.*[23] These causes are forms of spiritual, material, and psychological oppression. It is evident that freedom from these conditions is essential for the emerging realization of hope. We need only turn to the beatitudes to understand this connection. Beatitude is a state of fulfillment in which the blessings of God are comprehended and received.[24] It is also, however, a state that is anticipated and worked toward in imitation of the Christ, who announces God's blessings to the world.

The two accounts of the beatitudes in Matthew (5:3–12) and Luke (6:20–23) identify the blessings that Christ brings into the lives of his followers. In Matthew's Gospel these blessings convey spiritual happiness and promise the hope of a reward that will be great in heaven. Luke's Gospel emphasizes blessings of a more material nature and offers the same promise of a great eternal reward. Both stress that these blessings will begin to be received in this life even if their final fulfillment is eternal. In Matthew, the poor in spirit receive the blessings of the kingdom of heaven, those who mourn will be comforted, the meek will inherit the land, and the merciful will be shown mercy, all because Christ is already among us. In Luke, the poor receive the kingdom of God and those among them who are hungry will be satisfied, while the weeping will laugh. In both accounts hope is brought to those who are blessed, because their condition of suffering is addressed by the Christ, who has come into their lives. In Christ they see and are blessed to live in the kingdom of freedom *from.*

---

22. Ibid., no. 41. John Paul II used this term as an alternative to the idea of heteronomy. It meant for him "man's free obedience to God's law."

23. See Pieper, *Faith, Hope, Love,* 113–17, for a discussion of despair.

24. Ibid, 92.

The deacon is the bridge into this kingdom. With one foot in the sacramental order and the other in the world, he images all the freedoms that lead to hope. He can lead the way in not succumbing to the temptations of freedom to choose by affirming his vocation to the divine good. He takes advantage of civil freedoms in order to develop his skills and talents, which he freely enacts for the sake of others. Moreover, his sacramental character orients his vocation to the defeat of vincible want and despair. He is a man whose character, marked by the transcendence of the Christ of God, dedicates him to the virtues that anticipate and promote freedom from. In all these respects, the deacon is the icon of Christ in his own actions and as the witnessing image who may well draw many who encounter him into the imitation of Christ.

Justice is the comfort for which hope strives, and the common good is the hope that all will share in its benefits. Catholic social ethics speaks of three kinds of justice: commutative, distributive, and social. Commutative justice governs the relationships between individuals and groups in society. It is exercised by the state as a neutral referee and reconciles claims that private parties make against each other. It oversees the implementation of contracts ensuring that parties to them fairly receive the exchanges of goods for which they contract with each other. Distributive justice is also exercised by the state. It governs the relationships private individuals and groups have with the public authority. In modern Catholic social documents, this authority has the responsibility to ensure that social advantages and disadvantages are distributed fairly, that is, according to the principles of equity. These hold that all individuals receive whatever is considered to be their due by the social order of which they are part. They also demand that individuals similarly situated in society receive like advantages and disadvantages. The outcomes of distributive justice are to ensure that the conditions prevail in society such that all have access to the means to advance their own welfare according to the system of rules by which social goods are distributed, and that abiding by these rules is beneficial and breaking them is not. The term "social justice" was used for the first time in the modern social encyclicals by Pius XI in *Quadragesimo Anno*.[25] Here and elsewhere in the tradition, the documents understand social justice to be those conditions in which excessive differences in the distribution of goods are avoided. Excessive concentrations of wealth and poverty as between social groups or classes, a term also used by Pius XI in *Quadragesimo Anno*, is anathema to these conditions.

The deacon finds himself immersed in the conditions of all three forms of justice in ways that more closely resemble those of the laity than of his brother ordained. Like priests and the laity he is subject to the ways in which the state handles commutative and distributive justice, but he lacks the financial and legal protections afforded bishops and priests by their sacramental connection to the church. He is ordained, as they are, but his *gradus* leaves him, like the laity, more or less on his own to defend his rights. He is protected only to the extent that his circumstances in life, his employment, and his network of family and friends afford him protection and support. In other words, he images in his own life the conditions of vulnerability shared with the laity, while at the same time he iconically witnesses to the defense of the vulnerable in his actions on their behalf, actions that he shares with priests.

If the common good is to be the end of justice, the conditions must prevail that allow all members of a society to advance their welfare. The common good is variously defined in the social encyclicals and in *Gaudium et Spes*.[26] Its elements are as follows: All human beings have needs essential to their spiritual and material flourishing; these needs are grounded in human creation; they are imaged in the creator God; and they are privileged by the Christ, who is the first born of mankind and therefore the universal form

---

25. Pius XI, *Quadragesimo Anno* (On Reconstruction of the Social Order, 1931), nos. 57, 110. The phrase also appears in the encyclical *Iucunda Sane* by Pius X (On Pope Gregory the Great, 1904) and in a letter of social concerns by Pius XI, *Quando Nel Principio* (1923). See B. Kettern, "Social Justice: The Development of the Concept of 'iustitia' from St. Thomas Aquinas through the Social Encyclicals," in David A. Boileau, ed., *Principles of Catholic Social Teaching* (Milwaukee, WI: Marquette University Press, 1998), nn. 133, 134.

26. Vatican Council II, *Gaudium et Spes* (Pastoral Constitution on the Church in the Modern World, 1965), no. 26.

of humanity. The common good also holds that the needs of some are not intrinsically preferable to those of others. It requires that within the constraint of limited available goods, when these are distributed, the needs of all are satisfied. Here too the deacon is the icon of hope, because in his service to the lay people of God and to the world he seeks to draw everyone without favor or preference to the Christ, who is the sign of hope for all and not just the few.

In these communal actions, the deacon is the servant leader of people in solidarity with the Christ. Being in and so much of the world, he bridges the earthly yearning for communion with the Christ of God and the sacramental order in which that yearning finds its solace. This demonstrates the solidarity of the church and its sacramental origins in Christ with the yearning of the world for betterment.[27] It also, however, concretely signals that the deacon lives and works in and among the vulnerabilities of the laity in a way that enables him to understand their worries and joys. The unique opportunity to identify with the nonordained and to sacramentally lead them from the basis of an intimate and shared connection is something that priests cannot achieve, which is why the diaconate is so essential to the ministry of the church.

Finally, there is subsidiarity.[28] This is the idea that higher orders of social, political, and economic action should not subjugate lower orders of activity but encourage them to function when they can and protect their autonomy when they cannot, always with the common good in mind. This principle of localism fits perfectly the vocation of deacons. They are the ecclesial instruments through which the universal church is always present locally. Deacons are not usually moved from one community to another like priests, unless they excardinate. They are not moved upward in the hierarchy to become bishops. Ordinarily, they remain for their entire ministry attached to a local parish community. They are

---

27. See John XXIII, *Pacem in Terris* (Peace on Earth, 1963), nos. 98–100, 121; Paul VI, *Populorum Progressio* (On the Development of Peoples, 1967), no. 17; John Paul II, *Solicitudo Rei Socialis* (On Social Concerns, 1988), no. 38.

28. See John Paul II, *Centesimus Annus* (On the Hundredth Anniversary of *Rerum Novarum,* 1991), no. 48.

permanent servants of an ecclesial and a civic community, and through their servant actions they image the preference of the church that human needs be addressed and satisfied in them.

As the icon of the sign of the hope who is the Christ of God, the deacon is called to *sacramentalized* action in the church and in and for sake of the world. He witnesses for the rest of the church and for the peoples of the world wherever he ministers the call to action urgently announced by Paul VI in *Octogesima Adveniens.*[29] There, the Holy Father says that the church has several functions: first, to "enlighten minds" about the truths of social life; second, to envision creative and innovative solutions; third, to develop a disinterested will to serve the poorest; and finally, to "take part in action and to spread, with a real care for service and effectiveness, the energies of the gospel."[30]

Conclusion

As I have shown in this chapter, the deacon is uniquely ordained and situated in the church and in the world, in the transcendent and in the worldly orders—as the bridge and intermediary between the two—to "enlighten minds" and to be the icon of a "real care for service and effectiveness." His ordained status in the ministry of Christ, integrally combined with his worldly vocation, anchors the life of the deacon. It gives meaning to his service in the church to his fellow clerics and to the laity, and to his service to the world. As the living icon of the hope that Christ offers to the world that vincible suffering will be overcome, the deacon's charitable activities, so widely attributed to his role in the church by theologians in the past half-century, assume a deeper meaning that resolves the inadequacies of the traditional post–Second Vatican Council accounts of the deacon's witness to service.

---

29. Paul VI, *Octogesima Adveniens* (On the Eightieth Anniversary of *Rerum Novarum,* 1971), nos. 48–52.
    30. Ibid., no. 48.

CHAPTER 6

The Moral Life of the Deacon

Dcn. James Keating, PhD

The Sacramental Identity of the Deacon

In any virtue ethic, a person's character is formed by aligning one's actions with the moral truth so as to reflect one's inherent human dignity. Tending to the development of character, by enacting the diaconal duties to which virtue calls, is crucial to becoming a saint. Beyond this, the identity of the deacon as a sacramental sign of the servant-church gives some direction to the ethic he must live. Further, in the case of most deacons today, the sacramental reality of ordination must also be integrated with the sacramental reality of marriage. Within these two Christ-centered callings—marriage and diaconate—the deacon strives to be open to the moral truth as it is formed within him by practicing the vocational duties to which virtue and judgments of conscience call. The sacramental life of the deacon (sacraments of initiation and the sacrament of reconciliation), and his own sacramental identity as cleric and husband, becomes the essential source from which he draws spiritual power and, in so doing, makes himself available as *servant*.

The virtue of the deacon is formed within him by his deep participation in the life, death, and resurrection of Christ. What, then, is unique to the deacon, since this participation is the grace of all Catholics? In the deacon the Lord is invited to live his *servant mysteries* most particularly. The deacon desires to become vulnerable to the moral truths found within the foot-washing at the Last

Supper, as recounted in the Gospel of John, wherein the Christ becomes the servant. In the same manner that the priest desires to be configured to the life-giving reality of crucifixion and Christ's radical self-offering upon the cross (witnessing Christ as priest), and in the same manner that the layperson becomes a sign of moral and theological truth in and through public witness (witnessing Christ as prophet), so the deacon offers himself to be inhabited by the mystery of Christ's own paradoxical kingship: "I am among you as one who serves" (Luke 22:27).[1]

In a way, the deacon is called to symbolize the coming kingdom; he is an eschatological sign, not empowered with his own gifts and strength of will but infused with the power of Christ living his mysteries over again in and through diaconal ministry. Thus, the deacon looks to serve, placing the needs of others before his own and so testifying to the vocation of the whole church as it strains to be completed in Christ, the perfect man (Eph 4:13). In this servant-kingship the deacon takes the low place, as did Jesus in washing the feet of his disciples. What does it mean to be configured to the kingly servanthood of Christ?

Pope John Paul II noted that

> there are two degrees of ministerial participation in the priesthood of Christ; the Episcopacy and the Presbyterate. The Diaconate is intended to help them...yet [the degree of priestly participation and the degree of service] are all conferred by a sacramental act called ordination....In the sacrament of holy orders [*Catechism*, no. 1554]...the deacon receives a particular configuration to Christ...who for love of the Father made himself the least and servant of all (Mk 10:43–45, Mt 20:28, 1 Pet 5:3)....Deacons are ordained to exercise a ministry of their own, which is not

---

1. Here I am simply emphasizing the threefold office of Christ as it is underscored in these vocations; I recognize that these three identities unfold in various ways in all Christian vocations. The model of deacon as "king" has to be understood within the ironic and paradoxical statements from Jesus on the nature of leadership, for example, "Whoever wishes to be great among you must be your servant, and whoever wishes to be first among you must be your slave" (Matt 20:26–27).

that of a priest....The deacon is not a profession but a mission....By virtue of ordination [the grace of the diaconate] is
defined by the spirit of service....To fulfill his mission the
deacon needs a deep interior life.[2]

Specifically, then, this vocation to embody the paradoxical servant-
leader is lived out by the deacon in his identity as a "mission" and
by means of a "deep interior life."

Mission

How should we understand that the deacon is a mission? In
being a mission, the deacon points toward the central ethical task
of the church: embodying the spiritual and corporeal works of
mercy that are executed out of the power of the paschal mystery.
Here we approach the key diaconal virtue within the context of his
sacramental life and identity: the deacon possesses a dispositional
eagerness to serve. The deacon is disposed toward availability; he is
eager to be available for the needs of others. He is constituted in
this way by his ordination and, if married, by his husbanding
virtues, for both of these ways of being a disciple lead to eager
openness. He asks, "How may I help you?" In a real way the deacon
is entrusted with the office of service, so that in him the culture
can see the manifestation of Christ's own availability in and through
this bishop's emissary. Even if a great portion of the church's members no longer engaged in acts of service, the deacon alone, sus-
tained by his participation in the liturgy, would embody the hope
of service. Such service for the salvation of others is near the core
of the ecclesial mystery.

The core of the diaconal vocation, then, is to be sent to serve.
It is not a lifestyle, as one would have in a religious order or even
within the celibate priesthood. The deacon exists so as to enact the
church's mission of service deep within the secular culture. He
achieves such a depth because the deacon does not normally draw

---

2. John Paul II, "Deacons Are Configured to Christ the Servant" (November 30,
1995), nos. 3, 4; available at www.ewtn.com/library/PAPALDOC/JP951130.HTM.

his livelihood from ecclesial employment.[3] Rather, in normal circumstances most deacons seemingly lead the life of a layperson. He is sent to the culture not in a prophetic way, per se, but to be a servant of the gospel within the world, bridging altar and culture. The deacon's service is of course directed toward the poor—any and all poor, meaning anyone in *need*—by attending to them spiritually, economically, intellectually, and socially. This service is also directed toward the needs of the bishop. Through the authority of the bishop, in whose ministry the deacon partakes at a level consistent with diaconal ordination (that is, not at a priestly level), the deacon is sent by Christ to serve. The deacon's mission is the mission of the bishop as it is particularly configured in service. The deacon, like the priest, has an authentic ministry in its own right, but it is one that flows from his ordination as a share in the ministry of the bishop. Because of this unique ordained identity, the deacon has close ties to the paschal mystery of Christ and thus to the altar and ambo as well. He is not simply a social worker.[4] The deacon is a cleric—deeply embedded in the church—but a cleric who also participates fully in lay life—deeply embedded in the world.

Interior Life

How should we understand John Paul II's call for the deacon to have a "deep interior life"? Since the essence of the deacon is service born out of an ordained participation in the paschal mystery, his interior life has to be one of profound communion with the Holy Spirit. It is the Spirit that dwells at the deacon's core and prompts him to will the good of others beyond all selfish ego concerns. The ordinary

---

3. In some dioceses this may not be true, however, as there is movement to attach the deacon more and more to church employment. There is a danger to this move, I think, if church employment is mandated. To do so would undermine the very essence of the diaconate as clergy who bring church service to secular culture. Two of the primary ways to do this are through a married diaconate and by the deacon retaining his employment and civic ties to the secular arena.

4. See Walter Kasper, "The Ministry of the Deacon," *Deacon Digest* (March/April 1998): 19–27.

practice of the deacon is to communicate with the indwelling Spirit in a dialogue about one's diaconal call to minister. Such an interior life is a sign of fidelity to the diaconal vocation and as such should be treasured and preserved by lively prayer and regular spiritual direction. Such an interior life is a state of being—a profound openness to being affected by the indwelling Spirit, as the Spirit urges the deacon to serve those in need and also to simply rest in prayer, worship, and contemplation.

What signals such openness is the prayer life of the deacon, which is addressed in Owen Cummings's chapter (chapter 9) in this volume. One important fact to mention here, however, is that prayer only culminates in a state of being as a result of many discrete acts of lifting one's mind and heart to God. Only after a deacon wills to pray over a series of years can he *come to embody prayer.* Only thus is he able to truly live out of a deep interior life, because no service the deacon renders will be simply his idea; rather, it is the fruit of living in communion with the indwelling Spirit in the midst of the church, guided by fidelity to vocation.

For such a deacon, his interior life necessarily includes a conscience that has become adept at listening to and for the moral truth. This listening is a discerning obedience, one that is characterized by a prayerful distinguishing of the many voices clamoring for his attention and followed by a true and solid judgment by the mind as to where truth lies in the particular decision before him. The deacon with a deep interior life makes no separation between his prayerful soul and his conscience. He is what he is within his soul—within his identity as one who stretches out to unite with God and serve the needs of his community.

To be faithful to such an interior life of prayer, of appropriating moral truth by the conscience, and of rendering diaconal service to others, a deacon needs to live the virtuous life. The moral virtues stand as invitations to the gifts of the Holy Spirit to come and assist the deacon to live out of the soul rather than the passing ideologies of the present age. The gifts of the Spirit transform the church, its members and ministers, into a community of transfigured hope. This is sanctity: we are being made fit for heaven now,

so that in a sense members of the church, through their development of virtue and vulnerability toward the Spirit, become signs of
our future perfection. The deacon's vocation inclines him to manifest this perfection most characteristically by proclivities to service. One's reach and surrender toward the Spirit constitutes the
integrating disposition among the deacon's vocational identity, his
moral life, his interior life, and his hope for heaven. The deacon's
interior life is to be understood as that capacity within him to com-
mune with God, and in doing so it becomes the well from which
the deacon draws his spiritual energies and his focus in his work of
promoting the kingdom of God.

The Virtues Needed to Sustain This Identity

Out of the deacon's sacramental identity and his concomitant
interior life, the cleric strives to enact those virtues that facilitate
fidelity to his vocation. All the relevant virtues of any human person are, of course, relevant to the deacon, and traditionally these
were labeled the "cardinal virtues": justice, prudence, fortitude,
and temperance. Beyond these, however, what specific virtues
enable the deacon to better enter the depths of his vocation? In
answering this question we would do well to remember all that is
said by Mark Latcovich on the diaconate and marriage later in this
volume (chapter 12). In no way does one artificially split the two
callings a man receives to the diaconate and marriage. One can say
that a good husband and father will be a good deacon, and a good
deacon will be a good husband and father. It cannot suffice, however, to simply let such a summary statement stand, since there are
real orientations in each vocation that require unique attention.
For example, the husband needs to be emotionally and physically
present to his wife in order for communion to occur between the
two, but this virtue alone does not make one fit for ordination.
Alternately, a man may have a great capacity for attending to the
sick, or for organizing civic efforts to assist the poor, but these

virtues alone do not make him fit for marriage. For the purposes of underscoring the very real change that has occurred with ordination, then, I highlight the following virtues as specific for the character development of a man who is deacon: peacemaking, humility, and eager availability.

Peacemaking

The real strength *(virtus)* of the deacon is, in fact, his greatest weakness: he stands as a servant minister, promoting the communion of laity, priesthood, and culture. This is a weakness only in the sense that, for some, such an identity adds confusion to what are otherwise neat and tidy categories. In the Catholic world, a married man is rarely recognized as a member of the clergy; marriage is for the laity, in the minds of most Catholics. Alternately, *only* clergy preach and assist at sacraments. Who, then, is this married man, if such is the case, who is both employed "in the world" and yet assists at the sacraments? It is from just such a complex identity that a deacon develops his greatest virtue: from within this world of marriage, secular employment, and ministry, the deacon develops empathic insight toward both kinds of vocations, and so he can offer the laity and the clergy humble, limited wisdom about and service to both states in life. The deacon can facilitate the sharing of vital knowledge between both states, if and when both sides are open to listen to him. The frustration for the deacon is that at times—and this is the weakness of his complex identity—either the lay side of the church or the clerical side will reject him as not quite "one of us."

As with all emissary positions, the deacon must take care not to let the differing sides crush him altogether, and so he must patiently seek balance as he informs priests, laity, and popular culture of the truths that may heal misunderstandings. To be a peacemaker is first to be one who allows Christ to work his reconciliation within one's own mind and heart. It is Christ, then, who balances the deacon and keeps his focus upon the ministry rather than on personality or power conflicts. Seeking discerning advice from counselors and from Christ in his own prayer, the deacon aims to allow the truth to lead. Thus his mission involves sharing his own insights with both priest and laity, helping to articulate where and how the gospel is best furthered. A temptation for the deacon is to make his own complex vocation "easier" by simply situating himself more firmly with one or the other camp, priests *or* laity. To develop a character that prizes the virtue of promoting communion and therefore peace, however, is to endure some suffering. The deacon must share in the virtues of Christ up to and including the point at which his own life becomes cruciform.[5] In such a life the deacon sees his call to service as a call to seek the good of others above his own *in the very exercising of his diaconal ministry.* All Christians, by virtue of baptism, are called to be peacemakers. The deacon *uniquely knows this call in his vocation to bridge the states of life found within the church and between church and culture.*

In bridging the worlds of church and culture, the deacon knows his dignity as minister.[6] The complexity of the deacon's life is its very gift to the church and to the world. Any attempt to reduce this complexity—by unduly limiting the deacon's assistance at altar and ambo, for example, or by trying to make him "fill in" in the pastor-priest role—is dangerous in the long run to this great virtue of the deacon. He is the only ordained representative located deep within the secular world of commerce, medicine, arts, and education. It is this embedded-in-the-world quality that best serves the unique contribution of the deacon and solidifies the emissary quality of his reconciling gifts. He is among the laity as one of them, to ecclesially serve them, and he is among the clergy as one of them, so as to bring the weight of secular realities to them as they plan and exercise their pastoral authority and ministry. As William Ditewig has said so well, "The diaconate must be identified and judged for what it is: *a unique strand in the tapestry of*

---

5. See Livio Melina, *Sharing in Christ's Virtues* (Washington, DC: Catholic University of America Press, 2001), 115–36.

6. Paul McPartlan's caveat (chapter 3) about bridge language stands. I am presenting this term as one that evokes the deacon as agent of communion and/or solidarity (see page 69 of McPartlan's chapter).

ministry, not a partial exercise of someone else's ministry in the church or in the world."[7] Reconciliation, then, becomes an essential strength or *virtus* of the deacon.[8] Peacemaking is the living strand that the diaconate weaves within the tapestry of the church. The deacon lives out and articulates the tension between the traditional sense of the holy and its counterpart, secular living.

Humility

During the preparation of the gifts at the eucharistic liturgy, the deacon takes water and pours a drop into the wine-filled chalice, saying, "By the mystery of this water and wine, may we come to share in the divinity of Christ, who humbled himself to share in our humanity." Here again we see the deacon entering into the mystery of linking or connecting two mysteries, but here he is meditating upon the divine and the human, not simply the sacred and secular. The virtue of Christ mentioned in this short private prayer is that of humility, a humility that literally bridged the human and divine for the sake of our salvation. In this virtue also lies the key to how a deacon brings Christ from the altar to the world, and the needs of the world to the altar. How should we understand the virtue of humility, and how does its possession solidify the paradoxical truth of the power of service?

There are many ways to approach the virtue of humility, but for the purpose of contextualizing it within the life of a deacon, it is important to view it from the perspective of sharing in the virtues of Christ. How did Christ manifest humility? In what exactly is the deacon sharing? The humility of Christ can be profitably reflected upon through the lens of Paul's Letter to the Philippians. Here we see the kernel of Christ's own virtue, in which he wills for the deacon to participate.

---

7. William T. Ditewig, "The Deacon as a Voice of Lament and Link to Thanksgiving and Justice," *Liturgical Ministry* 13 (Winter 2004): 28.

8. One, of course, may think of other poles that are needed to be reconciled by the deacon within his ministry: rich and poor, healthy and ill, and so on.

> Do nothing from selfish ambition or conceit, but in humility regard others as better than yourselves. Let each of you look not only to your own interests, but to the interests of others. Let the same mind be in you that was in Christ Jesus, who, though he was in the form of God, did not regard equality with God as something to be exploited, but emptied himself, taking the form of a slave, being born in human likeness. And being found in human form, he humbled himself and became obedient to the point of death—even death on a cross. (Phil 2:3–8)

This passage is relevant for all the baptized but resonates within the diaconal vocation very deeply, because it reflects the deep servant status of Christ himself. It is this status into which the deacon is ordained, a status he embodies sacramentally in his ministry for the whole church. According to Paul, humility is about regard for the needs of others. He exhorts his listeners to "have this mind among yourselves," a mind that has become familiar with thinking of the needs of others. In this way the deacon takes on "the mind of Christ" (1 Cor 2:16). What is most captivating about Paul's view of humility is that it was this virtue that led Christ to fully share in the lot of humans all the way to death itself. It is humility that leads us to embody compassion for others and to serve their needs out of such compassion. It was humility in Christ that gave birth to his committed presence among us. The deacon can draw great strength from the reality of this mystery of Christ, who shared in the full life of human beings even unto death, as the deacon is asked to endure the sufferings of his ministry while not abandoning the persons who seek his assistance.

Much of this assistance is given to others not simply in accord with the "job description" ministry of a deacon. Many deacons have found that being faithful to the assigned ministry leads others to call him to further spiritual or corporeal works of mercy. It is within these situations especially that the deacon finds the need to call upon this virtue of the Lord, so that he can either render such supererogatory service himself or enlist the help of others. Whichever response is discerned, the deacon needs to share in the humility of Christ in order to execute the decision faithfully. To say no to a particular call to assist can be as humble as saying yes; each call has to be considered individually.[9]

As with all virtues, humility inheres within a person through practice. How does one practice humility, however? Such a question raises the old conundrum of how one might avoid becoming proud in attaining humility! Humility is not achieved strictly by choosing to be humble; it is not a virtue gained by having it as an explicit goal. One becomes humble by knowing and faithfully executing the duties inherent within the vocation of the diaconate. The call to take the interests of others as seriously as one takes one's own interests is key to growth in humility and, if executed correctly, takes the focus off of the achieving self and places it upon the needs of the other. One never totally extinguishes the awareness of the ego (how could one?), but over time one's focus shifts to the needs of others without counting the cost to the self in any inflated way. Beyond this, Mother Teresa was known to say that the only way to become humble was to endure humiliations. When the humiliations come in the course of one's ministry, this indeed speeds the course of humility to the heart, but to do so one has to *receive* the humiliation and not be defensive. To be defensive about one's faults or mistakes only later breeds regret about one's overreaction in the face of having been corrected by another. Defensiveness does not give rise to humility.

The true bedrock of diaconal humility, however, is located in the deacon's consciousness of being one who is called to public ministry. The giftedness, and some would say Spirit-filled randomness, of the gift of holy orders can overwhelm the chosen man on occasion. The consciousness that such a vocation is a gift, not an earned crown of competency for any single aspect of talent or character, invites humble prayer and praise from the deacon. The vocation has come from God, and now through virtuous living,

---

9. One pastoral note here is vital: Even if someone calls the deacon to some form of service that is better rendered by another, it is best to meet with the petitioning person at least once and fully listen to his or her needs. Many graces have been given to parishioners or coworkers simply through the kindness of hearing out their problems or questions fully before referring them to another more competent minister.

service to others, and receptivity toward the gifts of the Holy Spirit, the deacon returns the vocation back to God. Out of such humility a powerful selfless ministry can emerge.

In the end the virtue of humility stands near the core of the diaconal vocation as it shares in the paschal mystery of Christ. To be ordained is to have the life of Christ lived over again in the cleric in a public and unique ministerial way. The deacon is not simply a humble man, one who takes the lowest place. He is a man becoming conscious of how to facilitate the ministry of Christ within the church today. This facilitation is always best achieved through an eager readiness to be concerned with the needs of others. The more the deacon uses his gifts and senses in order to seek out the needs of his people and to find ways to serve them, the more such people will see the humble Christ acting within his ministry. They may not call it such, and the deacon may not recognize it as such, but the fruits of such humble compassion will prove it to be such. In light of such humility, the deacon's ministry may with the help of the Holy Spirit deepen faith in others.

Through the sacrament of ordination the deacon shares in the mysteries of Christ's own humility. The humility of Christ was simply the public expression of his great and deep trust in the Father. It was this trust that led him to come "not to be served but to serve" (Matt 20:28) and to take up his cross. For the deacon who has been captivated by the truth of Christ, a developing sense of trust in God's providence consumes him. The deacon does not have to "exalt" himself in anxiety or fear, motivated by some sense of not "getting recognized" for his ministry, because slowly it dawns on him that God will not forget his servant. In this act of trust in divine providence lies the key to diaconal humility as it participates in Christ's own trust in the Father.

Eager Availability

A recent International Theological Commission document, *From the Diakonia of Christ to the Diakonia of the Apostles,* speaks of ready helpfulness as the diaconate's "distinctive element."[10] It is the deacon's readiness to assist that carries the force of his own sacramental identity. Flowing from his share in the humility of Christ, this eager readiness to assist blooms as the hallmark of the deacon's public ministry. The deacon is—by virtue of his Spirit-filled ordination—an image of the availability of God's love to the community. The deacon is, as it were, pushed out to the community in service to its physical and spiritual needs. The virtue of availability is essential for the deacon to receive as gift and develop as virtue. This virtue-gift is handed over to the deacon not because others in the community are to remain inert in the face of the community's needs, but rather because it is the deacon who symbolizes in his actions the reality of the whole church becoming an available servant of the truth.

In his availability the deacon embodies the Spirit's agency of effecting communion between persons. Thus the alert deacon who is available to the needs of parishioners and citizens externalizes the work of the Spirit, who seeks to end alienation and loneliness, the seedbed for all sin. The deacon is always ready to hear the people's pleas. He is one who listens to prayers and can therefore articulate them to the priest or bishop. Without the deacon's willing readiness to listen to the prayers of the people, some of their voices might go unheard, and the liturgical prayers of the faithful would echo only a hollow universalizing of human needs rather than the needs of a concrete parish in a particular time, place, and culture. To pray is to entreat, so the Catholic population gives their pleas, yearnings, and hopes to the deacon, who is to be available to receive them. In turn the deacon beseeches other clergy to serve these needs and, through the prayers of the faithful, leads the community in calling out to God so God can attend to these needs as God sees fit.

The deacon is sent by the Holy Spirit to the forsaken. This is why it is crucial for the diaconate to remain a liminal

---

10. International Theological Commission, *From the Diakonia of Christ to the Diakonia of the Apostles* (Chicago: Hillenbrand Books, 2004), 95.

vocation.[11] The deacon lives at the doorstep between the culture and the liturgical mysteries *so that he can see and hear the cry of the poor* and lay these needs at the foot of the altar and the pastor. The deacon is also an *ecclesial porter,* opening the gates of mystery to those who desire to have their spiritual needs satisfied by God, and unbolting the doors of society to other clerics who may want to more deeply understand lay life. The virtue of availability develops most effectively in a deacon who learns to listen to people's hearts even while they struggle to articulate their needs in a cogent fashion. In this empathic availability, the deacon underscores the dignity of the person, even if the problem being articulated cannot be practically or immediately solved.

According to Khaled Anatolios, the Holy Spirit is "the one who effects the outward availability (giftedness) of the sonship of the Son by drawing us into the reciprocal availability (mutual love) between the Father and the Son." Within the church, the Spirit produces a mutual availability among the members of the church: "At Pentecost...the Spirit is experienced as the one who effects the reciprocal availability (mutual love) of the disciples of Christ by drawing them into the reciprocal availability of the Father and the Son."[12]

If this gift-virtue of availability is welcomed by the deacon, he will no longer see others as obstacles to his welfare but rather *a place where "I" can dwell, at the intersection of receptivity and self-donation.* In other words, over the long term a deacon's vocation will be to live in service. The deacon will, under the power of the Spirit, come to dwell in the activity and disposition of receiving others and giving himself away to them in response to their needs. This is who the deacon is to become. This is the way the deacon develops into a saint. This is so because the standard of holiness, the Holy Spirit, is communicating himself to the deacon through the sacrament of ordination in a particular way: the Spirit enables and

---

11. For a profound meditation on the role of the Holy Spirit in the context of the virtue of availability, see Khaled Anatolios, "Divine *Disponibilité:* The Hypostatic Ethos of the Holy Spirit," *Pro Ecclesia* 12, no. 3 (Summer 2003): 287–308.

12. Ibid., 290.

sustains the receiving of servant power and its expression in diaconal ministry. As the deacon receives his ordination in and
through the power of the Holy Spirit, he is becoming something
similar to what he has received—he is becoming holy. The deacon
becomes a man who is vulnerable to the divine rhythm of receptivity of life and its self-donation in loving service toward the needs
of others.

The true mark of an established virtue of eager availability is
known in the deacon's attraction to service. Over time and in the
active reception of his vocation, a deacon will become enthusiastic
toward service and will simply become joyfully present to any and
all in need. In this way the deacon reflects the interior disposition
of one of the church's greatest deacons, Saint Francis of Assisi.
Service was Francis's way of being, not just a task to fulfill.

> St. Francis' whole soul went out to the sick and poor; where
> he could not offer material assistance he lavished affec-
> tion....In every poor person he met, he saw the image of
> Christ and he insisted on giving them anything which had
> been given to him...indeed he believed that he was bound to
> give it to them, just as if it belonged to them....He wanted
> nothing more than to spend and be spent himself, in order to
> fulfill the duty of being compassionate toward others.[13]

Saint Bonaventure is careful to mention the very essence of who
Saint Francis had become—a deacon. Saint Francis was one who
spent and was spent in the context of compassion toward others.
Truly, this is the hallmark of the Spirit-inspired deacon who is
receiving and choosing to cooperate with the virtue of eager availability. In the end the deacon is attracted to those in need. He
delights in such service. This stage may take many years of penance
and ascetical practice to come to fruition, because the whole diaconal vocation is against the grain of the natural man, the man born
into a condition that makes choosing the needs of ego more

---

13. Bonaventure, "Minor Life of St. Francis," in *St. Francis: Omnibus of Sources of the Life of St. Francis,* ed. M. A. Habig (Chicago: Franciscan Herald Press, 1973), 809.

delightful than working to alleviate the suffering of others. It is by no accident that much of Francis's life was spent in penance. How shall such an anthropological and sanctifying necessity be applied to the life of a deacon? This is the key question for moral conversion within the diaconal vocation. Francis had his own disciplines to temper the relentless selfish ego. In what manner shall a contemporary deacon do the same?

The most penetrating arena of ascetic living, which assists in the killing off of the selfish self in any married deacon, is the vocation of marriage itself. It is here that the deacon, over many years of commitment, learns availability to the needs of others. Herein lies the wisdom of ordaining only middle-aged men, an age where one is often old enough to have suffered the death of the fattened ego at the hands of teachers, employers, wives, and children. In and through the many years of married love, and the deacon's secular study and work, the diaconal self finally begins to triumph, yielding a character that possesses an enthusiastic receptivity toward others in need. Of course the ascetical fruit is not automatically given simply by being married, employed, and/or a father; rather, one has to actively seek the death of the ego in and through the duties inherent in such commitments.

Here availability takes on the character of hospitality. The deacon begins to be a man who allows others in need to lay a claim upon him. This claim is not experienced as an imposed *duty,* because the deacon is experiencing the transformation of character wrought by his faithful prayer life. In prayer and in service, Christ is changing the deacon into one who seeks and rests within the active welcoming of other persons. This type of character is formed by a steady commitment to prayer, rest, study, and time with spouse and family, and by a realistic knowledge of the limits one's marital and parenthood status puts on the deacon's ministry to those in need. Nevertheless, the unrelenting movement of grace fashions a man who can never again be indifferent to the cry of the poor. The deacon's disposition is habituated toward dwelling in community and sharing the gift of being loved by God in the form of service. In sharing this gift the deacon edifies himself and lends support to the affection found in fellowship.

Pastoral Duties and the Formation of Conscience

Much of what was said previously constitutes the formation of conscience for the deacon. Specifically, however, for the deacon the conscience is best formed within a matrix of attention given to revelation, doctrine, marriage (if applicable), and relevant secular sources of truth. The most vital function for the conscience of a deacon is its capacity to judge fidelity to vocation in specific circumstances for which ethical determinations are called. Choosing what is morally good is always good for the diaconal vocation. Generally speaking, once a judgment of moral truth has been made, it would appear to always also further one's diaconal vocation. Concretely, however, in discerning what is good for one's marriage and family, one's ministerial assignment, one's relationship to other clerics, and one's professional activities, a prudent course ought to be taken, as these commitments cut to the very heart of one's vocation. Here the conscience is best formed within spiritual direction, spiritual reading, and consultation with affected parties, primarily one's spouse.

Beyond this and above all, the conscience of a deacon has to be molded according to the teachings of the Catholic Church. Upon ordination the deacon can only give witness to and teach what the bishop teaches. The faithful have a right to hear doctrine taught persuasively and with love. If they reject certain teachings, that is left to their own consciences. Clerics, on the other hand, have a duty to teach only what the church teaches, so that the laity can form their consciences according to the Catholic identity that has claimed them since baptism. In pastoral settings the deacon must be able to passionately teach doctrine. If he is struggling with a moral doctrine, he is obligated to seek further formation, and competent guidance by his pastor or other spiritual leader, before trying to teach it to others.

To say that a deacon can only teach what the bishop teaches seems severe to some people. It appears to take away conscience from a deacon rather than liberate it. In fact, however, the deacon was liberated on the day of his ordination. By virtue of being chosen by Christ, he now knows the privilege and burden of teaching and preaching only what the magisterium identifies as the "mind of Christ" for our present age. There is no freer mind than one conformed to the truth of Christ (see John 8:32). Of course some doctrine may develop over time, but all development must be recognized as such by the magisterium, not by singular, so-called prophetic deacons speculating from the ambo or classroom lectern. This form of obedience to magisterial teaching is often or can be a true cross for many deacons who were educated expecting the ideas of their classroom teachers to herald a new development of doctrine, especially in the areas of sexual and health care ethics.

Obviously, what was said previously regarding obedience to church teaching in the public forums of ambo and classroom holds also for the counseling office as well. The moral counsel given by deacons in marriage preparation sessions and other pastoral forums must be in accord with church teaching. The counselee may wish to reject teaching, but it ought not be with the tacit or overt permission of the counseling cleric. To fracture the teaching of the church into a private and a public realm undermines all doctrine, and it sends a false message that people do not have to discern moral teachings with clerics, that in the end parishioners can always "do what they want" anyway.[14] A deacon is required to send parishioners away with something more robust than the "American cultural conscience" that they might have possessed at the beginning of their time with the deacon. Conscience formation needs to be imbued with the sacramental life, with doctrine, prayer, the lives of the saints, and service to the poor; otherwise one may simply possess a

---

14. For more details on these ideas, see Anthony Ciorra and James Keating, *Moral Formation in the Parish* (New York: Alba House, 1998).

popular conscience (born of popular media), a political conscience (born of attention to partisan politics), or an ideological conscience (born of attention to academic camps).

What happens when a class full of adults or an individual taking a deacon's counsel reacts negatively to a church teaching? What should be the proper response from the deacon? First, the deacon needs to listen to the objections, and in doing so real empathy will be born for their situation of suffering or ignorance. Parishioners should not be shunned or shown the parish door simply because they disagree with the moral doctrine of the church. The opposite is also true: Church teaching remains church teaching even though some parishioners cannot or do not assent to it. In many cases, deacons and parishioners end up agreeing to disagree, while still holding out hope for conversion—the deacon for the parishioner, and the so-called prophetic parishioner for development of doctrine.

Second, the deacon needs to amend where he might have been in error, if necessary. Deacons cannot always teach or preach with such specificity as all would like. Sometimes he might generalize too much or simply get an aspect of doctrine wrong. Articulate and well-studied laity abound and will challenge the deacon's expression of doctrine. For example, some deacons teach that the church is against capital punishment as if such a stance is now a moral absolute. This is usually asserted in conversations with pro-life advocates as if the two doctrines—prudence on capital punishment and absolute rejection of abortion—are morally equivalent, which is not true. Such teaching errors are best acknowledged and then corrected in later classes or homilies.

Finally, a deacon can recommend that parishioners do further study, employ various approaches to conversion, and make use of institutional outlets such as writing to the bishop. The deacon should offer himself for further conversation. With classes and homilies that involve controversial material, the deacon needs to be prepared for the message to be questioned; presenting the teaching irenically, the deacon will be more effective if he avoids communicating out of anger or contempt. Many of the problems associated with teaching complex or ill-received moral doctrine are found in the way *the deacon* comes across in his expression, not only in the doctrine itself.

There is a complexity to moral decision making in the concrete lives of people, who must consider many things in order to have the courage to live the truth. Deacons are to assist in pointing the way toward that truth with courage. The main goal is to be a helpful, clarifying presence in facilitating moral conversions. This demands an ascetical stance from the deacon—not all doctrinal rejection is because of the way it was presented, nor is all moral conversion toward truth because of the deacon's many competent gifts. Deacons do the best they can, become competent, and realize that grace and human freedom cannot be manipulated to any end.

Conclusion

The conscience formation of the deacon culminates in this obedience to church doctrine and worship, because he—like the servant-Christ he wishes to allow to operate in and through him—must turn his ear only to the truth, to the Father. In this first duty the deacon abandons his ministry to grace. In so doing he can become a conduit for reconciliation between the altar and the world, humble in regard to the needs of others, above his own, and eager to be available to those to whom he has been sent, asking, "How can I help you?" The moral formation of the deacon is not about anything other than growth in holiness, and such growth is most fundamentally about detaching the self from the passing values of this world and attaching the self to the eternal Word of the Father, who is Jesus Christ. The deacon serves the moral growth of his people by giving clues to how such a detachment is made effective in one's clinging to the sacraments, engaging in service, and practicing rapt listening to the moral truths taught by Christ's church.

PART TWO

Pastoral Foundations
for Diaconal Identity

CHAPTER 7

Theological Education and the Diaconate

Dcn. Charles A. Bobertz, PhD

When I was ordained to the diaconate for the Diocese of Saint Cloud, Minnesota, in 1997, I had already been teaching theology, mainly New Testament and patristics, to seminarians, deacon candidates, and lay people for four years. At that time it would not have occurred to me actively to consider the importance of a theological education for diaconal ministry. After all, I spent most of my waking hours somehow involved in theological education; I was committed to its importance. In the months and years since my ordination, however, now actively engaged in parish ministry as well as teaching theology, I have come to see its importance in new ways.

My first encounter with some resistance to theological education as a prerequisite for diaconal ministry came after my ordination at my first quarterly meeting of the diocesan diaconate community. A proposal from the diocesan office of ministry, calling for a change in the diaconate formation program, had begun to be circulated amid the community for its insights and comments. Formation, as now proposed, would effectively take four years and culminate in both ordination and a master's degree in pastoral ministry. St. John's School of Theology, where I teach, would offer the degree to deacons through evening and weekend courses, and the degree would consist of forty-eight graduate credits in theology. I was delighted with the proposal and thought it would surely win unanimous approbation from the diaconal community. Instead it

141

was met with hesitation, some consternation, and even outright resistance. Why? When I probed my new deacon brothers about their attitudes to the new proposal, there emerged two primary lines of argument: (1) Diaconal ministry is primarily about service and goodwill, and one does not need extensive theological education for those activities and attitude; and (2) theological education occasionally leads one to question church teaching. Deacons need to be faithful and to follow church teaching. I hardly knew what to say at that meeting because I was surprised and even a bit angry— but these attitudes were then and are now common enough to warrant a thoughtful response, in writing, seven years later.

The first argument, like the second, has some immediate plausibility. One hears continually of the equation of the diaconate and service in both official church teaching and formation events. If the diaconal vocation is one of service, an enactment of Jesus the servant, as it is often described, then what is the need for extensive, or even rudimentary, theological education? Why not just get out there to *be* the servant and *do* the service? We might, as Jesus used to do, answer such a question with a question: Why then does one need sacramental ordination? Surely every Catholic Christian is called, by virtue of baptism and strengthened by confirmation, to serve others? What is the necessity of ordination to follow the universal Christian call to serve? It is, I think, the obvious answer to that last question that sets us onto right thinking about the role of theological education in diaconal ministry. Sound theological education would tell us that one need not be ordained to serve others within the church and in the world. *All* Christians are called to this.

The difference is that deacons *are* ordained, set apart and commissioned by the church with a sacrament of orders. Many deacons I know are a bit squeamish about this, not wanting to draw attention to themselves by highlighting their ordination. This is understandable. Many deacons are truly humble. It is precisely a good theological education, however, that would help them to understand ordination and show them that, far from a formality that places them in a position to accomplish what all Christians are called to accomplish (service), ordination goes to the very heart of what the Catholic Church is as *church:* the sacramental presence of God in the world, a visible symbol of the relationship of love between God and his good creation. Ordination is not given so that the one ordained can do what all Christians are called to do; ordination is given so that all Christians can visibly see and experience the presence of the triune God in our world. At the heart of that experience of God is service: "the Son of Man came not to be served but to serve" (Matt 20:28), and the church's ordained ministry exists to make that concretely known in our world. That is why ordination is uniquely and indelibly tied to the church's liturgical service, because it is from the reality of the liturgy, its concrete and physical enactment in our world, that we come to know both the reality of God (his sacred presence) and what God would have us do—how we ought to live in and for his good creation.

Every aspect of our lives as Catholic Christians emerges from the reality of our liturgy, and ordination literally makes liturgy possible. Some men are called out by Christ and his church to be the visible and concrete presence of Christ, especially in the liturgy but from the liturgy to the world. Thus, now from some good theological education we can respond to the first question posed by my own diaconal community: diaconal ministry is primarily about service and goodwill, but it is *ordained* ministry. It is the church's service visible and concrete in the world; it is present on the altar of Christ so that it can be present in the whole world. We need good theological education to know this about who we are as ordained deacons and to insist that our deacons serve in our liturgies whenever possible.

We also need a good theological education to address that second concern posed by my fellow deacons, namely that theological education often leads one to question church teaching and sometimes results in the outright loss of faith. This is the more serious of the two responses I heard on that day, and it is a concern I have heard expressed in other venues as well. I address it by telling my own story. When I was eighteen years old I lost my Catholic faith. In the fall of 1976, having come from a small public high school and small Catholic parish in rural South Dakota, I entered Davidson College as an eager freshman excited about my first college-level religion class. I left that class with my faith fundamentally shattered: The stories of the Bible were not *true;* religious faith was a crutch for the weak-minded who were unable to face up to Nietzschean reality. I stopped going to church. I felt both pity and disdain for those who still did. How did this happen to me and so many others who first encounter critical theological education? Should we not be suspicious of such "education" as preparation for the diaconate?

In *The Eclipse of Biblical Narrative,* a study devoted to how the Bible came to be understood and interpreted in the seventeenth and eighteenth centuries, Hans Frei describes the then-dramatic change in how the Bible came to be interpreted in the universities of Europe.[1] In the period prior to the seventeenth century, there was a perceived unity between the literal sense of scripture and what we usually think of as the historical world. If the Gospel of Mark depicted Jesus curing a man with a withered arm on the Sabbath (Mark 3:1–6), then the episode pretty much must have happened in exactly that way. In the period after the Reformation, there came to be a detachment of the "real" historical world from its literal biblical description. The early Christians were telling stories about Jesus in order to make theological points: the story about Jesus' cure of the withered arm was told to proclaim that "Jesus is Lord of the Sabbath," rather than to report what actually happened. At the center of this change there arose a question that I am still asked in my scripture classes more than any other question: whether or not such a biblical story is true history, a question that itself implies that the meaning of a scripture text is in fact detachable from the specific literal story. A usual response, given in theology classes time and time again, is that the story does not have to be "true" to be a "true story."

---

1. Hans Frei, *The Eclipse of Biblical Narrative* (New Haven: Yale University Press, 1974). For what follows see especially Frei's introduction, 1–16.

Frei recounts that, prior to this turn of events, the figurative meaning, sometimes referred to as typology or allegory,[2] was united with the literal historical reading and provided a sense of unity to the canon of scripture. After the Enlightenment, however, such complex reading offended against the prevailing notion that propositional statements had only one meaning. A biblical story was either true historically or it was not true. Typology or figuration could not function as an historical factual argument, nor could such reading sit in judgment over the ordinary referential way in which statements using ideas of sensation make sense. Indeed, the reverse is the true situation.[3] Any historical information gleaned from the text would eliminate the usefulness of typological and figurative reading altogether.[4]

As the scholarly arguments began to take shape, the realistic quality of the narrative was taken by more conservative scholars to be an indication of historical factuality. The story sounds as if Jesus was in the synagogue on that Sabbath, so Jesus was in the synagogue on that Sabbath. Liberal scholars, on the other hand, generally denied the factuality of the literal narrative and tended to deny the importance of the realistic narrative. Hence, biblical stories were always caught up in the arguments over whether an event or saying actually happened. In sum, the early post-Reformation centuries witnessed the pressing of an absolute divide—literal historical reading from historical nonliteral reading—that lasted until

---

2. An example of this sort of reading might be the baptism of Jesus in Mark being read as a "type" of the journey of Israel through the Red Sea to the Wilderness of Sinai, or Israel's crossing of the Jordan to the promised land. A deacon might recall the current rite of baptism wherein there is a litany that describes biblical "water" from creation to Jesus' own baptism.

3. Frei, *Eclipse*, 84.

4. Allow me to offer a brief example. Much has been said and written about the current search for the "historical" Jesus. Say what you will about the effort to uncover the historical Jesus, it is by definition an attempt to find, in Luke Timothy Johnson's recent title, "the real Jesus." The real Jesus is a Jesus *not* synonymous with the literal presentation of Jesus in the Gospels, both canonical and noncanonical, but rather a literal historical figure comprised only of those aspects and texts of the Gospels deemed to be factual (historical). The Gospels, in other words, include material that is not "real," that is, factual.

the first inklings of true narrative criticism of the Bible in the latter twentieth century.[5]

Once the arguments over meaning were framed in these terms—literal historical or historical nonliteral (that is, there might well be references in some manner to historical events, but this must be found through exegesis rather than through a simple acceptance of the literal story)—the next logical step was to question whether or in what way a belief in presumed historical events was necessary for biblical interpretation. There is no doubt in my mind that when I walked into the classroom as a naïve freshman at Davidson College in 1976 that Frei's description of the way the Bible was interpreted prior to the modern era, a perceived unity of literal and historical in the biblical narrative, fit my own understanding of the Bible. The Bible, I recall vividly, was exactly what it said it was. The stories were "true" in the way I understood truth, that is, they were historical. Later I came to realize that I had framed an understanding of the world and of all of reality in a manner that Clifford Geertz would describe as powerfully pervasive and meaningful.[6] The fit between the reality of the religious stories of the biblical narrative and my worldview, steeped in the necessity of historical truth, was darn near

---

5. It is out of place here to describe extensively narrative criticism, but at its most basic level narrative criticism treats the stories of the Bible as within their own temporal and spatial world. Like novels, they do not necessarily refer to anything or anyone in "real life." For further reading see Robert Alter, *The Art of Biblical Narrative* (London: G. Allen & Unwin, 1981); Hans W. Frei, "Narrative in Christian and Modern Reading," in *Theology in Dialogue,* ed. Bruce Marshall (Notre Dame: University of Notre Dame Press, 1990), 149–63; C. W. Hedrick, "What Is a Gospel? Geography Time and Narrative Structure," *Perspectives in Religious Studies* 10 (1983): 255–68; Mark Alan Powell, "Narrative Criticism," in *Hearing the New Testament,* ed. Joel B. Green (Grand Rapids, MI: Eerdmans, 1995), 239–55; Garrett Green, *Scriptural Authority and Narrative Interpretation* (Philadelphia: Fortress Press, 1987); R. Alan Culpepper, *Anatomy of the Fourth Gospel: A Study in Literary Design* (Philadelphia: Fortress Press, 1983); Frank Kermode, *The Genesis of Secrecy: On the Interpretation of Narrative* (Cambridge, MA: Harvard University Press, 1979); Robert Fowler, *Let the Reader Understand: Reader Response Criticism and the Gospel of Mark* (Minneapolis: Fortress Press, 1991); Ole Davidsen, *The Narrative Jesus: A Semiotic Reading of Mark's Gospel* (Aarhus, Denmark: Aarhus University Press, 1993).

6. Clifford Geertz, *The Interpretation of Cultures* (New York: Basic Books, 1973), 87–125: "Religion is a system of symbols which acts to establish powerful, pervasive

perfect: The wholesale destruction of the latter was bound to wreak havoc on the former.

I no longer recall the details. The professor relentlessly took the class on a sharp historical-critical exegetical tour of the Bible that highlighted, as I now recall, the sharp distinction between the literal narrative and the historical facts. My conclusion—and I do not recall the professor disputing this in any way—was that the Bible as written was not true (if it was not true historically then it was not true) and therefore could not function in any way to establish or describe faith in God. Worse, God himself was called into question, since my main source for knowledge about God—the Bible—had been utterly discredited. After one semester of such education I was left to my own wits, my own rational reason. I stopped going to Mass. I distinctly remember thinking that those who still went to any sort of church services were dupes, fools who did not know the truth, which, however painful, had been revealed to me.

What happened to me back then still happens to some theological students. Theological education "for the church" sometimes results in leaving the church, and candidates for the diaconate at times find a crisis of faith rather than a strengthening of faith. My diaconal friends sense this, and some perhaps even think it is better to be naïve and faithful than smart and lost. Does anyone, however, really think that leaders in the church ought to stay ignorant? That the church wants to ordain ostriches with heads in the sand? Modern biblical criticism is not only "out there" at Amazon.com and *Newsweek;* it is used and accepted by the magisterium of the church as well.[7] How

---

and long-lasting moods and motivations in men by formulating conceptions of a general order of existence and clothing these conceptions with such an aura of factuality that the moods and motivations seem uniquely realistic" (90).

7. See, for example, Pontifical Biblical Commission, *The Interpretation of the Bible in the Church* (Rome: Libreria Editrice Vaticana, 1993): "The historical-critical method is the indispensable method for the scientific study of the meaning of ancient texts. Holy Scripture, inasmuch as it is the 'word of God in human language,' has been composed by human authors in all its various parts and in all the sources that lie behind them. Because of this, its proper understanding not only admits the use of this method but actually requires it" (I, A, quoting Vatican Council II, *Dei Verbum* [Dogmatic Constitution on Divine Revelation, 1965]).

can deacons, who will be called upon to preach and administer the church's sacraments, encounter a theological education that will strengthen and vivify their faith rather than destroy it? The fact is that it takes more and better theological education than ever before to authentically present the church in the modern world. The task now is to provide for our ordinands a way of understanding modern theology that leads them both to understand theological criticism and to critique the criticism. In other words, the same scholarship that led us into this dilemma can and does guide us out. Moreover, as with Israel and the Jordan, the new place is better than what we have left behind. I explain what I mean here by telling another story.

I had found my way back into the church (another long story) when I began my teaching career in 1987 for one year at St. Michael's College in Vermont and then at Loyola College in Maryland. I was sure that I wanted to address concerns of faith in the midst of standard historical-critical courses in scripture. How was I to accomplish this, however, in such a way that I would not recreate with my students the same crisis I had experienced as a young undergraduate? How could critical theological education not lead to such crises of faith? In ten years the students and culture had not radically changed; the methods of study that had affected me so powerfully in the 1970s were bound to have a similar effect on students in the late 1980s. Some of my faculty colleagues were convinced that this was just something "people had to go through" in order to reach a certain level of religious maturity. I could not then accept such an answer. I still cannot.

I began to think through "a criticism of criticism" from the position of being a Catholic theologian. What is the relation of historical-criticism to the church? How would teaching this material from within a Catholic institution, from within the Catholic tradition, potentially change the manner in which a theologian might approach the subject? Slowly but surely it dawned on me that what is fundamental to the Catholic tradition is liturgy, what scholars often describe as "ritual," and that ritual had to have something to do with the way one understands the world. I began to spend a great deal of time reading cultural anthropology and theories of ritual—

Catherine Bell, Raymond Firth, Roy Rappaport, Nancy Jay, Clifford Geertz, and Victor Turner, to name a few.[8] I came to the quite unsurprising conclusion that ritual is often at the heart of religious expression. More important, ritual matters because it has the power to create and sustain a worldview all by itself. In other words, ritual, which Catholics encounter most especially in eucharistic liturgy, has the power to create, through speech-acts, an alternative reality.[9] We really are there at the cross of Christ during the Mass; time is suspended; Christ is present because time is not. Ordinary rules of space and time are lifted. What might happen, I wondered, if we began to think of the biblical narrative as an expression that comes from such a place, from the heart of liturgy?

As I thought about this more in preparing my biblical studies classes, I carefully noted that modern biblical study emerged in the seventeenth and eighteenth centuries and was largely dominated by Protestant scholars working within increasingly secular university settings. Prior to the 1943 papal encyclical *Divino Afflante Spiritu,* Catholic scholars played virtually no role in modern biblical criticism. As a result, very little attention had been paid to the

8. Nancy Jay, *Throughout Your Generations Forever: Sacrifice, Religion and Paternity* (Chicago: University of Chicago Press, 1992); Geertz, *Interpretation;* Roy A. Rappaport, *Ecology, Meaning and Religion* (Berkeley: North Atlantic, 1979); Raymond Firth, *Religion: A Humanist Interpretation* (London: Routledge, 1996); R. A. Rappaport, *Ritual and Religion in the Making of Humanity* (Cambridge: Cambridge University Press, 1998); Catherine Bell, *Ritual: Perspectives and Dimensions* (Oxford: Oxford University Press, 1997); Catherine Bell, *Ritual Theory Ritual Practice* (Oxford: Oxford University Press, 1992); Mircea Eliade and Charles J. Adams, eds., *The Encyclopedia of Religion* (New York: Macmillan, 1987), s.v. "Rites of Passage," by Victor Turner; Victor Turner, "Passages, Margins and Poverty: Religious Symbols of Communitas," *Worship* 46 (1972); Victor Turner, *The Drums of Affliction: A Study of Religious Processes among the Ndembu of Zambia* (Oxford: Clarendon Press, 1968); Victor Turner, *The Ritual Process: Structure and Antistructure,* Lewis Henry Morgan Lectures (Chicago: Aldine, 1969); on qualifying Victor Turner's work, see also Bobby C. Alexander, *Victor Turner Revisited* (Atlanta: Scholars Press, 1991).

9. See Wayne Meeks, *The First Urban Christians: The Social World of the Apostle Paul* (New Haven: Yale University Press, 1983), 140–63; the importance of speech-act theory emerges largely from the work of J. L. Austin, *How to Do Things with Words* (Cambridge, MA: Harvard University Press, 1962).

importance of the liturgical gathering (ritual) for interpreting the New Testament in general and the Gospels in particular.[10]

Thus, what would it mean to my biblical classes if I put more of an emphasis on ritual and liturgy in interpretation? Would this help to prevent the crisis of faith I and many others had experienced in theology class? To do so would make necessary not only a revised historical claim about the nature of the New Testament and the importance of ritual location in the creation of the texts, but I would as well have to emphasize, in the face of a hostile, largely Protestant exegetical tradition, that a Catholic reader, reading from the heart of the liturgy, would read these texts differently, and with different effect, than one reading from a different location.[11]

As I contemplated my classes for the following term, the conversation in my mind between liturgy and historical criticism became more intense. What about the Catholic *location,* specifically

---

10. The reasons for this were many: The Reformation premise of salvation by faith alone (over and against any Catholic claim for the necessity and efficacy of the sacraments); a Christocentric theology highlighting Romans 10:4 (Christ as the *telos* of the law not in terms of goal or fulfillment, but in terms of supersession over legal and cultic practices); and the influence of nineteenth-century comparative studies in religion that charted religious "progress" from primitive utilitarian and *superstitious ritual* to reasonable and rational religion based on ethics and morality. See Mark McVann, "Introduction," *Semeia* 67 (1994): 7–8; the history of scholarship on this perception of the split between law (ritual) and gospel can be found in Howard Eilberg-Schwartz, *The Savage in Judaism: An Anthropology of Israelite Religion in Ancient Judaism* (Bloomington: Indiana University Press, 1990). Mary Douglas surveys this development in comparative religion studies in *Purity and Danger* (London: Routledge, Kegan and Paul, 1966), 7–28. Douglas quotes Robertson Smith to good effect: "The Catholic Church had almost from the first deserted the Apostolic tradition and set up a conception of Christianity as a mere series of formulae containing abstract and immutable principles, intellectual assent to which was sufficient to mold the lives of men who have no experience of a personal relation with Christ" (18). Barth's emphasis on the word of God along with Bultmann's priority on the existential stand of faith carried this emphasis forward into the heart of twentieth-century biblical scholarship—see especially Karl Barth, *The Word of God and the Word of Man* (Gloucester, MA: P. Smith, 1978); Rudolf Bultmann, *Theologie Des Neuen Testaments,* 3, durchgesehene und ergänzte Aufl. ed., Neue Theologische Grundisse (Berlin: Evangelische Verlagsanstalt, 1959); and Rudolph Bultmann, *The Gospel of John: A Commentary* (Philadelphia: Westminster, 1971), 218–37.

11. One notes, of course, that I would be making both a historical argument for the importance of liturgy in the formation of the gospel narrative and a second argument

the liturgical location, of reading scripture typologically? Why during the Christmas feast do we read Isaiah 60:6, "A multitude of camels shall cover you, the young camels of Midian and Ephah; all those from Sheba shall come. They shall bring gold and frankincense, and proclaim the praise of the LORD," before the story of the magi? If such figurative meaning is somehow not real, if there is no real prophecy here, is the liturgical setting in which scripture is proclaimed also not real? If there is a reality here, however, are there reasons why such figurative readings should *not* be included in a Catholic university course in the New Testament? I was moving toward a liturgical reading of the New Testament, which would take account of the historical dimension of Christian faith by placing that dimension within liturgy. I proposed to my classes that it was possible to consider the liturgical setting, ancient and modern, as a *historical* location, a gathering that constitutes its own temporal world within which the divine drama—which constitutes the core of the biblical story—unfolds. Put differently, I began to present to my classes the argument that the literal narrative form of the Gospels may be not so much history mythologized, but a mythology, built upon the symbolic structure of ritual, historicized. Rather than measuring the biblical story as less or more historical in relation to a secular temporal world, we Catholics might see a temporal world unfolding within the liturgical setting, a world that is constitutive of the biblical way of telling the story.[12] Historical description does not tell the story of liturgy; rather, liturgy tells the "story" of history.

Catholics have always had a wide-angle lens for truth. We experience the truth of Christ's real presence in bread and wine when others see bread and wine. We claim to be present at the sacrifice of Christ on Calvary when others claim it was two thousand years ago. We are not, however, fundamentalists or literalists. We know about and accept the rightful claims of modern science and modern critical-historical study. Rather, we take these claims back

---

that, by its very nature, did not rely on a historical claim, namely, a claim about the location of the reader as determinative of meaning.

12. Frei, *Eclipse,* 3.

to the future to incorporate them into the ever-deepening mystery of God's concrete presence in our lives and world. We do not have to stand and refute the historical judgment that Jesus was, most likely, not in that particular synagogue on that particular day curing a man with a withered arm. We might instead discover the ancient liturgical gathering that believed that the body, with its pain and suffering, matters to God. Furthermore, because that gathering was the body of Christ in the world, it began to care about bodies, about food and clothing and proper burial, and then expressed the reality of that actual, concrete, historical caring in the form of a story about Jesus' cure in a synagogue. That same gathering is now the communion of saints, bound with that Christ on this altar, bound with Christ in today's caring about bodies, food, and clothing.

Every deacon entering into active ministry, especially in preaching and teaching, will encounter the two worldviews I have outlined here. On the one hand there will be an assumption that understanding the Bible is akin to understanding a historical book in which one looks for historical facts in order to find the truth about Israel, Jesus, and the church. On the other hand, Catholics are also experienced in liturgy: they feel and know deeply that sacraments are more than mere physical objects; they bless themselves with baptismal water as they enter the church; they acknowledge the holiness of the place by genuflection; they bow their heads before receiving the body and blood of Christ in the form of bread and wine. Our people are ready to understand the Bible as they intuitively understand the liturgy, as a text filled with the possibility of touching them with God's love and grace, as a word from God that speaks to us today just as it did to our ancestors in the faith. They need deacons to lead them into this deeper understanding, deacons whose special place in the liturgy is the proclamation and preaching of the gospel.

How is a diaconal candidate to prepare for this role? What sort of biblical and preaching education and training should he seek from his formation program? Each diocesan formation program is different and offers different opportunities, so only generalizations are possible here, but there are things to look for in any formation program.

First, pay attention to the method employed in any biblical studies course. If it is strictly historical-critical and your sense of piety is challenged, do not hide your head in the sand or stop learning from the course. Recognize that a historical and scientific approach to scripture is a valid part of how the church understands and reads scripture in the modern world. Keep in mind that you yourself, most of the time, understand the world in a scientific and historical way. After you have studied what the text meant in its historical context, open yourself up to what the text has meant and continues to mean in the life and liturgy of the church. Look at scriptural commentaries that include how the fathers of the church in the first centuries understood the text (they often provide deep spiritual readings of texts), commentaries that are finally becoming more available and that belong in the deacon's library.[13]

---

13. The interpretation of the Bible in the church fathers is now more widely available in English than has been the case in the recent past. For a general introduction see Manlio Simonetti et al., *Biblical Interpretation in the Early Church: An Historical Introduction to Patristic Exegesis* (Edinburgh: T & T Clark, 1994), and Frances Young, *Biblical Exegesis and the Formation of Christian Culture* (Cambridge: Cambridge University Press, 1997). New volumes that cover patristic interpretation of individual biblical books are now being produced in a series edited by Thomas C. Oden, *The Ancient Christian Commentary on Scripture.* As of this writing the following volumes in that series are available: Andrew Louth, Conti Marco, and Thomas C. Oden, *Genesis 1–11* (Chicago: Fitzroy Dearborn Publishers, 2001); Mark Sheridan and Thomas C. Oden, *Genesis 12–50* (Downers Grove, IL: InterVarsity Press, 2002); Joseph T. Lienhard, Ronnie J. Rombs, and Thomas C. Oden, *Exodus, Leviticus, Numbers, Deuteronomy* (Downers Grove, IL: InterVarsity Press, 2001); Steven A. McKinion and Thomas C. Oden, *Isaiah 1–39* (Downers Grove, IL: InterVarsity Press, 2004); Thomas C. Oden and Christopher A. Hall, *Mark* (Chicago: Fitzroy Dearborn Publishers, 1998); Peter Gorday and Thomas C. Oden, *Colossians, 1–2 Thessalonians, 1–2 Timothy, Titus, Philemon* (Chicago: Fitzroy Dearborn Publishers, 2000); Erik M. Heen, Philip D. Krey, and Thomas C. Oden, *Hebrews* (Downers Grove, IL: InterVarsity Press, 2005); Gerald Lewis Bray and Thomas C. Oden, *James, 1–2 Peter, 1–3 John, Jude* (Chicago: Fitzroy Dearborn Publishers, 2000). Available in a good library is an excellent volume on Origen: Richard Bartram Tollinton, *Selections from the Commentaries and Homilies of Origen,* Translations of Christian Literature (London: Society for Promoting Christian Knowledge, 1929). See also *Origen,* trans. Rowan A. Greer, Classics of Western Spirituality Ser. (New York: Paulist Press, 1979), and *Origen: Treatise*

Commentaries with a pastoral focus, such as the *Collegeville Bible Commentary*,[14] can be useful in exploring how a text might speak to the life of the church today. Above all, do not fall into the trap of thinking that historical meaning is the only "real" meaning of any text. Our liturgical worldview tells us that there is more meaning here than meets the eye.

Second, students often think about their theological education as so many discrete pieces of a larger puzzle. As much as you can, force yourself to look at the whole picture of the puzzle even as you take individual courses. The biblical text you study in one class was most likely created within liturgy and has certainly spoken within liturgy for two thousand years. The moral theology you learn emerges from the truth encountered in the authentic prayer and diligence of the church in attending to God's word and revelation in creation. The systematic theology you learn is the disciplined thought of a church that meditates on God's revelation in our world even while singing his praises. Church history is the story of the church, in all its humanness, encountering the world with the message and spirit of Christ, an encounter that still goes on. Your teachers might not always make these connections, but you can and you must, or else you miss the richness, depth, and awesomeness of your task as a theological student.

Third, especially, do not neglect the opportunity in your formation, if it is presented to you, to move beyond learning the rubrics of ritual (how you move, act, and speak during liturgy) to exploring the depth of liturgy itself in a liturgical theology course. Take the time to explore the depth of the world created in liturgy, the language of "new creation" and what it means that liturgy is literally a place without time. Then when you proclaim and preach the word it will be about *now* as well as about *then*. The Gospel of Luke tells the story of disciples' hearts burning as Jesus spoke to them on the road to Emmaus (Luke 24:13–32). The hearts of those

---

on the Passover and Dialogue of Origen with Heraclides..., Ancient Christian Writers Ser., vol. 54 (New York / Mahwah, NJ: Paulist Press, 1992).

14. Robert J. Karris, *The Collegeville Bible Commentary Based on the New American Bible* (Collegeville, MN: Liturgical Press, 1992).

first communities who wrote this story were also burning, and when I preach now my heart is burning. The liturgy makes it possible to be in all those places at the same time, and the deacon must both know and experience this reality.

Finally, there is the important task of preparing to preach. Every course in any formation program lands at this doorstep, for it is here that one puts it all together: knowledge of the Bible, doctrine, history, and liturgy, and pastoral application. Neglect nothing you have learned and nothing of your experience when you prepare to preach. When God calls you to empty yourself into the sermon, be sure there is something there to be poured out. Do your homework. Study. Read. Pray. Consult. Pray again. Learn carefully good techniques for preaching, and fill the sermon with content worthy of the mystery of Christ present in our world.

There is no substitute for knowledge and study. Ordination to the diaconate is not a reward for piety or loyalty to the church. You will be looked to as a leader and therefore servant of God's people, and ignorance is not what God's people deserve. Use your study to deepen yourself, to come to know yourself, as well as the faith professed by all of us in the church. Use your study to increase your heart *because* you are attending to the mind—then you can be certain that when your faith is challenged, whether in class or reading, it is larger and deeper than you now know.

Of course deacons should have expert theological education for a host of reasons that go beyond the limits of the present essay. I have focused mainly on only one aspect of that education here, namely, the liturgical imagination in interpreting the Bible. Because understanding the Bible plays such a crucial role not only in preaching but in conversations with Protestants and the wider culture, however, it is a pivotal point of a deacon's education. My own special prayer is that biblical studies draws my brothers not into crisis but into a deep and unique Catholic faith—one that finds the deacon every day more in love with the church, its liturgy, its history, and its people.

CHAPTER 8

Father and Shepherd

Most Rev. Gerald F. Kicanas, DD

Introduction

Several years ago I had the privilege of serving as chairman of the Bishops' Committee on the Diaconate. At that time in my home diocese of Chicago, formation of those in ministry—priests, deacons, and laity—was done separately and with little collaboration. Now Archbishop Francis Cardinal George, OMI, has established structures of collaboration in Chicago by which the formation of all in ministry flows from a common theological foundation with a distinct emphasis for each ministry. This bodes well for working together in ministry.

The three years I served as chair were a treasured time. I had the opportunity to meet many deacons from across the country: during summer sessions at the University of Notre Dame, at a national assembly of deacons at St. Mary's in Moraga, California, and with deacons from around the world at the Jubilee Year celebration for deacons and their wives in Rome. I preached to them, I taught them, dialogued with them, laughed, and had delightful times socializing with them. They taught me a great deal. I heard their joys in ministry, their frustrations, and their hopes. I listened to when they felt received and valued in the Catholic community and when they felt like parsley on a plate, undervalued, underutilized, underappreciated.

I came to realize that deacons and their wives are a precious blessing for the church in our day. Deacons remind all of us of the preeminence of service in the life of a disciple. As a bishop I experienced their loyalty, their dedication, and their burning desire to join with their bishop, the priests, and the laity of the diocese to build up the church. I witnessed the working together of deacons and their wives as a striking example of how clergy and laity can work together collaboratively.

During my term as chair, I had the opportunity to visit a number of dioceses that had not yet restored the diaconate. I talked with the bishops, presbyters, and others within those dioceses, clarifying how the diaconate could enhance the mission of that local church. Each diocesan bishop has the authority to decide whether to restore the diaconate in his diocese. In order to make that decision, a bishop is to consult with his presbyters and other diocesan leaders. The bishop is to engage in a process of education throughout the diocese in order to clarify for the people the role of the deacon and the kind of ministry in which deacons would be involved. That preliminary work is critical in order for the restoration to be successful. I was pleased that those consultations resulted in the restoration of the diaconate in several more dioceses of the United States. Those decisions by bishops to restore the diaconate have meant great benefits for their dioceses. I finished my term as chair with a deeper sense of my responsibility as a bishop to participate actively in the selection of candidates for diaconate and in their formation, to know the deacons of the diocese, to learn from them, to challenge them to maximize their gifts in carrying out the mission of the church.

In this chapter I reflect first on the meaning of the bishop as father and shepherd of the community. This has significant implications for the bishop's relationship to deacons and those preparing to serve as deacons. Then I discuss the bishop as minister of sanctification and how the deacons' participation in liturgical ministry amplifies and extends this core ministry of the bishop. I emphasize the role of the bishop in assuring proper formation of deacons for liturgical ministry. Finally I consider the bishop as promoter of justice and peace. This has important implications for the responsibility to serve that is at the core of diaconal ministry. The bishop calls deacons to service in the diocese in promoting justice and peace.

Father and Shepherd

The Second Vatican Council refers to the bishop as the father and shepherd of the community. He lives among the people of God as one who serves. Pope John Paul II titled his postsynodal statement on bishops *Pastores Gregis* (On the Bishop, Servant of the Gospel), emphasizing the biblical images of shepherd and servant.

Being pastor is one of the significant gifts in the ministry of a bishop (together with teacher and sanctifier). Vatican II directed bishops to

> govern the particular churches entrusted to them as the vicars and ambassadors of Christ. This they do by their counsel, exhortations, and example, as well, indeed, as by their authority and sacred power. This power they use only for the edification of their flock in truth and holiness, remembering that he who is greater should become as the lesser and he who is the more distinguished, as the servant (cf. Lk. 22:26–27).[1]

In fact, the council describes the office of bishop as "a true service which in Sacred Scripture is significantly called a *'diakonia'* or ministry."[2] The *National Directory for the Formation, Ministry, and Life of Permanent Deacons in the United States* emphasizes the teaching of the council, recalling that "the Council Fathers teach that the bishops, with priests and deacons as helpers, have by divine institution taken the place of the apostles as pastors of the Church."[3]

---

1. Vatican Council II, *Lumen Gentium* (Dogmatic Constitution on the Church, 1964), no. 27, in Walter M. Abbott, SJ, ed., *The Documents of Vatican II* (New York: America Press, 1966).

2. Ibid., no. 24.

3. United States Conference of Catholic Bishops, Bishops' Committee on the Diaconate, *National Directory for the Formation, Ministry, and Life of Permanent Deacons in the United States* (December 26, 2004), no. 2, citing *Lumen Gentium*, no. 26.

A key quality for one who serves as pastor and shepherd is "the ability to enter into authentic and constructive relationships with others, an aptitude for encouraging and developing cooperation, an innate goodness and patience, an understanding of and compassion for those suffering in body and spirit."[4] The bishop lives among his people. He serves to bring about a unity, a communion between all who are a part of the body of Christ. He holds the responsibility to recognize gifts, foster them, and to coordinate and evaluate the diverse charisms and ministries of those who make up the local church he governs.

> The Bishop will make every effort to develop within his particular church, structures of communion and participation which make it possible to listen to the Spirit who lives and speaks in the faithful, in order to guide them in carrying out whatever the same Spirit suggests for the true good of the Church.[5]

The bishop's constant preoccupation is to promote communion. "It is up to the Bishop with the help of the priests, deacons, religious and lay people to implement a coordinated pastoral plan which is systematic and participatory, involving all the members of the Church and awakening in them a missionary consciousness."[6]

Clearly the bishop serves as the father and shepherd of the diaconate community. This means he knows his deacons, their wives, and those in formation for the diaconate. He spends time with them. He prays with them. He serves with them. Among the numerous references in the *National Directory* concerning the relationship of the bishop and his diaconate community, that guiding document recalls the teaching of the Holy See that "in the formation of deacons, 'the first sign and instrument of the Spirit of Christ is the proper Bishop....He is the one ultimately responsible for the discernment and formation' of aspirants and candidates as well as

---

4. John Paul II, *Pastores Gregis* (On the Bishop, Servant of the Gospel, 2003), no. 43.

5. Ibid., no. 44.

6. John Paul II, *Ecclesia in America* (The Church in America, 1999), no. 36.

the pastoral care of deacons." Even more, while others will help the bishop in his responsibilities, the bishop should "commit himself, as far as is possible, to knowing personally those who are preparing for the diaconate."[7]

It is only right and proper that the formation, ministry, and life of deacons should be an interest of bishops. Deacons are key collaborators with the bishops in carrying out the mission of Christ. They are entrusted with key dimensions of the bishop's pastoral care of the particular church. In the early church deacons were bound closely to the bishop. They assisted him in his ministry. Deacons were entrusted with significant diocesan responsibilities. They were the right arm of the bishop, extending his ministry and his presence in the areas of the diocese. Pope John Paul II, in teaching about the diaconate, once observed that in an ancient text, the deacon's ministry is defined as a "service to the Bishop."[8] The *National Directory* takes note of this teaching, since it "highlights the constant understanding of the Church that the deacon enjoys a unique relationship with his Bishop. The Pope clearly has in view, therefore, the reason for not only the diaconate but the whole apostolic ministry: serving the discipleship of God's people."[9]

The bishop fosters communion by respecting each ministry and helping those who serve in the diocese to esteem each other's ministry. This is especially important for the deacon who, sometimes, feels ignored by the priests or the laity as an unnecessary minister who only gets in the way. On the other hand, some deacons may imagine themselves as "mini-priests" or somehow by ordination placed above the laity. Neither represents the true meaning of the diaconate. An earlier document, *A National Study on the Permanent Diaconate of the Catholic Church in the United States, 1994–1995,* suggested that a large minority of parishioners,

---

7. United States Conference of Catholic Bishops, *National Directory,* no. 266, citing the Congregation for Catholic Education, *Basic Norms for the Formation of Permanent Deacons* (Washington, DC: United States Catholic Conference, 1998), nos. 16 and 19.

8. John Paul II, General Audience, "Deacons Have Many Pastoral Functions" (October 13, 1999), no. 1, citing Hippolytus, *Apostolic Tradition.*

9. United States Conference of Catholic Bishops, *National Directory,* no. 30.

priests, and lay staff with whom deacons worked did not adequately understand the identity of the deacon.[10] Some see them as "incomplete priests" while others as "more advanced laity." The bishop teaches the diocese by upholding the place of each ministry within the body of Christ. He can do that by personal example and by confronting competitiveness when it appears.

While in most dioceses the bishop has collaborators who assist him in the pastoral care of the diaconate community, he must play an active and personal role. Presence communicates most powerfully that others are important and that they matter. Personal presence at diaconate convocations, retreats, and assemblies can make a big difference:

> The Bishop will seek in every way possible to know personally all the candidates for the diaconate. After their ordination he will continue to be a true father for them, encouraging them to love the Body and Blood of Christ whose ministers they are, and Holy Church which they have committed themselves to serve.[11]

The bishop has responsibility to choose those who will enter diaconate formation. A personal interview with candidates before they are selected can be helpful in assuring the bishop that this candidate has potential to serve. Likewise, the bishop can maintain contact with candidates during their formation by teaching an occasional class to them, by visiting them during their practicum experience, or by giving an occasional formation talk.

In the end the bishop has the responsibility to call a candidate to orders. This requires the utmost care and attention. The bishop's involvement with candidates and their wives during the years of formation can ready the bishop, as father and shepherd, to make wise judgments in calling candidates to the diaconate.

---

10. National Conference of Catholic Bishops, Bishops' Committee on the Permanent Diaconate, *A National Study on the Permanent Diaconate of the Catholic Church in the United States, 1994–1995* (Washington, DC: United States Catholic Conference, 1996).

11. John Paul II, *Pastores Gregis,* no. 49.

Minister of Sanctification

Through the sacred liturgy the bishop calls the community to holiness. This is his primary task. When he celebrates with his priests, assisted by deacons and united with all God's people, the bishop exercises his liturgical ministry. Just as the Eucharist is the source and summit of the church's life, so its celebration is the center of a bishop's activity:

> hence the importance of liturgical life in the particular Church, where the bishop exercises his ministry of sanctification, proclaiming and preaching the word of God, guiding prayer for his people and *with* his people, and presiding over the celebration of the Sacraments.[12]

The bishop has responsibility to see that the liturgy is celebrated with reverence and according to the liturgical norms of the church. Such reverence reflects the profound mystery that is being celebrated.

The latest Synod of Bishops, the Eleventh Ordinary General Assembly, had as its theme "The Eucharist: Source and Summit of the Life and Mission of the Church." The hope of this synod is "that the Eucharist maintain its central place in the eyes of the Church, at the universal and local levels…, that a necessary increase of faith in the Eucharist may result, and that the Church's teaching on the Sacred Eucharist might be taken up anew and more profoundly received in its entirety."[13]

Deacons play an important part in the celebration of the liturgy. They proclaim the gospel, they preach, they offer petitions expressing the needs of the community; they send parishioners out to live what they profess. They baptize and witness marriages. They conduct services for the deceased. To exercise these ministries, diaconate candidates need proper training and helpful supervision.

---

12. Ibid., no. 32.

13. Synod of Bishops, *The Eucharist: Source and Summit of the Life and Mission of the Church,* Lineamenta (2004), no. 3.

Bishops can encourage the presbyterate to utilize deacons in liturgical celebrations. He himself can make known his preference to have deacons serve with him at the altar.

The bishop in his oversight of formation should insist on adequate training for deacons in the rites of the church, their history, and a sound theology of liturgy and sacraments. Likewise the bishop needs to provide solid homiletic training. Poor and inadequate formation leads to celebrations of the Eucharist and sacraments that are less reverent than they should be.

Promoter of Justice and Peace

In every diocese, the bishop bears responsibility to reach out to the littlest and weakest. Christ himself said that he can be found and encountered there. This concern for justice and peace begins at home but reaches out to all the churches. Bishops extend their concern to the entire church. "Solidarity [concern for all] is thus the fruit of the communion which is grounded in the mystery of the triune God and in the Son of God who took flesh and died for all. It is expressed in Christian love which seeks the good of others, especially of those most in need."[14] Everywhere challenges exist to the dignity of human life. The church belongs with the most vulnerable, and the bishop can become the voice of the unborn, the vulnerable, the homeless, and those in prison.

> The Bishop is the defender of human rights, the rights of human beings made in the image and likeness of God. He proclaims the Church's moral teaching by defending life from conception to its natural end. He likewise proclaims the Church's social teaching, based on the Gospel, and he shows profound concern for the defense of all who are poor, raising his voice on behalf of the voiceless in order to defend their rights.[15]

---

14. John Paul II, *Ecclesia in America,* no. 52.
15. John Paul II, *Pastores Gregis,* no. 67.

The bishop has responsibility to preach the social teaching of the church and to invite people to become active in rendering service.

During the Holy Year 2000, Pope John Paul II gave a striking example of putting words into action: he invited the homeless of Rome to dine with him.[16] He sat next to a homeless woman at table, as Christ dined with those seen as outcasts in his day. Yes, even the Holy Father is called to serve. Bishops by their example and by their preaching can rally people to exercise discipleship. Deacons, who are icons of Jesus the servant, share closely in this ministry. They stand among us as continual reminders of the church's preferential but not exclusive option for the poor. "The Church in America must incarnate in her pastoral initiatives the solidarity of the universal Church towards the poor and the outcast of every kind. Her attitude needs to be one of assistance, promotion, liberation, and fraternal openness. The goal of the Church is to ensure that no one is marginalized."[17]

In the early church deacons served the bishop and not a particular parish. The scriptures tell us that deacons were entrusted with the responsibility of service to free the apostles for their pastoral oversight. In every diocese deacons can extend the ministry of the bishop to those in need. This happens in prisons, in hospitals and shelters, in nursing homes and among the homeless. A truck-stop ministry arose during my tenure as chair of the Bishops' Committee on the Diaconate, bringing the pastoral presence of the church to truckers on the move. The church reaches out to all. Deacons can make that happen. Archbishop Roger Cardinal Mahoney of Los Angeles was once asked, "Do we not have enough deacons?" He responded that we will have enough deacons when every prisoner is visited, every person in the hospital has someone at their side, and justice and peace are available to all.

While the majority of deacons serve in parochial ministry, even in some instances as pastoral administrators, bishops can invite some

16. See "Homeless Men and Women Dine with the Pope," available at www.ewtn.com/jubilee/news/poor2.htm.
17. John Paul II, *Ecclesia in America,* no. 58.

to take up diocesan ministries that involve the exercise of charity to a specific community. This has taken place in some dioceses where there are needs for an official presence of the church to a particular group. In the Diocese of Tucson there are many prisons and few priests to serve the spiritual needs of those men and women. Deacons have begun to minister through the Rite of Distributing Holy Communion outside Mass with the Celebration of the Word and to preach, to counsel, and to spiritually nourish those who are incarcerated. The response has been encouraging.

Deacons can serve as liaisons for the bishop to various groups that need pastoral attention. In our diocese there are deacons serving as spiritual directors to the Cursillo and to the Charismatic groups as well as acting as liaisons for life issues. In every diocese there are so many challenges, needs, and difficulties that cry out for a pastoral response. While this can seem overwhelming at times, the bishop finds strength in Christ and in his collaborators.

> Leaving behind his very self in order to proclaim Jesus Christ, the bishop takes up his mission with confidence and courage, becoming in truth a "bridge" which leads to every man and woman. With the burning love of a shepherd he goes out in search of the sheep, following in the footsteps of Jesus who says: "I have other sheep that are not of this fold; I must bring them also and they will hear my voice."[18]

Conclusion

Deacons are called to serve. They contribute to the ministry of the bishop by assisting in teaching the word, celebrating the Eucharist, and working for justice and peace. In each of these areas they cooperate with their bishop and further his work. The bishop bears responsibility to call those who will serve as deacons, to oversee their formation, to ordain them, and to assign them to share in his ministry. "As ministers of Holy Orders, Bishops also have direct

---

18. John Paul II, *Pastores Gregis,* no. 66.

responsibility for permanent deacons in whom the Synodal Assembly saw authentic gifts of God for proclaiming the Gospel, instructing Christian communities and promoting the service of charity within God's family."[19] Obviously the bishop needs to care for those who are preparing to serve as deacons and to guide them in their lives as deacons. He needs to strive to know them personally and to promote their involvement in the life of the diocese.

Christ has told us that "the harvest is plentiful, but the laborers are few" (Luke 10:2). The restoration of the permanent diaconate has provided the church with additional workers who bring great commitment and dedication to their ministry. Deacons, however, will be effective ministers of the gospel only to the extent that they are properly screened, well formed, and involved in ongoing formation for ministry. The bishop bears the responsibility for ensuring that this happens. It is encouraging to me to see how this gift of the restored diaconate is contributing to the mission of Christ, especially among the littlest and weakest.

---

19. Ibid., no. 49.

CHAPTER 9

<hr>

The Deacon and
Personal Prayer

Dcn. Owen F. Cummings, DD

Writing about personal prayer is dangerous and risky at the best of times, given our almost unlimited human penchant for self-delusion and pretense. We are so skilled at fooling ourselves. If the writer is a minister of the church, for example, a deacon, when it comes to prayer, he is also aware of the gaps and *lacunae* between his public ecclesial persona and his personal daily performance. I recall some words of Charles Davis (1923–2001), a popular theologian in England in the 1960s and a *peritus* at the Second Vatican Council. Davis was continually bombarded with requests to speak on all aspects of the conciliar decrees and the renewal for which they called, and he was generous in his response. I refer to the following statement as the "Davis Declaration":

> They come to talks by speakers like myself. They hear about the new liturgy, about the new understanding of the layman's role, about collegiality, about the Church and the world, about a thousand and one new and exciting ideas. They are duly impressed. But who will speak to them quite simply about God, as of a Person he intimately knows, and make the reality and presence of God come alive for them once more?
>
> Before such need, how superficial, pathetically superficial, is much of the busyness of renewal. We reformers know so much about religion and about the church and about theology, but we stand empty-handed and uncomfortable when confronted with sheer hunger for God. Holiness is less easily

acquired than fluency in contemporary thinking. But people who, after listening to our enthusiastic discourses, quietly ask us to lead them to God are, though they do not know it, demanding holiness in us. I fear they may find everything else but that.[1]

The declaration is immensely challenging. Prayer is about holiness of life. While deacons—indeed all Christians—are committed to and engaged in the multifaceted and ongoing renewal of the church subsequent to Vatican II, the question is, Are we men of prayer, or do we stand "empty-handed and uncomfortable when confronted with the sheer hunger for God" among our people? Elsewhere I have written about the dysfunctional trait of anti-intellectualism sometimes found in our diaconal communities, but it is easier to get a graduate degree in theology than to become holy through personal prayer.[2] The Davis Declaration, then, summons us both to the daily renewal of prayer and to an examination of conscience in respect of our diaconal prayer lives.

Our daily prayer begins with morning prayer (Lauds) in the Liturgy of the Hours, but perhaps even before that liturgical moment, our daily renewal of prayer might open, as our eyes open, with that splendid final strophe from Psalm 17:15: "As for me, I shall gaze upon your face in faithfulness; / as I awake, I shall be content in your presence."[3] The New American Bible uses the word *justice* and the New Revised Standard Version employs *righteousness* for "faithfulness." The Hebrew noun is *sedaqah* and is best translated as "faithfulness." The "just man" or the "righteous man" is the one who strives to remain faithful to God in all the circumstances of his life. In our strophe the psalmist gazes upon God's face in faithfulness. It is God's face that is faithful, God's countenance constantly turned toward us in love. The psalmist recognizes this, and from that recognition he is transformed and graced toward an increasingly more faithful daily response to this ever-faithful God.

---

1. Charles Davis, "A Hidden God," *America* 114, no. 5 (January 29, 1966): 173.

2. Owen F. Cummings, *Deacons and the Church* (Mahwah, NJ: Paulist Press, 2004), 108–9.

3. This is my translation, from the Massoretic Text.

As the psalmist wakes from sleep, immediately he finds himself "content in (God's) presence." What a way to wake up and start the day—to wake up with our first conscious thought that we are in God's presence, and more, that we are *content* and *satisfied* in this presence. Our daily prayer ends with night prayer (Compline) in the Liturgy of the Hours, introduced with a brief examination of conscience. This, needless to say, must be a very personal examination, but surely central to this examination must be our constancy in prayer. If we awoke "content in (God's) presence," were we aware of this presence throughout the busy complexity of the day? Was the day punctuated by such moments of awareness?

Saint Paul's Prayerful Awareness of God

It would seem that the earliest Christian writer, Saint Paul, regularly punctuated his day with moments of God-awareness. He was a God-saturated man, and this comes to expression throughout his letters. Consider the following passages:

> 1 Thessalonians 5:16–18: "Rejoice always, *pray without ceasing,* give thanks in all circumstances."

> 2 Thessalonians 1:3: "We must *always give thanks to God* for you, brothers and sisters."

> 2 Thessalonians 1:11: "To this end we *always pray* for you."

> Romans 1:9: "For God…is my witness that *without ceasing I remember you always in my prayers.*"

> 1 Corinthians 1:4: *"I give thanks to my God always for you."*

> 2 Timothy 1:3: "I remember you *constantly in my prayers night and day.*" (emphasis added)

Few of the apostolic witnesses of the first century could have been as busy as Paul. As an evangelist and missionary, he founded and/or nurtured Christian communities in Damascus, Antioch, the various regions and provinces of Asia Minor, Greece, Cyprus, Malta, Rome, and perhaps even Spain. He supported himself as a worker in leather, probably especially tent making, so as not to be a burden to the communities among whom he worked. To have produced his magnificent corpus of letters full of wisdom and theological insight into the entire Christ-event must have demanded vast amounts of time given over to personal reflection, meditation, and analysis of biblical texts. The passages noted, however, show him constantly praying for, remembering, and giving thanks to God for his fellow members of Christ's body. Rather than thinking of Paul's prayer activity as discrete actions at discrete times, it is probably more fruitful to understand it as a constant and regular awareness of God-in-Christ's presence, an awareness punctuated by bursts of spontaneous doxological expression, of praise and thanksgiving, but always rooted in this acknowledgment of corporate union with others in Christ's holy body.

Notice also in these references to constant prayer the absence of language of personal satisfaction. There is not the slightest hint that this outpouring of prayer engenders within him an accompanying sense of personal satisfaction or emotional well-being. There must have been some sense of satisfaction flowing from his living with constancy in God's presence. It would be difficult to imagine it otherwise, but there is no dwelling upon this. He just gets on with his day punctuated with praising and thanking awareness.

One is reminded of some sentiments on prayer of the late English Dominican, Herbert McCabe:

> I usually don't find praying a deeply satisfying experience. It is true I hardly ever get a kick out of it, it almost never takes my breath away, but if you are deprived of, say, a decent liturgy for a fairly long period of time you discover an important gap in your emotional life. I might as well say at this point that I think there is a mistaken tendency, more especially in the United States but to some extent in the United Kingdom, to design the liturgy for too immediate a satisfaction.[4]

---

4. Herbert McCabe, OP, *God Still Matters* (London and New York: Continuum, 2002), 64–65.

McCabe is speaking of liturgical prayer as well as personal prayer, but his point holds. It simply is not the case that prayer always yields this "deeply satisfying experience" or "takes [our] breath away." While this happens from time to time, as it must have happened for Saint Paul, the point is that it cannot be engineered. To design our prayer lives to provide such instantaneous satisfaction is to make of prayer a therapy. Prayer does have therapeutic effects, but such effects stem from the prayer of ec-stasy, the moving out of ourselves to the acknowledgment of God, not from the prayer of self-concern. What does ec-static prayer look like? What shape does it take?

The Fourfold Shape of Ec-static Prayer: ACTS

Many of us learned in school long ago an acronym that provides us with a picture of ec-static prayer, ACTS: *A* stands for adoration, *C* for contrition, *T* for thanksgiving, and *S* for supplication. Prayer in which we move out of ourselves, in which we stand out of or away from self-preoccupation, takes the fourfold shape of adoration, contrition, thanksgiving, and supplication.

Adoration

First, *adoration* comes from two Latin words that imply movement out of oneself: *ad,* meaning "toward," and *orare,* meaning "to pray." Adoration is a movement out of egocentricity toward theocentricity. It is an acknowledging of God as God. It is a cumulatively intense awareness of and concentration on God as sheerly present. The patristic theologian, Brian Daley, SJ, writes, "The heart of Christian prayer, both for the individual alone and in the gathered community, has always been worship, adoration, the disinterested and preoccupying acknowledgment that at the heart of our reality lies a good and loving and self-dispensing Mystery who is Truth itself."[5]

---

5. Brian E. Daley, SJ, "How Should We Pray? Five Guiding Principles," *Crisis* 12, no. 3 (March 1994): 29.

Thus, both personal prayer and corporate-liturgical prayer find their heart in this self-transcending movement that is ad-oration. More needs to be said than this, however. This ec-static movement out of ourselves in ad-oration is only possible in response to our ec-static God who has moved out of himself into us in creation-redemption. God has made us for communion within his own being as Communion, as Father-Son-Spirit. Our ec-static response in adoration is made possible by God's ec-static initiative.

There is a wonderful phrase attributed to Saint Paul in the Acts of the Apostles that summarizes the meaning and the effect of adoration: "In [God] we live and move and have our being" (Acts 17:28). Behind this phrase, and indeed throughout our entire Catholic theological tradition, lies the axiom that God is not an object in the world of objects, not even the supremely divine object over against all created entities. Rather, God is the originating ground of all that is, and the final *telos* or goal of all creation. To be is to be *presenced* in God. Adoration is the graceful recognition that it is so, that I am so. That changes a person. The Anglican priest-theologian, John Macquarrie, comments, "The person who loses himself in the wondering contemplation of God begins to reflect something of the divine glory so that the image of God in which he was made becomes more manifest in his being."[6] Adoration, or what Macquarrie terms "the wondering contemplation of God," has consequences for the one who habitually adores: he or she begins to reflect something of the divine presence in the self. This reflection is not our own doing or achievement so much as it is the initiative taken by God, responded to by the person, having transformative consequences. An analogy may be offered in the person of Moses, or in the person of the Lord in the Transfiguration. After Moses communed with God on Mount Sinai, his face was shining (Exod 34:30–35), and as Jesus communed with his Father, his clothes "became dazzling white" (Mark 9:3). Moses' and Jesus' intimacy with God

---

6. John Macquarrie, "Adoration," in Gordon S. Wakefield, ed., *A Dictionary of Christian Spirituality* (London: SCM Press, 1983), 308.

made them glow, and our closeness with God makes us glow, perhaps not through the skin of our faces or in dazzling clothes, but in producing a deep, inner serenity. We are "content in God's presence," and it shows. Adoration transforms not only ourselves but our way of envisioning, of seeing reality. We see all reality theocentrically. One spiritual writer sums it up like this: "Prayer discovers the presence of the divine within the ordinary. It is part of the whole process of turning to God, of seeing all things in God, and of being transformed according to the likeness of God. It is a kind of transfiguration."[7]

Contrition

Second, *contrition* is saying, "I'm sorry." It is taking ownership of our moral failures, our sins before God, not in the direction of excessive guilt and anxiety so much as recognizing that in the enveloping presence of God whose best name is Love, we are so unlovely. It is the recognition of George Herbert (1593–1633) in his poem, "Love III": "Love bade me welcome: yet my soul drew back,/Guilty of dust and sin."[8] It is not easy to be contrite, to own our unloveliness. It is natural to wish to appear as good as we can to our peers and fellows, and to see in our reflection the fairest of them all. Honesty and integrity demand of us so much more. As Esther de Waal says, "It is humbling to stand before God with our failures, wounds, chaos, vulnerability. I think we all know deep down that it is only by facing them that we can hope to enlighten the darkness. This means that we must start by grieving honestly and without pretence or excuse."[9] Contrition is humbling prayer, but humbling prayer that keeps us honest and prevents our being reduced to a spiritual immobility. Turning again to George Herbert, but this time to his poem "Discipline," we read: "Though

7. Peter Baelz, *Does God Answer Prayer?* (London: Darton, Longman & Todd, 1982), 15.

8. John Tobin, ed., *George Herbert: The Complete English Poems* (London: Penguin Books, 1991), 178.

9. Esther de Waal, *Lost in Wonder* (Collegeville, MN: Liturgical Press, 2003), 102.

I fail, I weep: / Though I halt in pace, / Yet I creep / To the throne of grace."[10] Our failures before the love that is God should make us weep, but realizing that we may not be spiritual athletes does not prevent us from moving ahead in response to God. Not with confident running, but with honest and humble creeping, we move closer to God.

Thanksgiving

Third, *thanksgiving,* to say "Thank you," is to acknowledge a gift and a gift giver. A gift is never a right, never something to which one is entitled. A gift is purely gratuitous, and it is that which elicits our thanksgiving. Moreover, when someone gives us a gift, a gift that is free of manipulation and any hope of return, it is a symbolic way of giving themselves to us. It is an expression of love. This understanding is what leads Herbert McCabe to describe thanks-saying as follows: "To say thank you for a gift (or as the Greeks would say, to make a eucharist of it) is to recognize it, to think of it, as a communication of love."[11] Probably, thus far most people would find themselves in agreement with this description of thanks-saying. A Christian, however, would go much further. A Christian sees all of reality under the legend of gift. All reality comes from God as gift, initially with the first moment of creation. God's gift giving continues through the course of salvation history until reaching its climax in God's gift of self, the Word made flesh, Immanuel, perpetually rendered sacramentally in the Eucharist-making-the-church. Creation is an intentionally eucharistic, freely given gift eliciting from us as the voice of creation the words "Thank You," the action of Eucharist. In practical terms on the personal level, this eucharistic understanding of creation invites us to count our blessings, to count them one by one. Look back over the past day, the past week, the past month, the past year, and see how God has in fact upheld you, brought you through, gifted you. Sunday by Sunday we ought to collect a list of our thanksgivings

---

10. Tobin, *George Herbert,* 169.
11. McCabe, *God Still Matters,* 68.

and throw them gratefully into the great and global stream of thanksgiving that flows up to God in the Eucharist. As Oliver Davies has it, "In the Eucharist, the dynamic that we might call Eucharistic perception becomes the ideal ground of all human perceiving."[12]

Supplication

Fourth, *supplication* is the mode of prayer in which we ask God on behalf of others or for ourselves. This is an urgent matter, according to Jesus:

> Ask, and it will be given you; search and you will find; knock, and the door will be opened for you. For everyone who asks receives, and everyone who searches finds, and for everyone who knocks, the door will be opened....If you, then, who are evil know how to give good gifts to your children, how much more will your Father in heaven give good things to those who ask him! (Matt 7:7–11)

Supplication or petition is grounded for us in the teaching of Christ, and the Matthean passage is confident of the divine response. While there is a very strong sense of the faithful to pray for one another, and with trust to place all our needs in God's providential hands, there is also an awareness that our requests to God should not be superficially egocentric or obviously trivial. Our unease with trivial supplication has been well captured by the Catholic scientist, Chet Raymo:

> For many people, the entire purpose of prayer is to invoke God's intervention in the course of their daily lives, to adjust the tilt of the universe in their personal favor, to redirect the stream of time ever so marginally so that benefices flow their way....I struggle to shed the shabby shawl of petitionary and formulaic prayer that I inherited as a child—to reject the default syllables "Me, Lord, Me"—so that I might attend to

---

12. Oliver Davies, *The Creativity of God: World, Eucharist, Reason* (Cambridge: Cambridge University Press, 2004), 145.

things—to swallows and auroras—to the voice that whispers in *all* of creation, to the voice that *is* all of creation.[13]

We can probably readily identify with the first part of Raymo's statement, that is, the complaint that puerile petitionary prayer seeks "to adjust the tilt of the universe in [our] personal favor." Are we as comfortable, however, with the latter part of his statement—that attendance "to the voice that whispers in *all* of creation, to the voice that *is* all of creation" is incompatible with less egocentric forms of petition or supplication? I doubt it. Apart altogether from the Lord's teaching about petitionary prayer, there is a powerful ecclesial impulse to lift up our needs and those of others to God in prayer. To regard this kind of prayer as shabby and as simply tilting "the universe in [our] personal favor" seems excessively rationalistic. Brian Daley seems closer to the mark when he affirms:

> We cannot explain how prayer "works" any more than we can explain Who or what God is. But if we have some dim apprehension that the reality we share finds its source and norm in a Holy Mystery whose name, for lack of a more precise term, is Love, we *must* reach out to that Mystery with our own love and longing—Love summons love in return.[14]

What Daley has that is missing in Raymo is naming and trusting as Love the voice that whispers in all of creation, the voice that is all of creation. Recall the words cited by Saint Paul earlier: "In [God] we live and move and have our being." God, this mystery of love, not only transcends creation as its originating source, but is the within of its within. This is Daley's understanding, and to trust this mystery with our deepest needs is not only no bad thing, nor no selfish thing, but, like the prayer of thanksgiving, a primal Christian instinct.

Theologian John Macquarrie comes at the prayer of petition in somewhat different but no less helpful terms than Daley:

---

13. Chet Raymo, *Climbing Brandon, Science and Faith on Ireland's Holy Mountain* (New York: Walker & Co., 2004), 157, 167.

14. Daley, "How Should We Pray?" 32.

> [Intercessory prayer] provides, as it were, openings into the dense texture of the human situation through which can come the creative and healing power of the reality we call God; and because within that human situation our lives are all bound together in a mysterious solidarity, then God's power is able to operate far beyond the particular person who offers the prayer, though through him. Prayer, as petition and intercession, helps to make the human reality porous to the divine reality—the whole human reality, and not only that part of it actively engaged in prayer.[15]

It seems to me that two key ideas emerge from this interesting passage. First, if God is the one in whom "we live and move and have our being," prayer of petition for Macquarrie makes us porous to this divine milieu. Second, human lives are all bound inextricably together in relationality, so that one person is no person. We are person-ed in and through and for one another. We are not discrete units of humanity, and this embodiment, strengthened in Christ, is a mysteriously powerful ecology of divine action. Without overreaching ourselves we may say with confidence that mature supplication works wonders.

Other Forms of Personal Prayer

Lectio Divina

A tried and true monastic practice that provides an excellent conduit for adoration, contrition, thanksgiving, and supplication is *lectio divina,* or divine reading. More often than not the scriptures are the object of *lectio divina,* but the reading may also be from the Roman Missal, other liturgical books, or even poetry. Whatever one is reading in this style of prayer, the four steps of the process remain the same: *lectio*/reading, *meditatio*/thinking, *oratio*/praying, and *contemplatio*/silence. The first two steps are well described by

---

15. John Macquarrie, *Paths in Spirituality,* 2nd ed. (Harrisburg, PA: Morehouse Publishing, 1992), 27–28.

a deacon who is also a professor of English and a published poet, Chris Anderson:

> Reading the Bible isn't a matter of receiving simple lessons for living once and for all, immediately, full grown, so that no thinking ever has to be done again. No, reading is slow, it's a process, it happens over time and only with cultivation, and it all depends on how the reader works and what the reader does. The fruit isn't handed to us.[16]

Talking about scripture, Dcn. Anderson is emphatic that the reading must be slow—we might even say extra slow. Sometimes it helps to do the reading aloud, since that slows us down. Depending on the actual text, more than one reading may be demanded. This is *lectio*. Slow and careful reading is a fairly rare skill, but when it is practiced, new insights emerge, new questions, a higher level of intellectual curiosity. This is *meditatio*. The reading raises questions for us, ranging from fairly straightforward questions of fact that may not be immediately intelligible to questions that search through ambiguities and subtleties and possible layers of meaning that occur to a particular reader. This may continue until a point of satisfaction with *meditatio*/thinking has emerged. This is what Anderson means when he refers to "how the reader works and what the reader does."

Moving to step 3, *oratio*, we burst into prayer, prayer with words, the fourfold shape of ec-static prayer: adoration, contrition, thanksgiving, supplication. Usually, relative to our mood, circumstances, and the text we have been reading and thinking about, one of these prayer styles will predominate. We may feel called simply to adore God, or to supplicate God on behalf of someone or a problematic issue, or the experiences of the day may produce in us a litany of thanksgiving or an act of contrition. The important thing is not to fake it, but to go with the flow of our mood and the text. How long are we to do this? As long as it takes. It may be over in

---

16. Chris Anderson, *Teaching as Believing* (Waco, TX: Baylor University Press, 2004), 55.

seconds; it may take much longer. It is over when one reaches a point of satiety. Then comes the last step of *contemplatio/*silence, when one lapses into silence, free of words, even inner words and inner noise, free of images and associations, just deep silence. This requires cultivation. We live in such noisy contexts—almost as if, terrified by silence, we need to fill every waking moment with auditory and visual stimuli. Silence seeks to eliminate such stimuli, less through intense effort and striving on our part, and more through a process of letting go. In the beginning we probably will find it somewhat difficult to endure too much silence, but as we move along, we will come to relish longer periods of silence in which we encounter the God who lures us into a relationship of communion. If a deacon were to practice *lectio divina* on a regular, even daily basis, it would make an enormous difference to his prayer life. The entire process can take a few minutes or a much longer period of time, depending on the circumstances of the day and our commitments, but the cumulative impact of divine reading will be very significant indeed.

Prayer Journal

Many people like to write in a journal. I do not mean a detailed and intimate diary or exact historical record of our everyday lives. Rather, I mean putting into writing our thoughts and reflections, the ideas that occur to us during quiet times. This too is a form of prayer. The four steps of *lectio divina* may be applied here as well. Step 1 is writing, 2 is thinking as we write and about what we have written, 3 is prayer, and 4 is silent contemplation. Our temperaments and backgrounds are all different, but if one likes to write, this is a powerful medium of prayer. Dcn. Chris Anderson likes to write, and he offers this reflection: "Writing can't save us. Writing can't take the place of prayer. But when prayer comes first, joy and sadness and tenderness well out in waves, and those waves are the condition of any writing that matters. Writing becomes possible in the wake of prayer, a side effect, possible because no longer necessary or important, pure play, pure praise."[17] Here Anderson differentiates writing from prayer. Perhaps he is referring to the kind of professional writing that he does, but in my analysis, existential and deeply personal writing not only "becomes possible in the wake of prayer" but is itself a form of prayer. The last sentence, however, seems to go far in the direction of writing *as* prayer when he asserts that it is "pure play, pure praise." This is prayer with a pen or a journal—prayer even with a laptop!

Toward a Practical Conclusion

In a very insightful essay on prayer, the late Bishop of Saginaw, Michigan, Kenneth Untener, states forthrightly the first axiom of prayer: "The relationship with God remains key. Without some continuing conversation in a relationship, you lose your friend; you lose your wife or husband; you lose your God. The depth of relationship equals the depth of communication."[18] Relationship is impossible without communication; indeed, depth of relationship and depth of communication are synonymous. True of our human relationships, it is true *a fortiori* of our relationship with God. This chapter has been but a very limited teasing out of this axiom.

In conclusion I want to stay with some of Bishop Untener's reflections, because they seem right on target for a deacon. Some structure for our daily personal prayer is absolutely necessary; otherwise it will fall by the wayside. We need, however, to exercise some caution in this respect. Too many deacons experience the temptation to measure themselves by a model of spirituality that can make them appear second rate when it comes to prayer. During retreat time or days of recollection, for example, one feels strongly the resolution to redo one's schedule to allow time for more prayer. This is no bad thing, as it helps us to situate our priorities more appropriately. Surely, however, although he is describing the

17. Ibid., 84.
18. Kenneth Untener, "Using the Wrong Measure?" in Donald B. Cozzens, ed., *The Spirituality of the Diocesan Priest* (Collegeville, MN: Liturgical Press, 1997), 25.

situation of priests, Bishop Untener is not telling us something we do not already know as deacons when he writes, "Regularity in any-thing, even meals, falls apart sometimes. If the ideal is a regular schedule, regular time for prayer, regular asceticism (or even exer-cise), regular community, (even regular meals), they cannot man-age it. It turns into the regret, 'I'm not praying as I ought.'"[19] Most deacons are working full time and are married with familial respon-sibilities, as well as being ministers of the church. This makes for very complex schedules and can also invite guilt about our prayer lives. That kind of guilt is utterly useless. We need to recall with Bishop Untener: "Adding on to busy lives usually does not work. What does work is taking what is already present in our lives and turning that into the ongoing conversation with God....We would do better to take the pattern that is there...and find ways to build into it an attentiveness to God that runs from morning till night."[20] Which of us deacons would disagree? Scheduling our prayer lives is important, yes, but it is also important to do so realistically and in such a fashion that we find ourselves increasingly attentive to God, an attentiveness and an awareness that runs from our waking "con-tent in His presence" to our falling asleep in his peace.

Let me end with the wise words of a skilled prayer practi-tioner, Esther de Waal: "The commitment to the time of prayer is the keystone [to the spiritual life]. It is so easy and attractive to read about prayer and to talk about prayer. But unless we go to pray there is no prayer."[21]

---

19. Ibid., 24.
20. Ibid., 26.
21. de Waal, *Lost in Wonder*, 49.

CHAPTER 10

The Deacon and Work

Dcn. Thomas Baker, MBA

Most deacons have at least one funny story about how a well-meaning parishioner has been shocked or at least momentarily silenced by the discovery—usually through the sudden, well-timed appearance of the deacon's affectionate spouse or squalling baby—that deacons may be married. The observer's dumbfoundedness is often followed by an interesting discussion about the positive value of being married on a deacon's ministry, and how the busy, demanding life of a husband and father can make his preaching and general attitudes a helpful addition to the parish scene.

While awareness that deacons are married is slowly but surely growing, thanks in part to these often comical encounters, what I suspect even fewer people realize is that not only are deacons married, but generally speaking deacons go out and earn a living in the secular world, just like everyone else does. When people do discover that deacons work full time outside their parishes, often the follow-up discussion focuses on "how we do it"—manage, that is, to fit in a full-time job with what seems like a substantial parish schedule. A far more interesting conversation (and the subject of this chapter) is "*why* we do it"—that is, why it is a good and even necessary thing for deacons to make their lives so apparently complex.

Sometimes this discovery that deacons are also earning a secular living leads people to conclude that we are not serious, full-time ministers, perhaps something more like glorified lay volunteers. Furthermore, at times I also wonder (uncharitably, I admit) whether one of the reasons deacons are asked to earn their own sustenance is simply that the church has found a great way to recruit some wonderful ministers without having to pay most of them. The fact is, however, that for me and for many other deacons, there is something much more positive to deacons' working lives than simple economic necessity.

There are certainly some deacons who at times see their daily work as an impediment to their ministry, and maybe even to their general happiness. After all, deacons are just as likely as anyone else to face oppressive bosses, boring jobs, draining schedules, ruthless corporate cutbacks, or periods of career disillusionment. Then, too, there are deacons who have become so attached to their church leadership role that their secular employment has gradually come to seem a form of time serving, a source of income that makes their ministry possible, but a poor second as a focus for their passion and excitement.

Heaven knows I have not been happy in my work all the time—few people are—but I have come to embrace this duality of work and church in my life. Despite the full-time nature of diaconate ordination and ministry, many of us spend many, many more hours working outside the parish than in it. Most deacons serve in parishes in one way or another, but our role is not focused solely there: many of us work in the parish *and* outside of it, working in the church *and* in the world, and our mission is not to lead two separate lives but one integrated life, where the interaction between our work and ministry is near the very heart of our identity as deacons.

In his book *Diakonia,* John N. Collins provides a fascinating historical review of the word *diakonia* in both sacred scripture and the other literature of the ancient world.[1] He sets forth the thesis that the many layers of meaning in this Greek word suggest a person who is not simply "servant" but "go-between" or "ambassador"—one whose role it is to move back and forth between two places, relaying messages and acting as a helpful, communicative

---

1. John N. Collins, *Diakonia: Re-interpreting the Ancient Sources* (New York: Oxford University Press, 1990).

183

emissary. This special flavor of the deacon's identity found expression, in time, in the ancient thought that the deacons served as "the bishop's eyes and ears"[2]—informing the community about the concerns and desires of the bishop, and reporting to the bishop the needs and situation of his people. From the outset, it seems that at least in part, deacons have been seen as intermediaries, people who by nature function in two spheres at once, conversant with what is going on in each, playing a role as interpreter, observer, and creative catalyst in both church and world.

Most diaconate formation focuses on the deacon's "church" identity: theology, sacramental ministry, preaching, and pastoral endeavors. This is all to the good, but as a result few deacons have had much chance to reflect on how their diaconate might find expression in their work, and how their work experiences can enrich the church. This chapter offers a few beginning reflections on this topic, along with some thoughts that might help stimulate thinking about some new future directions.

Work: A Blessing, Although a Mixed One

All the studies prove it: Americans are hard-working people. We like to work, and we are good at it. "What do you do?" trumps almost any other question we want to ask when we meet a stranger, and despite some occasional studies decrying our workaholic American natures,[3] in general it does not seem as if our love affair with work and accomplishment is going to fade anytime soon.

Fortunately, our church has also taught that work is, by nature, not only a necessary thing but a powerfully good one. In a Catholic theology of work, the fundamental assumption is that work not only provides the necessities of human life but also

---

2. Cited in the National Conference of Catholic Bishops, Bishops' Committee on the Permanent Diaconate, *Permanent Deacons in the United States: Guidelines on Their Formation and Ministry* (Washington, DC: United States Catholic Conference, 1985), no. 35.

3. Among others, Arlie Russell Hochschild's *The Time Bind* (New York: Henry Holt, 1997).

enables us to take part in carrying on God's work of creation: we are called to make this world, through our work, a shining place of prosperity and justice, a result we may never achieve but toward which we are called continually to strive.

> Through work man must earn his daily bread and contribute to the continual advance of science and technology and, above all, to elevating unceasingly the cultural and moral level of the society within which he lives in community with those who belong to the same family....Man is made to be in the visible universe an image and likeness of God himself, and he is placed in it in order to subdue the earth. From the beginning therefore he is called to work.[4]

There is still another reason why we work, however, one that goes beyond both economic necessity and theological *should.* Work, done well, is its own reward. For many people, it is the most powerful way they have of expressing their God-given talents and interests. The experience of doing what we do best and love best, whether it is writing a novel, leading a group, or building a table, gives us a deep sense of rightness and well-being. As the sociologist Mihaly Csikszentmihalyi has written, through work we can experience a nearly transcendent state of "flow": a state in which our engagement with work is so natural and so deep that we lose track of time.[5] Those of us who are believers know that when that happens we are doing what we were meant by our Creator to do.

This might be a good time for me to disclose that I have been extraordinarily lucky in my working life—not that I have been made terribly rich from it, but because I have been able to do work that I love. As a writer and editor, I have worked at eccentric publishing companies and been around smart, amusing colleagues; as a manager, I have had the enormous pleasure of seeing how a group

---

4. Opening blessing of *Laborem Exercens* (Pope John Paul II, On the 90th Anniversary of *Rerum Novarum,* 1981), the church's foundational encyclical on the question of work and workers.

5. In, among other works, Mihaly Csikszentmihalyi, *Finding Flow: The Psychology of Engagement with Everyday Life* (New York: Basic Books, 1997).

of people, working together, can accomplish great things while building on and respecting one another's talents. I like the work I do, and the unexpected call I experienced to be a deacon has not changed my sense that a secular career is somewhere I very much belong. Given a choice between working full time in a parish and being around a magazine or a newspaper, I will definitely take the newspaper—yes, even if the salaries were the same.

Even, however, for those of us who have been fortunate in our working lives, we all know that work is not always a joy. In fact, work can damage us: the people who oversee it, the workers who do it, and the world from which it draws its resources. As humans, just as we can misunderstand and misuse the other glorious gifts we have been given by God, we can end up getting work very, very wrong.

The story of how work can betray us is a complex one, but in many ways it all comes down to whether we consider ourselves owners or stewards of that with which we are working. That same theology of work that sees us entrusted with the care of the Earth makes it perfectly clear that though we may be here to "subdue" that Earth, it is not our possession. We are accountable to God for what we do with it, in the same way that the tenants in Jesus' parables are called to give an account to their landlord of what has been accomplished in his absence. This one unfortunate reversal of perspective, where we forget that we are only tenants of this world and not owners of its possessions or people, accounts for much of what goes wrong in our relationship with work. *Laborem Exercens* devotes nearly half its length to an analysis of all the things to which these mistaken ideas about work and our relationship to it can lead, from the oppression of workers to indifference to the natural environment. Work and business, uninformed by love or a desire for justice, can undo us all.

Thus on the one hand, work offers us deep psychological rewards and often money as well; on the other hand, the pursuit of these rewards often goes off the rails when we forget our role as stewards of creation. Given that tension, perhaps it is not surprising that we all so easily erect walls between work and the rest of life, and perhaps especially between work and faith. Work is in many ways so rewarding that it can easily begin to make up an absorbing world of its own. It is not at all unusual for people to divorce their career choices from considerations of their faith (much less their personal preferences or hopes), instead choosing a direction based on material concerns; it is also not uncommon for a successful business or corporation to decide (sometimes unintentionally) that its survival and growth are so valuable that it is free from some necessary restraints or responsibilities.

Into this working world, which we so easily divorce from our lives as "religious" people, come deacons, called to be ambassadors from one world to the other. Is this really an integral part of our role as deacons?

Deacons and Working

The groundswell of interest and research that helped lead to the restoration of the diaconate at the Second Vatican Council was not primarily an American effort. Instead, as William Ditewig noted in chapter 2, much of the thought and writing that underlies this revival began in Germany—and originally, the men who advocated the return of the diaconate had very different assumptions about how deacons and the world of secular work would be connected. In this movement[6] that ultimately gave birth to the diaconate, it is surprising to realize that most of these pioneers assumed that deacons would, like priests, be employed by the church. Their vision saw the deacon identified closely with full-time ministries of charity, especially social work and what we might today call community development. Many of the men who hoped to see the diaconate revived were themselves already pursuing careers completely devoted to charitable work, and they saw the diaconate as recognizing and strengthening that way of life.

---

6. Deacons with a historical bent may enjoy seeing a selection of these articles, in translation, in National Conference of Catholic Bishops, Bishops' Committee on the Permanent Diaconate, *Foundations for the Renewal of the Diaconate,* trans. David Bourke et al. (Washington, DC: United States Conference of Catholic Bishops, 1993).

Even Karl Rahner, the famous Jesuit theologian whose work on the diaconate (and many other topics) was so influential at the council, saw a sharp division between the idea of a revived diaconate and secular employment:

> Ordination…is meant to stamp a person permanently and completely and should claim the whole person, with all his internal and external powers….In view of this fact, the ordained deacon must fundamentally be someone who normally receives his livelihood from the Church in basically the same way and with basically the same "titles" as canon law envisages for the priest.[7]

While this passage might seem to be harboring a relative contempt for secular life as a second-class "distraction" from pastoral work for the ordained person, part of Rahner's thinking reflects the contemporaneous revival of the role of the laity as having the primary responsibility for the transformation of the world. It is the laity, in Rahner's and the council's view, who are called by Christ to evangelize and reshape the world, not as followers but as leaders. The primary place of deacons, in this view, is not in duplicating the role of the laity but in a more specialized and distinctive role focused on full-time service and charity.

In Germany, many deacons do in fact work full time for the church as their primary employer,[8] much as the founders of the movement envisioned. In the United States, however, things have developed very differently. Seventy-three percent of American deacons are not paid at all for their ministry, and a significant majority of deacons of preretirement age work in secular employment.[9]

---

7. Karl Rahner, SJ, "The Theology of the Restoration of the Diaconate," in National Conference of Catholic Bishops, Bishops' Committee on the Permanent Diaconate, *Foundations,* 173–74.

8. Walter Cardinal Kasper, *Leadership in the Church: How Traditional Roles Can Serve the Christian Community Today* (New York: Herder & Herder, 2003), 206–7, n. 33.

9. Cited in Center for Applied Research on the Apostolate, "Profile of the Diaconate in the United States," CARA Working Papers Series 6 (Washington, DC: Georgetown University, 2004).

Perhaps driven by a quintessentially American practicality, American deacons seem to have embraced a clearly dual model of the diaconate, one in which a deacon's presence in a secular work-place is the norm rather than the exception.

Is this a good thing? The ultimate answer to that depends on the creativity and energy with which deacons embrace and explore this ministry. Perhaps inevitably, parishes have presented deacons with an enormous amount of pastoral and charitable work to be done, and many deacons have embraced the parish as a headquar-ters for their work. Deacons have an equally important role *outside* of traditional parish-centered ministries, however.

> It is the deacon's special call to be on the front line, an atten-tive listener and a pioneer who leads the church's response to these [contemporary] challenges....Many of these tasks can be done only by full-time professionals, others by a non-stipendiary [not employed by the church] deacon, whose main opportunities lie in his professional activity where— like the French worker-priests—he should represent the church locally in his work and be present in spheres of life to which no one else from the church has access.[10]

Deacons who are employed in the secular world, and who embrace their roles as "go-betweens," may see their work lives gen-erating a dual identity: as ministers from the church to the world of work, and as interpreters of the world of work inside the church. The remainder of this chapter explores these two facets of the deacon's relationship to work and suggests some creative ways in which deacons might think about and address them.

Bringing the Church to the Working World

My wife's late grandfather was an Irish Philadelphia lawyer, Catholic to the bone, with strong opinions about religious obser-vance and no reservations whatsoever about imposing his routines

---

10. Kasper, *Leadership,* 36, 42.

and devotions on others. His family still tells the story of how at noon each day, everyone in his law practice stopped whatever he or she was doing and got down on their knees to pray the Angelus, after which business as usual could resume. In general, though, we all recognize that our American workplaces are much more secular affairs, where even the discussion of religion, much less its active observance, has long been a relative taboo. In many ways, we should be very glad. Through our reluctance to introduce religion as a daily factor in work life, American culture has helped create places where (at least in theory) we can offer everyone who is a part of our country an equal chance at success. Part of offering that opportunity is ensuring that success is based on accomplishment and ambition only, not who people are, where they are from, or what religion they follow. We want religion, like race, not to be a factor in business decisions about promotions, salaries, hirings and firings, and other employment issues.

Thus, with the best motivation in the world, we have made sure that religion as a source of pressure or discomfort is mostly absent from the places we work. As a business manager, I support this reticence: workplace openness and toleration is an admirable goal. Of course, this divorce of religion from the workplace has also had some unfortunate results: namely, a tendency for people to regard their work as an area of life completely separated from religion's call for justice and generosity. If we do not talk about faith at work, we ever so gradually may come to feel that faith has no role there at all. There is obviously work to do helping Americans reflect on, and act on, what their faith has to say about their working lives. What form will that take?

Some recent trends suggest surprising ways in which this will happen. In recent years even this intensely secular American workplace has seen a rather dramatic shift in its openness to a peculiarly American form of religion: A new willingness to talk about work in spiritual, if not religious or sectarian, terms. Books, workshops, discussion groups, and speakers, all focused on looking at work from the perspective of our spiritual fulfillment, are breaking down the traditional resistance to thinking of work as anything other than a series of economic choices. Such monumental best-sellers as Ken Blanchard's *The One-Minute Manager* and Stephen Covey's *The 7 Habits of Highly Effective People,* although written by deeply religious people, are not explicitly religious books—they allow for their readers to be nonbelievers—but the authors do push their readers to consider the spiritual significance and effect on others of what they do. Thanks to this new wave of interest in "spirituality and work," many working people now think about their actions and future in terms where religion, if not explicit in the discussion, is at least lurking beneath the surface.

Many of these "spiritual" but nonsectarian approaches to reflecting on work and vocation have done much good: they help people make decisions about their work lives, direct them into careers in which they are happier, and even help people consider whether their deepest values have found adequate expression in the work they have chosen to do. It is true that some of these so-called spiritual books have more to do with a gospel of self-empowerment than the gospel itself, and they often neglect the self-questioning and concern for justice that traditional Christianity brings to any moral issues. Nevertheless, it is a start and, for the traditional churches, a new and exciting opportunity for new forms of ministry.

What might deacons be called to do in the midst of this hunger for seeing a deeper significance to work on the one hand, and a reluctance to be too overtly "religious" in the workplace on the other? Here, clearly, deacons will be on the "front lines" of developing a new frontier for ministry. Among the possibilities for deacons to reflect on when defining their workplace ministry are the following.

Simple Presence and a Visible Identity

Most deacons find that once the rumor spreads around the workplace that they have a "secret life" as ordained ministers, that alone will create significant, unpredictable opportunities for pastoral work. Deacons are still rare enough to be the subject of curiosity and conversation among Catholics and non-Catholics alike. Even marginal or alienated Catholics in an office generally want to hear a little bit about deacons (even if only as another ideal opportunity for them to vent some more about the church's past or current failings). It is not at all unusual, even for deacons who do not actively market their availability for "religious" conversation, for deacons to gradually become the unofficial provider of the religious point of view on any topic during rambling lunchtime or airport conversations. Perhaps more important, people who discover that a church minister is in the workplace often come forward for suddenly and surprisingly frank, private one-on-one conversations: on their marriage relationships, their vocational concerns or futures, their status or relationship with the church. Again, laypeople can and do have these discussions with their coworkers as well—but deacons, as official church emissaries, often flush out some who are ready to talk simply because of this identity.

Deacons generally avoid using their presence in the workplace as an excuse to become religious busybodies. They respect the privacy of their colleagues and take no for an answer when someone clearly does not want to talk about a personal or religious question. Even low-key deacons, however, will find that just being on the premises, subtly identified as a minister of the gospel, is a ministry they never expected to discover.

Modeling an Integrated Work Life

A second challenge for deacons as working people is to serve as a model of people who do not build walls between their lives as workers on the one hand and their lives as Christians on the other. Erecting those walls is a tempting proposition, because being a Christian person in a workplace is not a task that comes without problems. The fact is, Christian values and business values, while not completely incompatible, are not identical, and no one in business can lose sight of it. After all, business rewards winners, while Christianity calls us to bend over backward for life's "losers." Business values success; Christianity nags us with the thought that we can easily become blind to what we are neglecting in the pursuit of that success. Being a Christian anywhere, but perhaps especially in certain types of businesses and occupations, requires a level of self-awareness and moral sensitivity that many more people need help developing.

Deacons, along with the laymen and laywomen who are on the front lines in the workplace each day, help people live not by one rulebook for weekdays and a different one for Sundays but by one integrated approach to life. We do it not always by preaching about it but by the decisions we make at work, the advice we give, and the actions from which we refrain. Like anyone living a Christian life, this means deacons may occasionally find themselves in trouble with their work authorities; they may fight for policy changes, or refuse to participate in objectionable or dishonest practices, or make sacrifices to protect the workers for whom they are responsible. On the other hand, deacons have tremendous opportunities to be forces for good in the workplace, people who stand out through their commitment to hiring a diverse workforce, to honesty in communication, and to fairness in treatment. Deacons, like all Christians, need to find the ways that a genuinely Christian approach to life can transform the places people work; there is plenty of work to do.

Chaplaincies and Other More Formal Workplace Ministries

According to recent reporting in the *New York Times,* many churches—particularly evangelical churches—are now establishing formal workplace-focused ministries.[11] Some companies, even major global firms, now permit employees to form overtly religious organizations that meet using company facilities. Some companies

---

11. Russell Shorto, "With God at Our Desks: The Rise of Religion and Evangelism in the American Workplace," *New York Times Magazine,* October 31, 2004. The story emphasizes some of the more aggressively sectarian forms that religiously focused workplaces can take.

have themselves actually formed relationships with "corporate chaplains" (paid or unpaid) who make themselves available systematically for interaction with employees.

Most of these "official" workplace religious activities, like Bible study, are ecumenical in nature, with evangelicals, Catholics, and others participating equally. Others have a much more sectarian flavor, focused on the evangelization and Christian conversion of souls. With the aggressive expansion of evangelical churches into this form of outreach, there may be both an increase in workplace conflict but also, clearly, an opportunity for other, more traditional churches to respond with their own approaches and experiments.

The Catholic Church has traditionally not expended much apostolic energy toward formal workplace outreaches such as these. In part this reflects an overly parish-centric view of where ministry takes place, but it also reflects a natural and intelligent reluctance to create sectarian conflict. This reluctance is now being challenged. The fact is that there are people who will come to a Bible study group or morning prayer in an office conference room who might never set foot in a parish on Sunday, and the workplace has become yet another setting in which newer, more aggressive Christian churches may attract away marginal Catholics who feel unconnected with their church. Deacons are particularly well positioned to experiment with new roles as the church's official ministers in workplaces, and to create new (and perhaps successfully ecumenical) ways to reach out to people in settings well outside of the parish.

Bringing the World of Work to the Church

Churches generally (and not just the Catholic Church) have historically had an ambiguous relationship with the business world. On the one hand, wealthy businesspeople have long been actively pursued as donors and behind-the-scenes advisers to pastors, bishops, and other leaders. On the other hand, however, many businesspeople of goodwill feel that the church undervalues and denigrates their lives as laypeople and businesspeople. They hear homilies focused on work's excesses and evils, and little about the creativity, passion, and societal benefits that working brings.[12] The churches, they feel, "don't get it"—and, as a result, they fail to offer working people opportunities to put their skills and insights to work in the service of the church's future. Here, too, deacons have the opportunity to map out some new territory, acting as official interpreters of the world of work to the church at large. There are several ways that deacons can bring their experiences and talents to bear.

Preaching about Work and Its Value

Most adults in every congregation spend most of their weekdays working, and I have found that acknowledging that fact from the pulpit, and perhaps even addressing it head-on, generates interest and gratitude. Sometimes this effort simply involves occasional homiletic examples that suggest that the preacher knows and understands how working people's time is spent each week. Dull meetings, exhausting travel, tough economic conditions—deacons, like their congregations, spend their weeks there, and establishing a rapport on these matters helps produce homilies with a real-world flavor that other homilists may not command.

More important than amusing or sympathetic examples, however, is preaching that affirms secular work as *itself* a vocation—a primary place in which the vast majority of Christians live out their baptismal promises and work out their salvation. Deacons especially need to preach that involvement in the parish, valuable and indispensable as it is, cannot be held out as the only goal of the Christian life. Surely we need to tell people far more often than we do that the transformation of the world through the passionate work and evangelism of laypeople is also something the church exists to support. Many preachers only mention work when they want to tell people how important it is to get away from it for

---

12. An outstanding overview of the relationship between businesspeople and their churches is Laura Nash and Scotty McLennan, *Church on Sunday, Work on Monday: The Challenge of Fusing Christian Values with Business Life* (San Francisco: Jossey-Bass, 2001).

prayer and quiet. Certainly this is one possible message for working people, but deacons can take on as their own special responsibility to preach about embracing and transforming work, not just the need to step away from it.

Encouraging Vocational and Moral Reflection

Many people in our assemblies are facing choices about their work, often difficult ones. They wonder whether they chose their career for the right reasons and whether it is time to rethink how their work lives are being spent. They may be facing a shrinking paycheck or significant discrimination or undue pressure to perform, and they wonder how they should respond. In some cases, these moral choices and decisions are stark and serious ones: executives needing to decide whether to cut benefits for employees, salespeople resisting the idea of fudging the sales figures the way the boss wants them to, middle managers agonizing about whether to fire the devoted but less competent longtime employee.

In general, homilies and adult faith formation neglect issues such as this, and yet working people are generally eager to find settings to reflect on them and discuss them, both one on one and in informal discussions with one another. Deacons can clearly take a leading role in helping people through the process of making difficult work decisions and the vocational choices that will bring them greater happiness and a greater sense of their own personal missions as Christians.

Conclusion

If deacons are "ambassadors" of the church to the world, there is plenty of work to do on the return trip: helping the church learn from and benefit from the insights and talents of its members who work outside of the church and parish. The church's need for insight and leadership from deacons and laypeople experienced in secular affairs has never been greater. This need goes far beyond repairing the flaws in church governance and oversight that became apparent in many dioceses as a result of the sexual abuse crisis of recent years. As the church looks to the future, it needs new models for governing and administering parishes; new approaches to recruiting and training people for (and paying people for) new forms of parish leadership and ministry; new ways to make and implement decisions about the church's resources (parish closings, administration of Catholic schools, and so on); and new ways to articulate and preach its message to an increasingly indifferent surrounding culture. These are all hard problems, and all issues where deacons, as the church's official "go-betweens," could play an innovative role in tapping the experience and talents of the secular world.

The church has been naturally—and rightly—reluctant to turn even its secular affairs entirely over to people whose primary experience has been in a worldly, perhaps for-profit environment. The church is not, after all, in a profit-making business, and it will always (in the interest of its mission) make at least some choices that a business would never elect. Here, too, however, there is a clear leadership role for deacons: we know both the church and its priorities on the one hand, and we have some insight into the benefits that strong management, good governance and leadership, and common sense have brought to institutions in the secular world. For deacons, using the insights and experience we glean from secular work is a challenging assignment to which our exciting, still-evolving ambassadorial role is calling us.

CHAPTER 11

The Sacramental Ministry of the Deacon in Parish Life

Dcn. Ray R. Noll, Doct. ès Sc. Rel.

Introduction

One of the fine accomplishments flowing from Vatican II was the revision of the formal sacraments of the Catholic Church. Granted that for some the revision was not enough and for others too much, still the council's *Sacrosanctum Concilium* paved the way for a new attitude toward worship,[1] and permanent deacons gradually came to be a part of this. Directly related to the sacramental revision was the work of some of the great theologians at the council, such as Karl Rahner and Edward Schillebeeckx. They taught us to see sacraments and sacramentality in a much broader context than simply the seven official rituals of the church. They taught us, for example, to see Christ himself as the sacrament of our encounter with God,[2] and in turn to see the church as the fundamental sacrament[3] of Jesus, and the actions of the church—those seven official rituals—as sacraments in a derivative sense because they are in fact the

---

1. Vatican Council II, *Sacrosanctum Concilium* (Constitution on the Sacred Liturgy, 1963).

2. Edward Schillebeeckx, OP, *Christ, the Sacrament of the Encounter with God* (New York: Sheed & Ward, 1963).

3. Karl Rahner, SJ, *The Church and the Sacraments* (New York: Herder & Herder, 1963).

actions of a sacrament, the church. They taught us that these formal sacraments can transform us through the working of the Holy Spirit so that we become living sacraments in our world, effective signs of what the rituals themselves signify, namely signs of acceptance, commitment, thanksgiving, forgiv(en)ness, preparedness, and service. In short, it is not directly that God is revealed to us, but indirectly through signs, through Jesus, through the church, through the actions of the church, and ultimately through the Christians themselves functioning as living sacraments of God's love. With this the sacramental economy of salvation has come full circle.

The Deacon as Symbol

Today the most common question people ask about deacons is "What do they do?" To this we need to answer, Deacons do all that the church asks them to do today, and whatever the church might ask them to do in the future. In short, the Second Vatican Council never intended to define the functions of deacons, only to point out the areas of their ministry, namely service in liturgy, word, and charity. The church is certainly free to explore further the function of deacons in relation to the needs of the church in the contemporary world.

Vatican II did spell out a few of the deacon's liturgical tasks in the *Lumen Gentium:*

> For strengthened by sacramental grace, in communion with the bishop and his group of priests, they [deacons] serve the People of God in the ministry of the liturgy, of the word, and of charity. It is the duty of the deacon, to the extent that he has been authorized by competent authority, to administer baptism solemnly, to be custodian and dispenser of the Eucharist, to assist at and bless marriages in the name of the Church, to bring Viaticum to the dying, to read the sacred Scripture to the faithful, to instruct and exhort the people, to preside at the worship and prayer of

the faithful, to administer sacramentals, and to officiate at funeral and burial services.[4]

Nonetheless, as Douglas LeClair and many others since the council have pointed out:

> The Fathers at Vatican II did not restore the permanent diaconate for its functions. Arguments were put forth at the Council that the roles could be fulfilled by others such as lay ministers, acolytes, and others in the Church. Nor was it restored to fill the dwindling ranks of the presbyters.... However, the arguments against restoration did not take the day because the diaconate was restored not so much for what it does as for what it is, a visible sacrament of Christ in the world.[5]

Michael Himes, in his *The Sacraments of Vocation,* places the church offices into a broad context by showing how the ordained ministries of bishop, priest, and deacon are related to our own baptism.[6] He notes that there are three ministries in the church in which we all share by our baptism: responsibility for the unity of the church, responsibility to and for the Word of God, and responsibility to serve others. Because these ministries pertain to all of us by virtue of our baptism, however, there is a need that someone, somewhere, personify these ministries full time in an ordained fashion, as a concrete sign to us all and as a remembrance of our share in these three ministries. The person who personifies the ministry of responsibility for the unity of the church we call the *bishop.* The one with full-time responsibility to and for the Word of God is the *presbyter* or *priest.* The one responsible for the special ministry of service to others we call the

---

4. Vatican Council II, *Lumen Gentium* (Dogmatic Constitution on the Church, 1964), no. 29, in Walter M. Abbott, SJ, ed., *The Documents of Vatican II* (New York: America Press, 1966).

5. Douglas M. LeClair, *The Deacon as Icon of Christ* (Phoenix, AZ: Catholic Sun Publishing, 2001), 50.

6. Michael Himes, *The Sacraments of Vocation* (Jefferson Valley, NY: Fisher Productions, n.d., videocassette).

deacon. These are the ordained personifications of the ministries that redound to each Christian person by virtue of his or her baptism. This is a reality we sometimes forget.

All three of these ancient ministries go back to New Testament times, back to the time when deacons were permanent members of the early church order. As time went on, the ancient order of deacons, for a number of historical reasons, devolved into simply a step for those preparing for the presbyterate. With Vatican II and the *Motu Proprio* of Pope Paul VI, *Sacrum Diaconatus Ordinem* (1967), the permanent diaconate was restored. In April 1968, the U.S. Catholic Bishops requested permission to utilize permanent deacons, that is, married and unmarried men of mature years, in those areas where needed; by August the Vatican had granted the permission.

With this restoration of the diaconate in the United States now nearly forty years old, it is still important to underline what J. M. Barnett pointed out again—namely, that "deacons are not ordained essentially in order that they may perform the distinctive functions of their order, but to hold up *Diakonia* as central to all Christian ministry."[7]

It may be asserted that the diaconate and the deacon are more a symbol than a function, even though their symbolism is made visible in one or other of their functions, and this is certainly not limited to liturgical functions. Happily, the deacon's ministry of charity is not at all as circumscribed as his liturgical tasks. The real freedom for diaconal creativity lies there in the ministry of charity in the world.

The Three *Munera*:
Priest, Prophet, and King

One of the things we sometimes forget is that Vatican II made a rather radical realignment of ordained ministry in the Catholic

---

7. James Monroe Barnett, *The Diaconate: A Full and Equal Order,* rev. ed. (1981; Valley Forge, PA: Trinity Press International, 1995), 141.

Church. It was not just bringing the permanent deacon back into the ancient triad of bishop-presbyter-deacon. From the time of Thomas Aquinas until Vatican II, *the* holy order was priesthood—*not* the bishop. The bishop was simply a priest who had been consecrated with three additional powers of authority, namely to govern his own diocese, to be its major teacher in matters of faith and morals, and to ordain other bishops. Episcopacy was not seen as a separate sacrament, nor was diaconate or subdiaconate. Priesthood was *the* sacrament. Vatican II changed that when it redefined the office of bishop. Kenan Osborne, OFM, explains this quite well:

> With a clear change in the theology of bishop, the theology of presbyter has to be reconsidered as well. There is, however, much more need for rethinking bishop-priest-deacon because Vatican II rejected the Scholastic view of priest, which had dominated our theology for almost eight centuries and chose instead to base all ministry, ordained and unordained, very clearly on the ministry of Jesus himself. The bishops did this by using as we all know today the *tria munera* description. Jesus was prophet, priest and king. Jesus preached and taught, sanctified and healed, shepherded and led.
>
> In the second chapter of *Lumen Gentium,* on the People of God, the bishops in a very full way present each baptized Christian as one who has been called and commissioned by God himself to share in the ministry of preaching/teaching, sanctifying, and leading.[8]

Osborne also makes the point that "ordained ministry forms an organic whole."[9] In other words, change one ministry and something happens in all the other ministries. Thus it is virtually impossible to focus solely on the renewal of the diaconate without in some way also considering the renewal of the priesthood and the episcopacy.

---

8. Kenan B. Osborne, OFM, *The Diaconate in the Christian Church: Its History and Theology* (Chicago: National Association of Diaconate Directors, 1996), 58.
9. Ibid., 60.

The Ministry of Charity: *Munus regendi*

While we recognize the liturgical and the preaching/teaching ministries of the deacon as the genuine help for which most pastors these days are quite grateful, it is the ministry of charity in our world—the ministry that the deacon has with all his fellow Christians—that many of us feel will ultimately define the diaconate in our day, and the deacon in his life. We see today more and more examples of deacons, mature men with leadership skills and solid backgrounds in business, industry, science, and education, speaking out on the real problems of injustice in our world and in our society, especially on the plight of the poor and deprived, and stepping forward to rally the means of help. In our American society today there is an enormous need for strong justice leadership, and today there are many deacons who have found unique, compassionate, creative ways to serve others in our world. We can find deacons managing food banks in cities, running programs for the rehabilitation of alcoholics, working in all types of community service and renewal projects, serving as chaplains in hospitals and prisons, developing apostolates to the handicapped, visiting residents in care facilities, working in ecumenical apostolates, and serving as pastoral associates and even as diocesan administrators. This is the key area of the future of the diaconate: a fellow Christian serving in the world as a sacrament of God's love. Our mutual hope is that given his training, prayer life, and closeness to his bishop and pastor, he will have the courage to reach out and embrace creatively the challenges he sees.

The Ministry of the Word: *Munus docendi*

The bishop, during the rite of ordination, gives the Book of the Gospels to the deacon, saying, "Receive the Gospel of Christ, whose herald you have become." The challenge for the deacon is now to learn the prayerful art of communicating the faith effectively and integrally to persons in diverse stages of life and in many different cultural circumstances.

The Sacramental Ministry of the Deacon in Parish Life

The deacon is a herald preaching the gospel of Christ. How should he best do this? The age-old axiom attributed to Saint Francis is that one should preach the gospel day in and day out without ceasing, and to "use words if necessary." Francis—himself a deacon—had it right: Nothing preaches more eloquently than personal example. This, too, is in keeping with some of those earlier comments that it is in *being* a deacon, not just in *doing* diaconal things, that a deacon can be an enduring sacramental sign. That does not in any way diminish the challenge of the heralding. In the church community the deacon is both a homilist and a catechist.

How challenging it is to serve consistently as an effective homilist! It is one thing to compose a homily using scripture commentaries, personal stories, homily helps, contemporary events, and humorous anecdotes to illustrate gospel passages. It is another thing, when having done all of this, to present it in a way that truly touches the hearts of the people and challenges them to grow in faith and to love God more through Christ our Lord. This latter usually happens after lots of effort, plenty of humility, self-critique, and the honest help of others. My experience is that compassionate wives, my own included, are the ones who so often provide the sincere help and the critical sounding board that leads to consistently effective homilies.

The deacon is also expected to be a catechist. He is the one who is called upon to offer the workshop for parents bringing their first child to baptism, or the one who is asked to speak to the confirmation class as they prepare for their sacrament of personal commitment, or to design and participate in a penance celebration. In some parishes it is the deacon who is asked to direct the RCIA process or to be one of its regular presenters.

In my St. James parish in Petaluma, California, we have one pastor, three deacons, twenty-four different ministries, and 2,200 families. In many ways we are a rather average American parish. The deacons are all involved with our pastor in the RCIA process, either as director or as presenters, along with a number of other parishioners who also serve as sponsors or presenters. It is one of the truly great post–Vatican II additions to parish life.

Often the deacon is the one who is asked to help young couples prepare for their marriage. Many of the deacons I know join with their wives in leading a parish marriage preparation program, and the programs come in many different designs. In our town there are two Catholic parishes: St. James and St. Vincent's. The deacons were able to convince both pastors that a single marriage preparation program in town could work. The engaged couples complete the FOCCUS Inventory and the subsequent counseling at St. Vincent's; then about a month later they do the marriage preparation weekend at St. James. My wife, Jean, holds the doctorate in education; Jean and I designed a Friday evening and all-day Saturday program that offers ten interactive sessions covering family of origin, our story, our communication, intimacy and sexuality, spirituality, covenant and sacrament, finances, planning the wedding, and a "Question Box" session with the pastors and the whole team. The couples then attend the 5:30 p.m. Saturday evening Mass, at which they read scripture, lead the prayers of the faithful, and come forward together to receive their certificates of completion and the applause of the whole congregation. After Mass they process out with the celebrant and servers right into the parish social hall to a candlelight supper prepared by the Knights of Columbus or one of the other service ministries in the parish. We do this four or five times a year with the help of both pastors and a group of twelve trained and experienced married couples, three couples serving per weekend so that no couple gets overburdened or burned out. It turns out to be a joyful catechetical experience for our two parishes.

The Ministry of the Word also includes the healing ministry, although it often also involves bringing the person holy communion. Healing, of course, has to do with physical ailments, with forgiveness, with family and personal troubles, and with grieving for those who have died. It surprises me sometimes how many of my fellow deacons are involved in healing ministry, because the deacon does not administer the anointing of the sick nor dispense sacramental absolution. There are times, however, whether he chooses it or not, that he ends up listening to a person's confession of sin or praying with a very penitent or broken-hearted parishioner. A good number of us regularly visit the sick and bring them holy communion.

These days deacons also participate in penance services that parishes generally sponsor during Lent and Advent. A well-planned penance service, with a homily on the message of forgiveness in the scriptures and often a community examination of conscience, helps parishioners as a group prepare for personal confession to the priest.

Liturgical Ministry: *Munus sanctificandi*

Liturgically the deacon is primarily an assistant to the bishop and priest in all the matters assigned to him in the various rites. At the celebration of the Eucharist, the deacon is assigned to carry in the Book of the Gospels held high; lead the penitential rite; proclaim the gospel; present the prayers of the faithful; prepare the altar and gifts; raise the cup as the celebrant raises the consecrated bread at the end of the eucharistic prayer; bid the community to offer one another the sign of peace; help with the distribution of holy communion; return unused hosts to the tabernacle; and dismiss the community. This is no small part in the celebration!

When it comes to the place of the deacon at the Eucharist, it might be appropriate to note that one of the first movements for the restoration of the diaconate was started by a group of priests of various nationalities imprisoned in Block 26 of the Dachau concentration camp in Nazi Germany. They meditated together often and asked themselves how the church and humanity would again find their identity once the horrors of World War II were over. "It was one of their proposals that blue and white collar workers as well as businessmen should place themselves at the service of the Church and the parishes the way deacons had done in the Early Church. They were to help people in need, but they should also serve at the Lord's Table at the celebration of the Eucharist."[10] As a group, in papers smuggled out during their imprisonment and by

---

10. Hannes Kramer, "Diaconia and Diaconate," *Worldmission* 26, no. 4 (Winter 1975–76): 26.

their writings and speeches after their release, they urged the ordination of permanent and married deacons. They saw from the beginning the need for the deacon, as a minister of charity in the world, to be seen at the right hand of the celebrant at the Sunday Eucharist—the deacon as symbol of the church in the world.

Other eucharistic ministries of the deacon are to bring holy communion to those not able to attend the Sunday celebration, especially to bring viaticum to the dying, and to give benediction of the Eucharist either with the monstrance or ciborium. One highlight of my week is a Sunday afternoon communion service at an extended care facility near my home, where about a third of the residents as well as a good number of nurses and certified nursing assistants (CNAs) are Catholic. When I get there, a nurse announces that there will be a Catholic communion service at 4:00 p.m., and those who are able begin to make their way by wheelchair or walker and gather around two large tables placed together in the day room. I vest in alb and stole. Sometimes I have the help of a young Baptist minister who brings his mom, a Catholic resident, to the service. He is often happy to read the second reading from the Sunday Mass, after which I proclaim the gospel and give a brief homily. After that we all join hands for the Our Father, and I distribute holy communion to the Catholic residents, nurses, and CNAs. Afterward we do a group thanksgiving, pray for the intentions of those present, and conclude. By this time the CNAs have identified a number of bed-bound "parishioners" who also wish to receive communion, so I make the rounds. To witness the profound faith of these residents, many of whom are terminally ill, is enormously inspiring to the staff, to one another, and certainly to me.

Every deacon, with the pastor's delegation, can preside at the sacraments of baptism and marriage; in our parish all three deacons take turns with our pastor in presiding at the Sunday afternoon baptisms, very often to a full church. When we celebrate confirmation it is a genuine parish event. At least two deacons assist the bishop and the pastor, one often holding the chrism oil stock as the bishop anoints. Vigils, funerals, and burials, though not sacraments in themselves, are also a part of the deacon's liturgical spectrum. The deacon in a parish is probably called upon more regularly to preside at the vigil service than at the funeral, although very often the deacon will also be asked to assist at the funeral Mass. My experience is that the deacon is more readily asked to preside at a funeral and burial when the funeral is held at the funeral home with the burial directly thereafter. After celebrating both vigils and funerals, it becomes very clear that the most meaningful are when the deacon facilitates a wide participation in the ceremony by the grieving family and friends of the deceased.

Sacramental Life in the Church/World

If the notion of sacrament is expanded and placed into a context broader than the confines of a sacramental ritual, many more actions take on the properties of sacrament than previously imagined. We can look at the first covenant and see that the Hebrew prophets, perhaps the greatest institution in Israel or any other nation in history, were the persons who spoke with the voice of the living God, calling and drawing the people back to the true worship of the heart. They are among the personal sacramentals of the first covenant.

For the second covenant, God sent his only Son. Jesus is the unique personal sacrament, standing in the long line of the prophets. For us, he is the sacrament or primordial sign of God's love for all humankind. Consequently his ministry in the world, his healing, forgiving, and sending, can be called sacraments in a derivative sense: they derive from him. After his death and resurrection, Jesus gave the world a sacrament of himself: the church, the community and assembly of followers he had nurtured over the years of his public life. He sent them forth into the world to preach, teach, and baptize. They are to be himself in the world, the fundamental sacrament of himself.

Over the centuries, this fundamental sacrament, church, developed words and actions that ritualize the words and deeds of Jesus for the world, what you might call the basic attitudes or values of Jesus: baptism (acceptance), confirmation (commitment),

Eucharist (thankfulness), reconciliation (forgiveness/forgiven-ness), anointing of the sick (preparedness), marriage (service to spouse, family, and the larger secular society), and orders (service to the local faith community).

To say that there are just seven formal sacramental rituals, how-ever, does not deny the possibility of recognizing what we might call "sacramental moments." That handshake, hug, or kiss from a friend or one-time enemy could be realized as an outward sign somehow coming from God, showing God's favor for that person. It could be the most powerful experience of God ever to enter a person's life, even if it were not in any way a formal sacrament as such.

Nonetheless, with the ministration of the formal sacraments, the sacramental economy of salvation is still not complete. These words and actions are done for real people, and, because through them the Holy Spirit is given, these persons are in fact trans-formed. They themselves become living signs in their world of the acceptance, commitment, thanksgiving, forgiv(en)ness, prepared-ness, and service mentioned earlier. God is revealed to people pri-marily through word and sacrament, especially the Holy Eucharist, but also to many in the world through Christians themselves func-tioning as living sacraments of God's love.[11]

It is into this circle of Christians that the deacon is called as an example for his fellow Christians. The stole he wears over one shoulder symbolizes the towel with which Christ continues (through the deacon) to bend and wash the feet of the sick and imprisoned, the young and the old, the alienated, the victimized, and the marginalized.[12] The gospel passage "The Son of Man came not to be served but to serve" (Matt 20:28) remains the heart of all ministry, and the towel that Jesus used to wash the feet of his dis-ciples remains the icon of all ministry.[13]

---

11. Ray Robert Noll, *Christian Ministerial Priesthood: A Search for Its Beginnings in the Primary Documents of the Apostolic Fathers* (San Francisco: Catholic Scholars Press, 1993), 40–42.

12. T. C. Foley, "The Servanthood of Christ," *Deacon Digest,* part 1, vol. 3, no. 4 (November 1986): 15.

13. Osborne, *Diaconate,* 62.

PART THREE

Sociological Foundations
for Diaconal Identity
and Marriage

CHAPTER 12

The Diaconate and Marriage: A Sociological Reflection

Rev. Mark A. Latcovich, PhD

This chapter was born out of research begun in 1994, when the diaconate community of the Diocese of Cleveland participated in a research project that sought to describe how ordained ministry affects the marriages of deacons. We began by convening a focus group, and then nearly 204 deacons and their spouses participated in a lengthy survey that asked some rather frank questions about their ministry and marriage.[1] The focus of this study demonstrates that the diaconate ministry can be a positive environment in which deacons and their wives live out their commitment to each other in marriage and their commitment to the church. While the study's findings are from a particular diaconate community, the practical wisdom shared may be helpful to both current and future deacons and their spouses in many other dioceses who embrace the challenges of ministry and marriage.

The literature that guided the original 1994 research project addressed some of the issues surrounding clergy marriages of Protestant ministers and their spouses. For years, mainline Protestant denominations explored salient problems and stressors for the minister and spouse. Clergy marriage studies highlighted the role of the ordained minister within congregational life, role

---

1. Mark A. Latcovich, "The Effects of the Ministerial Environment on Roman Catholic Permanent Deacons and Their Spouses" (PhD diss., Case Western Reserve University, 1995).

expectations developed by the self or congregation, boundaries between ministry and family life, and the management of time for marital and family obligations.

The Roman Catholic deacon offers a new avenue of study, because his role in the Roman Catholic community differs slightly from the full-time married minister of the Protestant church. Within many Protestant communities, ministers serve as the only pastor, with a secretary, board of trustees, and many volunteers. Most Catholic deacons hold a full-time job in addition to church-related ministries. Furthermore, the deacon serves with priests and lay ecclesial ministers in a ministry with canonical definitions and guidelines. Few deacons have administrative responsibilities for the total parish community, but, like lay ecclesial ministers, they feel the effects of the ministerial sector within their marriages and family life and vice versa. Family responsibilities combined with ministry create an environment that must always be reviewed by the Catholic deacon and his spouse. Early in the formation process, and certainly in postordination life, this environment requires ongoing evaluation by the deacon, his wife, and their family. Clergy families, like other professional families, are subject to heavy strains and demands on their marital and family life.[2] The family environment for married ministers is viewed in the literature as having both negative and positive effects on their spouses and families.[3]

---

2. C. Lee, "Toward a Social Ecology of the Minister's Family," *Pastoral Psychology* 36 (1988): 249–59. See also C. L. Lee and J. Balswick, *Life in a Glass House: The Minister's Family in Its Unique Social Context* (Grand Rapids, MI: Ministry Resource Library, 1989).

3. Some of the classic studies of clergy marriages have looked at the family unit and examined various stressors that have strong effects on the minister and his wife: S. W. Blizzard, *The Protestant Parish Minister: A Behavioral Science Interpretation,* Monograph Series 5 (Storrs, CT: Society for the Scientific Study of Religion, 1985); D. Mace, "Introduction: Clergy Families in Transition," *Pastoral Psychology* 30, no. 3 (1982): 139–40; D. Mace and V. Mace, *What Is Happening to Clergy Marriages?* (Nashville: Abingdon, 1980); D. Mace and V. Mace, "Marriage Enrichment for Clergy Couples," *Pastoral Psychology* 30, no. 3 (1982): 151–59; and J. T. Walker, "What's Behind the Stress in Clergy Families?" (paper presented at the Summer Missouri Area Pastor's School, Columbia, MO, 1978).

Negative Effects

Research has identified specific issues of strain and conflict that may have negative effects on clergy marriages, including schedule and time conflicts between family commitments and church activities[4]; expectations of the minister with regard to ministerial commitments that often result in conflicts with the spouse[5]; burnout in ministry[6]; unhealthy personal involvement with the pains and crises of congregants[7]; unrealistic expectations from parish staff members[8]; higher moral standards imposed on the spouse and children[9]; and tension and stress in family life caused by placing the ordained minister's "call of service" over personal needs (for example, affection with spouse, time with family). The literature has frequently noted that the lack of family priorities by clergy negatively impacts marital and family life.[10]

---

4. C. Prestwood, *The New Breed of Clergy* (Grand Rapids, MI: Eerdmans, 1972); W. H. Willimon, *Clergy and Laity Burnout* (Nashville: Abingdon Press, 1989).

5. W. Presnell, "The Minister's Own Marriage," *Pastoral Psychology* 25 (1977): 272–81; R. M. Oswald, *Clergy Self-Care: Finding a Balance for Effective Ministry* (New York: Alban Institute, 1993).

6. J. A. Sanford, *Ministry Burnout* (New York: Paulist Press, 1982).

7. W. E. Hulme, *Managing Stress in the Ministry* (San Francisco: Harper and Row, 1985).

8. D. C. Houts, "Marriage Counseling with Clergy Couples," *Pastoral Psychology* 30, no. 3 (1982): 141–50; D. Schaper, *Common Sense about Men and Women in Ministry* (New York: Alban Institute, 1990).

9. G. J. Jud, E. W. Mills, and G. W. Burch, *Ex-Pastors: Why Men Leave the Parish Ministry* (Philadelphia: Pilgrim Press, 1970); E. W. Mills and J. P. Koval, *Stress in Ministry* (Washington, DC: [Ministry Studies Board], 1971) (Ministry Studies Board, 1717 Massachusetts Ave NW, Washington, DC 20036); Lee and Balswick, *Life in a Glass House;* G. Noyce, "The Tensions of Our Calling," *Christian Ministry* 11 (1980): 18–21; L. J. Richmond, C. Rayburn, and L. Rogers, "Clergymen, Clergywomen, and Their Spouses: Stress in Professional Religious Families," *Journal of Career Development* (September 1985): 81–86; L. E. Whybrew, *Minister, Wife and Church: Unlocking the Triangle* (Washington, DC: Alban Institute, [1980/1984]).

10. C. Alexander, "The Interface of Marriage and Ministry: A Survey of Conference Directors of Pastoral Care" (paper presented to the Consultation on Clergy Marriage, Lake Junaluska, NC, 1980); P. W. Blanton, "Stress in Clergy Families: Managing

To explain further, sometimes a "holier-than-thou" façade elicits a messianic attitude in which the minister perceives himself to be superhuman. This attitude negatively impacts the minister's interactions and relationships with others.[11] In some instances, both the minister and the spouse report that their marriage and ministry are measured by superhuman standards of behavior.[12] Moreover, regarding clergy burnout, Sanford's study indicated that when the minister has limited resources of external support, family life and marriage often become the only vent for anger and frustration, leading to unresolved tension and stress. While family is a key support for clergy, it is also important to have the support of colleagues and denominational leadership.

Responses to Negative Aspects

In the sample of Cleveland deacons and their wives, the negative stressors listed in the literature about Protestant clergy were noted and affirmed as areas that were addressed in formation and addressed by individual families from time to time. The group did identify some negative stressors that seemed significant: (1) unrealistic expectations from the pastoral staff (rather than parishioners), (2) levels of communication between spouses, and

---

Work and Family Demands," *Family Perspectives* 2, no. 3 (1992): 315–30; B. J. Niswander, "Clergy Wives of the New Generation," *Pastoral Psychology* 30, no. 3 (1982): 160–69; J. E. Norrell, "Clergy Family Satisfaction," *Family Science Review* 2, no. 4 (1989): 337–46; Walker, "What's Behind the Stress?"

11. Jud, Mills, and Burch, *Ex-Pastors;* Mills and Koval, *Stress in Ministry;* Lee and Balswick, *Life in a Glass House;* Noyce, "The Tensions of Our Calling"; Richmond, Rayburn, and Rogers, "Clergymen, Clergywomen, and Their Spouses"; and Whybrew, *Minister, Wife and Church.*

12. Blanton, "Stress in Clergy Families"; Episcopal Family Network, *Episcopal Clergy Families in the 80s* (Hartford, CT: Episcopal Family Network, 1988); R. A. Hunt, "Clergy Families Under Stress" (paper presented at the Seminar on Clergy Marriage and Divorce, United Methodist Church, Oklahoma City, OK, 1978); Lee and Balswick, *Life in a Glass House;* M. Mattis, *Pastors' Wives Study,* Report of Research Division of the Support Agency (New York: United Presbyterian Church, 1977); and Presnell, "The Minister's Own Marriage."

(3) sensitivity to the inclusion of the deacon's wife as an invited guest to clergy gatherings.

A few deacons named their biggest stressor as expectations of their coworkers in ministry (their pastor and/or lay ecclesial ministers), who assumed they would be available at nearly every parish function. One deacon shared his dissatisfaction with the parish liturgical schedule:

> My pastor always schedules me for Christmas and Easter liturgies to assist him. While I am honored to share in this liturgical role, I wish that he would realize that my wife and I often want to visit our children and grandchildren around the holidays…and too many times we need to cancel our plans.

Another deacon expressed his concern this way:

> I love my parish and my pastor. He is really supportive of my ministry and wants me involved in the parish. But I wish he would talk with me more about my family schedule. Sometimes we have to make big adjustments as a family because of events and activities I am expected to be at in the parish.

Another stressor for some deacons was their lack of involvement in the parish decision-making process. Many did not attend weekly staff meetings because the meetings were scheduled during the day, when the deacon needed to be at his secular job. A few deacons reported that they felt they were deliberately left out of the decision-making process. One deacon laments:

> I really feel out of the loop. Sometimes things are done in the parish and I really don't know what's going on. I feel like I am a second-class minister because I am not full time on the staff. My wife keeps telling me that I was ordained to serve the people and should not get caught up in thinking this way. But it is hard to support parish decisions when those decisions are not communicated to you in the right way.

One deacon found that the lack of support from staff created a tension between his spouse and him, when he defended their priest's nonsupportive behavior.

> I know the priests at my parish are busy. The pastor tries his best to support me, but my wife keeps telling me that they are taking me for granted, and using me when they want to get out of something. I don't quite see it that way, but she does. Maybe it's intuition or something…but this causes real stress in my life.

One source of tension among some of the deacons' wives was the perception of how they were treated at social gatherings with priests. Several women felt that some priests seemed uncomfortable around them. One describes her sentiments of feeling out of place:

> When my husband gets invited to parishes for special dinners for "clerics only," he always feels bad leaving me behind. But I tell him that's all right, because the few times I do get invited, I really don't know where I fit in. Some of the clergy make me feel that I am intruding on their turf. They are cordial to me, but they let me know by their nonverbals that I am not one of the boys.

Most of the deacons and the wives in the focus group, as well as those who completed the survey, did not see the diaconate as their major stressor. Rather, they identified communication with each other, their lack of time for one another, and conflict in their personal schedules as the primary stressors. Nearly 60 percent of the wives and deacons felt that these stressors were already a part of their marriage prior to diaconate. Nearly 44 percent from that group felt that the diaconate formation program challenged them to work more proactively at communication and time management. The couples in the survey indicated that while formation and ministry present new challenges to the marriage, the formation period actually taught them new skills in communication and time management, as well as how to spiritually renew their family life.

The participation of both husband and wife in the diaconate formation process was seen as a unique contributor to enhancing skills in communication. The findings from the Cleveland study suggest that when formation programs address many of these potential stressors proactively, there is less tension in the marital relationship after the deacon is ordained. The Cleveland study had similar findings with *A National Study of the Permanent Diaconate of the Catholic Church in the United States,* which noted that couples in the formation process had "more enriching experiences, met more people and on deeper levels had more to share and talk about."[13]

Positive Effects

The ministerial environment also has the potential to serve as a vehicle for healthy growth and development for the ordained minister (and his or her family). The personal satisfaction one receives from doing ministry creates a positive equilibrium in family life. This satisfaction is cultivated through support systems and a clear description of tasks.

Church communities provide the minister with a support system,[14] and support from one's congregation positively affects the well-being of clergy families through friendship and affirmation.[15] Remuneration for ministerial services (for example, time off, continuing education allowance, and so on) and affirmation from

---

13. U. S. Bishops' Committee on the Permanent Diaconate, National Conference of Catholic Bishops, *A National Study of the Permanent Diaconate of the Catholic Church in the United States* (Washington, DC: United States Catholic Conference, 1981), 3–4.

14. B. Gilbert, *Who Ministers to Ministers: A Study of Support Systems for Clergy and Spouses* (New York: Alban Institute, 1992).

15. J. Warner and J. D. Carter, "Loneliness, Marital Adjustment and Burnout in Pastoral and Lay Persons," *Journal of Psychology and Theology* 12, no. 2 (1984): 125–31; C. Lee, "Toward a Social Ecology of the Minister's Family," *Pastoral Psychology* 36 (1988): 249–59; Lee and Balswick, *Life in a Glass House;* D. Mraz, *Ministry and the Family of the Permanent Deacon* (Collegeville, MN: Liturgical Press, 1987).

ministerial peers and superiors for various projects in ministry afford ministers a healthy sense of growth and development. Staff and parish support provide nurturing and supporting friendships that become important resources for the minister (and his or her spouse). Lack of resources for ministerial support has been reported to negatively affect the personal well-being of both the minister and his spouse.[16]

Reactions to Positive Aspects

Nearly 95 percent of the deacons in the study named support and affirmation from coworkers in ministry as highly significant for their personal growth and development as ordained ministers. One deacon writes:

> My parish staff and family treat me like a china doll…and offer me respect and reverence for my contributions to ministry. My wife is my number one support. The staff (of the parish) is quick to affirm and share their appreciation. It is a great environment to grow as a minister of the gospel.

The deacons and wives also noted that the diaconate offered them joint opportunities to collaborate as a married couple in various aspects of ministry (23 percent). Many led programs in the parish together. One deacon speaks on this regard, "I know that I did not get into this for kudos from the people I serve. My wife and I are really loved by the people we work with."

A good number of deacons found their greatest support in ministry coming from their spouse. A deacon of twenty years writes, "My wife has stood by me in the thick and thin of my ministry; she is my worst critic of my homilies and gives the best pick-me-up when I need something."

Wife respondents felt personal satisfaction with their spouse's role in the diaconate. Some reflected on the overall happiness and

---

16. R. M. Oswald, *Clergy Stress and Burnout* (Minneapolis: Ministers Life Resources, 1982).

pride of seeing their spouse minister as deacons. One wife writes, "My husband loves to visit the sick—this ministry gives him great joy, and gives me great satisfaction to see how the people respond to him." Another wife shares, "I get great satisfaction when he gets fired up about what he is going to do at church."

Many deacons as well as their spouses have found great support from their friends in the parish. One wife describes her new status within the parish. "Since ordination the people in our parish have been so supportive of us. They treat both of us like gold. Sometimes I feel like a celebrity." A newly ordained deacon shares this insight: "Our friends in the parish have rallied around us since ordination. They tell me how proud they are of my call to serve them through this special ministry."

Many deacons are active members in their parish communities before they begin studies for the diaconate. It is very clear that these ecclesial communities play a strong role in the discernment of the diaconate vocation. Hence, the support systems for the deacon and his family are often established prior to formation and ordination. While these systems continue after ordination, both the deacon and spouse have found this aspect vital for their marital satisfaction. The assimilation of diaconate ministry into marital life is necessary for the continued growth and development of the couple. One important integrating factor is the personal spirituality of the deacon (and his spouse).

Spirituality and Marriage

Studies in the sociology of religion have discussed the nature and effects of prayer and its correlation to life satisfaction, well-being, and happiness.[17] The literature has also noted that highly religious people

---

17. A. M. Greeley, *Religion as Poetry* (New Brunswick, NJ: Transaction Publishers, 1995); K. L. Woodward, K. Springer, D. Glick, M. Talbot, B. Fisher, C. Miller, and S. Lewis, "Talking to God," *Newsweek* (January 6, 1992): 39–44; M. M. Poloma and B. F. Pendleson, "The Effects of Prayer and Prayer Experiences on Measures of General Well-Being," *Journal of Psychology and Theology* 19, no. 1 (1991): 71–83; D. G. Richards,

have more satisfaction and affection in marriage[18] and adapt better to life's problems.[19]

D'Antonio, Newman, and Wright suggest that religious and family institutions reinforce one another in two different modes: social control and social support.[20] With social control, religion constrains deviant attitudes and behaviors that threaten traditional family values. Hansen concludes that religion viewed as a social support provides norms for familial love, self-esteem, marital stability, marital satisfaction, and family values.[21]

The institutions of church and family impact the deacon's life in a public and private dimension. Public prayer is an important part of the spiritual life of the deacon. He is required to pray the Liturgy of the Hours, lead public prayer, and assist with eucharistic celebrations. The deacon must also develop a personal spirituality of private prayer, as mentioned by Owen Cummings earlier in this book (chapter 9).

The spiritual life of the deacon is formed from the personal and professional life of his marriage and family life. The deacon's reception of two of the vocational sacraments has implications both on a theological and sociological level for his spiritual development. Theologians Karl Rahner and Walter Cardinal Kasper describe the sacrament of marriage in relationship to the church community by emphasizing the implications of the matrimonial mission within the church community. Karl Rahner, in his work

---

"The Phenomenology and Psychological Correlates of Verbal Prayer," *Journal of Psychology and Theology* 19, no. 4 (1991): 354–63.

18. W. V. D'Antonio, W. M. Newman, and S. A. Wright, "Religion and Family Life: How Social Scientists View the Relationship," *Journal for the Scientific Study of Religion* 21 (1982): 89–104; E. Filsinger and M. Wilson, "Religiosity, Socioeconomic Rewards, and Family Development: Predictors of Marital Adjustment," *Journal of Marriage and the Family* (August 1984): 663–70; and G. L. Hansen, "Religion and Marital Adjustment," in *Religion and Mental Health,* ed J. F. Schumaker (Oxford, UK: Oxford University Press, 1992), 189–98.

19. Filsinger and Wilson, "Religiosity, Socioeconomic Rewards," 664.
20. D'Antonio, Newman, and Wright, "Religion and Family Life."
21. Hansen, "Religion and Marital Adjustment."

The Church and the Sacraments, develops a theology of marriage that is rooted in Christ's union with the church. He writes:

> Marriage and the covenant between God and humanity in Christ can not only be compared by us, they stand objectively in such a relationship that matrimony objectively represents this love of God in Christ for the Church; the relation and the attitude of Christ to the Church is the model for the relation and attitude that belongs to marriage, and is mirrored by imitation in marriage so the latter is something contained or involved in the former.[22]

Walter Kasper presents the Christian understanding of marriage through an ecclesiological perspective.

> Marriage and family life are in a very special sense the Church in miniature—Vatican II spoke of the family as the domestic church.…They in fact make an active contribution to the building up of the church. That is why married couples have a special charism, that is a distinctive call, gift and form of service within the Church.[23]

The "special charism" of service in marriage and the deep love for the church are two traits that formation programs consider when they are screening married men for the diaconate. Nearly 87 percent of the study respondents offered comments about how their formation process gave them a new perspective on their marriage. One deacon writes, "My wife and I started praying and sharing our faith together in a concrete manner. We never did that before." Another deacon reflects on how he and his wife grew closer because of formation:

> Our marriage has changed since we became a member of the diaconate community. We have discovered something new in

---

22. Karl Rahner, *The Church and the Sacraments* (Freiburg, West Germany: Herder & Herder, 1963), 107 (see 107–12).

23. Walter Kasper, *Theology of Marriage* (New York: Crossroad, 1980), 38.

a level of discussion and prayer that wasn't there before. This has made us aware of what our marriage was suppose[d] to be. Diaconate for us seems to grow out of our marriage.

Many deacons and their spouses discovered the ministry charism of marriage through their formation process. They note how sharing prayer together provided a new level of spiritual communication. One wife shares this insight: "He never would share his spirituality with me. Formation made him more sensitive and self-revealing. Now he speaks on my level." This comment seems to reflect the overall satisfaction of many wives who felt that their spiritual formation created new venues for shared experiences and deeper communication. Forty-seven percent of the wives said they experienced growth in their spiritual lives because they attended formation with their husbands. Twelve percent of the wives said they prayed one of the hours from Liturgy of the Hours with their husband each day. Thirty-six percent noted the growth they experienced as a couple when they participated in retreats and days of recollection. Fifty-two percent of the wives report attending daily liturgy as part of their ongoing formation.

Ninety-eight percent of those responding stated that diaconate ministry has had many positive effects on their marriage. One deacon summarizes, "The diaconate has called me to service. Yet I am very aware that my wife and I are called to ministry in our marriage. Our family is a little church. I need to serve both of these churches."

Deacons described how spiritual formation has enhanced their marriages. They cited three areas that played an important role in this process. First, deacons felt that daily prayer gave them deeper insight not only in their relationship with God, but also with their wife and family. Many of the deacons felt that their prayer fueled their ministry. One deacon recalls how his relationship with God gives him a renewed sense of commitment for his family and ministry:

My commitment to daily prayer and meditation has given me a new focus in life. I have become very aware how important my wife, family and parish community are to me. The Lord abundantly blesses my daily routine so I can make a difference in the lives of the people I love.

Second, spiritual direction was essential for deacons' continuance in ministry and had significant effects on the way they related to their spouses. One newly ordained deacon writes, "I really can't believe how far I have come. My spiritual director challenged me and helped me recognize how God is acting in my life. I have found myself more open to people, especially with my family." Another deacon sums it up well. "The whole experience of entering into spiritual direction has radically altered my whole being. I am a better man, a better husband and father because of what the Lord has taught me. I've changed in my heart and soul."

Finally, many deacons said their ministry serves as a spiritual energy that renews them. Their ministry in parish groups, especially those who have regular contact with youth, older adults, and those hospitalized, seems to provide rich experiences for reflection. One deacon shares, "The people I serve on a weekly basis give me something in return that I can never give them. As Mother Teresa says, you can see Jesus' face in each of them....That's my spiritual food."

Deacons and Their Children

The focus group identified that having children younger than age twelve sometimes caused difficulties for the deacons and wives. This concern has been identified in previous clergy studies about children in the Protestant parsonage. London has found that church authorities (and congregations) hold clergy children to higher standards.[24] Bouma found that often children of clergy

---

24. H. London, *Clergy Families and Career Paths in the United Methodist Ministry,* A Report to the Board of Higher Education and Ministry (Nashville: General Board of the United Methodist Church, 1983).

households were "pressured to perform or act in a super spiritual way in public."[25] Perceived role conflict between the public and private sectors for children may create "a kind of schizophrenia," leading to experimentation with premarital sex, drugs, and alcohol, which represent conflicting lifestyles and values from those they are expected to uphold.[26]

Problems with children were reported in only a small percentage of the sample of deacons; however, many deacons and their wives felt that children needed to be included in parts of the formation process. The children of the candidates need to have opportunities for personal and family growth along with the candidates. Family weekend retreats and occasional formation sessions as families were viewed as proactive preventative measures. One teenaged son was overheard to lament after his dad's ordination, "While my dad is the one who gets to be the deacon, I'm seen by everyone else as the deacon's kid."

Of the 7 percent of deacon families that reported some problems with their children after ordination, those with children younger than age twelve felt that their children were often held to higher standards by their church community. One wife reported that she and her husband removed their daughter from the Catholic school because it appeared there was too much pressure placed on her. Deacons with small children often felt that their ministerial involvement at times conflicted with their spouse's need to have them home more often to help with domestic duties.

Many deacons in the study referenced page 4 of their handbook, which reads, "The first commitment of the candidate is to his family." This priority gave many of the deacons a balanced sense of freedom for their ministry. Their acceptance into the formation

---

25. M. L. Bouma, *Divorce in the Parsonage* (Minneapolis: Bethany Fellowship, 1979), 69.

26. S. P. Juergensen, "Growing Up as a Pastor's Child: The Pressures and Positives of Living in a Clergy Family System" (DMin thesis, Concordia Seminary, St. Louis, MO, 2000); D. L. Langford, *The Pastor's Family: The Challenges of Family Life and Pastoral Responsibilities* (New York: Hayworth Pastoral Press, 1998); London, *Clergy Families and Career Paths*, 147.

program depends on a strong marital relationship and support from their family. The deacons in this study did not provide strong evidence of their children feeling pressures from family members or parishioners to be perfect or held to higher standards.[27]

Marriage and Ministry

The service ministry of the deacon continues to play an important role in his marriage. His reception of the sacraments of orders and marriage becomes the source of his vocational holiness. What guidelines does the church provide to continually address this path to holiness? There is developed theology of marriage. Likewise there are documents on the spiritual formation of deacons. Owen F. Cummings notes, however, that the theology of marriage in relationship to the diaconate is "both undeveloped and underdeveloped."[28] Further theological reflection is still needed in official circles to clarify and define the fruits of matrimony combined with ordained diaconal ministry within the Roman Catholic Church.[29] Unofficially, however, deacons and their wives offer some very positive illustrations on how this theological integration occurs in their personal lives. Nearly all of the respondents in the study agreed that they could not compartmentalize their married

27. The popular literature refers to children of clergy as "pastors' kids" ("PK"), who often suffer from the "glass house syndrome" because their family or congregation place pressure on these children to be perfect and live up to positive stereotypes as clergy children. See Patrick Kemper, "Heaven Help Them," *Chicago Tribune* (August 18, 2002); Juergensen, "Growing Up as a Pastor's Child"; and Langford, *The Pastor's Family.*

28. Owen F. Cummings, *Deacons and the Church* (Mahwah, NJ: Paulist Press, 2004), 94ff.

29. Paul VI, *Sacrum Diaconatus Ordinem,* General Norms for Restoring the Permanent Diaconate in the Latin Church (Washington, DC: United States Catholic Conference, 1967); National Conference of Catholic Bishops, Bishops' Committee on the Permanent Diaconate, *A National Study of the Permanent Diaconate in the United States* (Washington, DC: United States Catholic Conference, 1981); National Conference of Catholic Bishops, Bishops' Committee on the Permanent Diaconate, *Permanent Deacons in the United States: Guidelines on Their Formation and Ministry* (Washington, DC: United States Catholic Conference, 1985).

lives from their experiences with ordained ministry. The blending of these two roles was perceived as a challenge that had creative outcomes. Most deacons said that their wives were their strongest advocates and confidants in ministry. They viewed their vocational call to marriage to be just as important as their ordained ministry to the community. At least 75 percent of the wives said that their marriage was enhanced through ordination. The data suggest that this sample has blended the Rahnerian notion that Christ is incarnate through the marital sacrament with Kasper's notation that the "special charism" of marriage is lived out through their service.

A number of the respondents reported that parishioners use the term "diaconal couple" as a reference for them. This term seems to capture the marital and ministerial realities that identify the deacon and his wife. This has been identified as a term of function and respect, as well as self-definition.

Sociologist Ralph Turner, who studied the dynamics of how roles are integrated into institutions, suggests that individuals legitimize, adapt, and formalize their roles when they are new to an organization or structured system.[30] Role differentiation tends to link role statuses in the organization through self-definition. This postulate by Turner seems supported by the diaconate community, who over the past forty years had to define the multiple roles of husband, father, ordained minister, and employee in the workplace. The wives define (and continue to define) what it means to be the wife of a deacon, and they feel that they have been incorporated into the diaconal lifestyle and in some ways are helping to form it.

Fourteen percent of the sample reported that they ministered together (that is, conduct family retreats, teach baptism

---

30. Ralph H. Turner, *Role-Taking: Process Versus Conformity, Human Behavior and Social Processes, an Interactionist Approach* (Boston: Houghton Mifflin, 1961). See also Turner, *International Encyclopedia of the Social Sciences* 13 (New York: Macmillan, 1968), s.v. "Role: Sociological Aspects"; Turner, "Rule Learning as Role Learning," *International Journal of Critical Sociology* 1 (September 1974): 35–48; Turner, "The Role and the Person," *American Journal of Sociology* 84, no. 1 (July 1978): 1–23; Turner, "Strategy for Developing an Integrated Role Theory," *Humboldt Journal of Social Relations* 7, no. 1 (1979/90): 123–39.

classes, do marriage preparation, work on RCIA teams). Most of the sample agreed that after ordination they discovered a new synergy of lived faith experiences from their charism of marriage and diaconal service. Deacons offer their lived faith experience from the perspective of their secular jobs, their parish ministry, and what they have learned living their marital sacrament. One deacon who works in a factory writes, "The guys I work with feel comfortable telling me things that they would not share with anyone else." Another notes, "Being married and having a family allows me to understand the majority of the parish's problems from experience."

Likewise, the women offer personal reflections from their own perspectives as wife, mother, and professional that are connected to the dynamics of diaconate service. One wife muses, "My life is changed since diaconate, and I feel I make a difference to people in small ways. We serve each other and witness our love to others by who we are." Another states, "My role with the diaconate is simple. I am the deacon's wife. What that means is that I share all that I am to the people I meet. They expect that of me."

A Service Perspective of Marriage: A Conclusion

While giving witness to the marital sacrament, these women and men give witness to the faith communities to which they belong. The data suggest that while the ministry of the deacon is appreciated, what a deacon does (in terms of ministry) is not as important as who a deacon is. His witness is paramount. Formation invites the deacon and his wife to begin a journey of marital rediscovery and ministerial formation.

Formation challenges the deacon and his wife to explore and renew their witness of faithfulness and fidelity of commitment. The years of formation require them to make personal sacrifices; it challenges their skills in time management and conflict resolution, and it helps them prioritize what is important in their family life. This level of commitment only intensifies after ordination. The deacon and his wife live a dual commitment: the one they made to each other in marriage, and the one they gave to the church at the time of his ordination. Most couples tell us that this process is ongoing and only fortified through grace and prayer. The formation process connected them once again to the renewing grace of their marital sacrament. Ordination requires them to live and cultivate that grace in community through a ministry of service, charity, and justice. Most couples confess that they have a deeper shared spirituality because of the very nature of diaconate.

Deacons were not shy in expressing how the diaconate intensified for them the sacredness of sexual loving. Several wives and deacons felt that their sexual life improved as a result of the diaconate. In formation, the candidate and his wife were challenged to explore their patterns of communicating on a physical and spiritual level. Diaconate ministry requires continuous self-giving by both of them to one another. This inherent dynamic can only intensify the couple's ability to connect their spiritual, emotional, and physical giving to each other. Perhaps the formational venues used to train professional church ministers may have something to also offer premarital preparation today. Nevertheless, deacons and their wives have a rich potential to witness to the sacramentality of marriage on varying levels.

The Cleveland sample clearly articulates high levels of marital satisfaction. Many responses suggest that this has been a lifelong process that still requires honesty, humor, humility, and the ability to ask for forgiveness. Many wives and deacons also cited the role that ongoing support by the diocese plays in their lives. One wife writes, "The letter from the bishop after my husband's illness made me realize we belong to the diocesan church." Others noted how yearly retreats and continuing education promote opportunities for reflection and dialogue on salient issues in marriage and family.

Deacons utilize spiritual direction and report that they are often able to find solutions to problems and maintain a peaceful equilibrium because of this discipline of dialogue with a spiritual mentor. Deacons and their wives practice a spirituality of workplace and parish. Their interaction with parishioners and other church ministers enables them to receive the communal support they need to continue in their ministry and to grow in their marriage. Deacons and their wives must continue to shape their roles in the church. The diaconate remains a rich resource that continues to enhance both holy orders and marriage through the lived faith of these couples. Their shared wisdom and experience will give hope and encouragement to those in formation.

CHAPTER 13

The Deacon's Wife:
An Emerging Role

Rebecca Meehan, PhD

Deacons' wives occupy an unequaled position in the Catholic Church structure in two distinct ways. First, they are married to ordained clergy: deacons. Second, the deacon's wife is expected to attend the formation process—a three- to four-year education and training process—with her husband.[1] During formation, deacons are required, and wives are *expected,* to fully participate in classes, read required material, make presentations, and write papers. At the end of the training, the deacon is ordained; the wife is not. Because of the relative newness of the restored permanent diaconate ministry, the roles of both the deacon and his wife are evolving. There are very few official requirements of the wife but many unwritten expectations; hence there is opportunity for the development of various types of involvement of the deacon's wife

---

1. This expectation evolved over the years. Since the inception of the Cleveland Diocese diaconate formation program, wives have always been invited to attend. During the late 1970s, wives were "encouraged" to attend; and by the mid-1980s, wives were "strongly encouraged" to attend. This "encouragement" was perceived as an expectation by most of the husbands and wives. In 2004, wives are expected to fully participate in the program, although no official church requirement has changed (personal communication with the Cleveland Diocese, Office of the Permanent Diaconate, 2004). *Editor's note:* The new *National Directory for the Formation, Ministry, and Life of Permanent Deacons in the United States* (Congregation for the Clergy and Congregation for Catholic Education [December 26, 2004]) simply states, "Wives should be involved in the [diaconate formation] program in appropriate ways....It is necessary to include specific resources and programming addressed to [the wife]" (nos. 138–39).

in the diaconate ministry. There is also the potential for role ambiguity. To provide the best opportunity for the wife's full contribution to the diaconate ministry, it is imperative to create formalized and meaningful methods of recognition for wives' participation in formation programs and continued contributions to ministry. This chapter continues the sociological reflection on the diaconate ministry discussed by Mark Latcovich in the previous chapter and examines the role of the deacon's wife based on that same research project conducted among the diaconate community of the Diocese of Cleveland, Ohio. In that study, deacons and their wives were asked questions about their experiences in the diaconate ministry, their marriage, and the roles they both occupy. It was the first study to examine *both* husbands' *and* wives' perspectives of the role of the deacon's wife, and it is also among only a few studies to examine the experience of the deacon's wife through her own words.[2] It is my hope that this chapter can offer deacons and their wives, as well as potential candidates for the ministry, pastors, and others, an opportunity to consider the great gifts these women bring to the diaconate ministry and to the church.

Following the renewal of the permanent diaconate by the Second Vatican Council in 1967, official guidelines for the diaconate ministry were published by the National Conference of Catholic Bishops in the United States in 1971.[3] The guidelines provided the fundamental regulations for diocesan decisions but left ample room for local decision making in a number of areas. For example, the implementation of the diaconate formation and subsequent ministry programs were not specifically outlined in the guidelines.

Only general guidelines for the deacon's wife were created, with the exception of the need for her consent to her husband's

---

2. Others include V. Ratigan and A. Swidler, ed., *A New Phoebe: Perspectives on Roman Catholic Women and the Permanent Diaconate* (Kansas City, MO: Sheed & Ward, 1990), and J. Fichter, "Wives of Catholic Deacons," in *Wives of Catholic Clergy* (Kansas City, MO: Sheed & Ward, 1992), 75–96.

3. National Conference of Catholic Bishops, Bishops' Committee on the Permanent Diaconate, *Permanent Deacons in the United States: Guidelines on Their Formation and Ministry* (Washington, DC: National Conference of Catholic Bishops, 1971).

participation in the process. The guidelines addressing the wife are that (1) a "wife must formally consent to her husband's ordination"[4]; (2) a wife is free to determine the extent to which she will be involved in her husband's ministry; (3) developmental programs for wives are necessary; (4) consideration should be given to the family's economic situation; (5) commitment to wife and family has clear priority over ministry; and (6) two-way communication between the diocesan office and the deacons' wives is crucial.

These general descriptions of the wife's role narrowly address role expectations. In the years subsequent to the publication of the official guidelines, and throughout the first decade of experience in the diaconate ministry, some trends became apparent. For example, it was clear that as married deacons became more numerous, the wife who was involved in the formation program and later shared in her husband's ministry was less likely to feel stress and more likely to express satisfaction with her husband's participation in the ministry as a member of the clergy, than the deacon's wife who did *not* participate in formation.[5] Essentially, the couples who shared in this growth experience of the diaconate formation program were much happier. For most couples, the presence of the wife at the formation resulted in less marital tension because they shared more common experiences. Later revisions to the guidelines[6] included a section on expanding the role of the deacon's wife; specifically, the guidelines called for an "openness to co-ministry" between spouses.

This conclusion was also supported by the results of a four-phased *National Study of the Permanent Diaconate in the United States,* undertaken by the Bishops' Committee on the Permanent

---

4. Ibid., no. 150.

5. S. Taub, "The Permanent Diaconate in Today's Church," in Ratigan and Swidler, *A New Phoebe.*

6. National Conference of Catholic Bishops, Bishops' Committee on the Permanent Diaconate, *Permanent Deacons in the United States: Guidelines on Their Formation and Ministry,* rev. ed. (1971; Washington, DC: National Conference of Catholic Bishops, 1985).

Diaconate.[7] The survey showed that most wives participated actively in the diaconate ministry. As a result, most dioceses around the country began to "strongly encourage" deacon's wives to participate in the formation process. In order for the diaconate ministry to succeed, attending to and defining the expectations of the wives became necessary. No change, however, occurred in official *recognition* for the deacon's wife's participation.

To date, there is no standardized way in which deacons' wives are acknowledged for their participation in the training process. Recent changes in the formation program in the Cleveland diocese, however, give the wives college credit for their participation in diaconate formation. Despite the fact that husband and wife are both aware of the ordination parameters at the beginning of training, either or both partners may expect more involvement than what may be possible for the wife after ordination. The philosophy of the bishop, the acceptance of the pastor, and the parish culture are all critical factors shaping the level of involvement of both the deacon and his wife.

Past Research

The *National Study of the Permanent Diaconate* was designed to include an assessment of the deacons' wives as part of a four-phased study examining the status of the restored ministry of the permanent diaconate. Deacons, supervisors, and bishops were the other three groups of participants in the study. The phase of the study that included the wives was designed with the primary goal of gaining the wives' assessments of their *husbands'* position in the ministry, however, not in expounding upon what the role of the deacon's wife is or should be. The sample size was substantial (696) and received a 54 percent response rate. More than 90 percent of the wives who responded had participated in their husbands' formation programs

---

7. Bishops' Committee on the Permanent Diaconate, *A National Study of the Permanent Diaconate in the United States* (Washington, DC: United States Catholic Conference, 1981, 1996).

and continued ministry. Effects of diaconal ministry were assessed in terms of stress, satisfaction, and recognition. The specific questions, however, did not address the experience of the wife in those three categories, but instead asked how she perceived her *husband's* stress, satisfaction, and recognition levels. Any questions that asked about the wife were in relation to her family and marriage. A follow-up national study by the same group (1996) was also conducted in four phases, and it again limited its questions to the wives by focusing on the *husband's* experience.

Past empirical research offers a glimpse at the experience of the deacon's wife. Fichter interviewed 109 deacons' wives and asked questions about their ministry involvement, and he found them to be very satisfied: they were very proud of their husbands, and all wives were somewhat active in the church.[8] There were, however, varying degrees of satisfaction in the ministry by each of the wives. Some wives who had participated in all of the formation classes and intended to participate in ministerial duties experienced a feeling of being let down after their husbands were ordained, because they expected their involvement would be greater than it actually turned out to be. Some indicated that the balance the deacons attempted to manage among family, work, and the ministry was difficult to maintain. The relationship that wives had with pastors of parishes varied and was the source of tension for some couples, resulting from reported clericalism or sexism. Generally, the support for the deacon's wife from the parish pastor is critical to her involvement in the ministry and her acceptance by the parish community.

In another study, Ratigan and Swidler conducted research using a mailed questionnaire, obtaining responses from 51 percent of its systematic sample of 243 deacons' wives from around the United States.[9] Many wives described the tremendous sense of satisfaction they had in participating in the diaconate. In contrast, others disliked being referred to as the "deacon's wife," because it was as though they

---

8. Fichter, "Wives of Catholic Deacons," 80.
9. Ratigan and Swidler, *A New Phoebe*, 47.

were no longer individual adult women in their own right in the church but were instead merely support people for one of the church's ministers. The majority of respondents indicated that "requiring" formation class attendance was important, while others felt that "recommending" attendance was a better choice, because it yielded some respect for those wives with other commitments.

The Diocese of Cleveland Study

In 1993, Father Mark Latcovich and I designed a survey to assess marital satisfaction and role development of deacons and their wives in the Cleveland, Ohio, diocese.[10] To more fully understand experiences of the diaconate couples, focus groups with diaconate couples, deacons, and deacons' wives were first conducted. Following the focus groups, all deacons and their wives in the Cleveland diocese were sent a questionnaire of both closed- and open-ended questions, to be completed individually. The mailed questionnaire yielded a 93 percent response rate, for a resulting sample of 103 deacons and 97 wives. The findings discussed here reflect the responses of the ninety-seven wives who responded to the questionnaire.

Some deacons' wives in the church are the liturgical and prayer leaders of the community, as well as spiritual directors. They counsel parishioners, conduct scripture studies, visit the sick, prepare and coordinate parish events, and facilitate their husband's ministries. Parishioners have sought out the deacon's wife—simply because she is the deacon's wife—in order to discuss family or marital problems that they feel would be understood by a woman or a person with a family.

Being a deacon's wife was perceived by the majority of the respondents to be an informal ministry unto itself. Wives explained that ministry could take the form of maintaining the household, taking care of children, and assisting the spouse. Because of the new and time-consuming demands made on their

---

10. Survey of the Deacons and Wives, conducted by Latcovich and Meehan, 1994.

husbands by the diaconate ministry, wives described their support of their spouse—their "ministry"—to involve not only patience and understanding, but also managing the day-to-day operations in the household when their husbands were occupied with their diaconate ministry.

The nature of the wife's informal ministry is described by almost half of the wives to be an "on-call, twenty-four-hours-a-day" type of ministry. Most respondents described the ministry as a lifestyle in and of itself. Wives wrote, "I serve the parish," "We minister to each other," "I do bereavement ministry," "People come to me for direction," and "I minister to families and couples going through hardship." The few respondents who indicated that they *did not* have a ministry related to the diaconate clarified that that was because they were not ordained. Others in this group indicated that they had no ministry at all.

In order to understand how wives perceived the relevance of their role in relationship to the future of the ministry, respondents were asked if they (as deacons' wives) expect to have an impact on the future of the church; the majority agreed. They wrote, "I'll impact as a silent partner," "My role will impact the laity," "Diaconate couples have a unique opportunity to impact the future of the church," "As a lay person I will impact the future of the church," and "[I am a] bridge between the priests and the laity." Some wives recognized that their role would be expanded in upcoming years by noting, "We'll play a bigger role in the priest shortage," and "[I] impact as married clergy in the church."

Of those who did not feel that they would have an impact on the future of the church, their responses were both unsettled and unobtrusive: "This should not be a political forum," "Changes take time," "I'm still working full time; I don't have an impact," "Move slowly, God is in charge, not me," "The church is in transition, too much 'I' over 'we,'" and "I'm satisfied with history in the making."

Rebecca Meehan, PhD

A New Role: A Typology of Identification and Satisfaction

The following typology allows the reader to consider how some deacons' wives in the Cleveland diocese approached and assessed the diaconate ministry. The typology was created in order to offer another way of describing the experience of the deacon's wife, and it was based on two dimensions of the wife's experience in the ministry: *identification* with the diaconate and *satisfaction* with her experience in the diaconate ministry and with her role as a deacon's wife. Responses are grouped into four types, summarized in Table 1.

The majority of the wives have high levels of identification (61 percent) and satisfaction (66 percent) with their experience in the ministry. The data reveal that high levels of identification with the diaconate ministry are strongly associated with being satisfied with the ministry. This supports impressions received from earlier research,[11] as well as the focus group sessions indicating that wives who were involved tended to stay happier and more productive in the ministry than wives who were not as involved. Still, there was some diversity in patterns of adaptation of the deacon's wife.

The typology allows the reader to understand how some deacons' wives experienced the ministry and the rationale behind how different women approach the ministry. While the following section describes general types of experiences, all deacons' wives will have unique perspectives.

Table 1. Satisfaction and Identification Typology of the Deacon's Wife

Type	Percentage of Respondents	Description
Type A	11%	Wife who *identifies highly* with the diaconate ministry but has *low satisfaction* with the ministry
Type B	50%	Wife who *identifies highly* with the diaconate ministry and has *high satisfaction* with the ministry

---

11. National Conference of Catholic Bishops, *Guidelines Revision* (1985).

Type	Percentage of Respondents	Description
Type C	23%	Wife who has *low levels of identification* with the diaconate ministry and has *low satisfaction* with the ministry
Type D	16%	Wife who has *low levels of identification* with the diaconate ministry but has *high satisfaction* with the ministry

Type A: High Identification and Low Satisfaction

This category represents the lowest proportion of respondents (11 percent). A deacon's wife who fits into the Type A category identifies strongly with the diaconate ministry but has a low level of satisfaction with her place in the ministry. Wives in this group wanted to participate in the ministry but could not or did not for a variety of reasons. Some wanted to participate more in the ministry but simply could not because of the demands of a career or a family at home; they just did not have enough time for ministry. Twenty-two percent of these respondents had children under the age of twelve, and 50 percent were working full time outside the home. Others perceived a lack of support from the parish pastor for the wife's participation and thus felt that they could not participate. Type A was significantly associated with one's husband being ordained fewer years (5.6 years) than the other types, perhaps demonstrating more time was needed to adjust to the role. These wives may have experienced a letdown after ordination; in general, they were expecting to have a different level of involvement and a better set of interactions than they actually received.

Type B: High Identification and High Satisfaction

This category was the most predominant in the group (50 percent of respondents). Type B represents wives who both highly identify with ministry and are highly satisfied with their role in the ministry. Open-ended questions yielded a multitude of positive responses from the wives. Respondents communicated that they felt "a sense of completeness" because of the ministry. Moreover, Type B category respondents revealed that their marriages had become better because of diaconate, because it brought them closer to their husbands. The ministry provided the couple a new chance to grow together. The responses within this category confirmed the success of the local diaconate ministry. Wives in this type had an average of more than nine years of ordained experience as a couple, perhaps allowing them more time to adapt to and find a niche in their ministry.

Type C: Low Identification and Low Satisfaction

Individuals in the Type C group can be described as those wives with low levels of identification and low levels of satisfaction. This group represented 23 percent of respondents. These wives did not identify strongly with the ministry, or could not or chose not to meet the expectations of the group to participate fully, and they were dissatisfied by this limitation or their experience in the ministry. Responses to open-ended questions among this group reflect the sentiment of frustration of the wives who want to participate more extensively but cannot; this reduced their overall satisfaction. The average number of years that husbands had been ordained for this type was ten years, the highest among the group; only 11 percent of this group had children younger than twelve years old, which is the smallest proportion among the four types. Wives in the Type C category provide areas for development for the diaconate ministry because of the low satisfaction levels coupled with low levels of identification. These are wives who have experience in ordained life and may have not found a niche for self-expression in the ministry. This is a group of which to be mindful, because there is potential for these wives to disengage, potentially influencing their marriage, family, and ministry.

Type D: Low Identification and High Satisfaction

The respondents categorized as Type D represented 16 percent of the wives. They expressed low identification with the diaconate ministry and high levels of satisfaction. These women are occupied with other obligations (for example, career or family) and are very pleased with the arrangement. The Type D deacon's wife is a person who has determined and found a niche for herself in balancing her personal life and the diaconate ministry but is not as involved in the diaconate ministry. As one of the wives indicated, "I am happy remaining in the background." These women are very pleased about being engaged in their own career, family, activities, and obligations, and they are happy to be a support person behind the scenes enabling their husbands to fulfill their ministerial duties.

Areas of Difficulty

Respondents were asked, in an open-ended format, "What is the most difficult aspect of the diaconate ministry?" Nearly one-third of the wives indicated that "balancing time for ministry with time for family" was the most difficult. Others described a similar experience by indicating that "saying no" to volunteering was problematic. One respondent detailed, "Whenever anyone from the church asks us to do anything for the diaconate, 'no' is *never* the answer; but when it comes to family demands, *too often* 'no' is the response." Some wives detailed, "Your life is not your own anymore," "You become a public figure," "There are feelings of guilt in this position," "[It's difficult] keeping a constant high energy level," and "The loneliness and patience [are difficult]."

Respondents were asked whether there were any roles in the diaconate ministry with which they were uncomfortable, and about half (51 percent) of the group said no. They wrote, "The diaconate has only brought our family together," and "The ministry is a blessing to my husband and me." Of those who did experience situations in which they felt uncomfortable, they indicated that they disliked "public speaking," "the unrealistic role expectations," "the pomp and circumstance," "educating others about deacons," "unequal areas of ministry," and "late meetings."

Overall, wives were very satisfied with the diaconate ministry and the roles they occupy; this general finding was anticipated in this group of women. Despite the difficulties mentioned, there are several explanations for the wives' reports: The first and most obvious conclusion suggests that the deacon's wife finds participation in the diaconate ministry to be a truly satisfying and enriching experience. This sentiment, expressed by a majority of respondents, was further supported by their responses to open-ended questions: "The diaconate has given me new purpose in life," "The diaconate ministry has given me the tools to reach people where I couldn't before," "This new shared role of diaconate couple keeps us on our toes—it's done wonders," and "My husband and I have had a new and deeper sense of love grow between us because of the diaconate."

Family Issues

In other religious traditions in which the leader of the congregation is married and has a family, there is a more defined set of expectations regarding the treatment of the family. In the Catholic Church, parishioners are still growing accustomed to a married clergy member and hence are still trying to find the right way to interact with his family. Moreover, there will be another layer of ambiguity because the deacon's wife is trained along with her husband in the formation process and is most often well schooled in ministry. Some wives shared, "There is tight scrutiny from the parish community," and "I'm ignored by other women of the church community."

Deacons' families with young children tend to experience role strain as the parents try to meet the demands of growing children and the demands of an expanding ministry. In general, the families whose daily lives were most affected by the diaconate ministry were those with children under twelve years of age. Some indicated that stronger expectations were made of the children in schools and in the community; this pressure to be better behaved than other children added strain to the family. Wives tended to be more likely to indicate family tension than their deacon husbands, but this is probably based on the fact that part of the wives' responsibilities included balancing the family issues while their husbands were active in the ministry. One wife wrote, "He doesn't become aware of his kids' school problems until I tell him." This phenomenon may be common to other dual-career families or families in which the husband is involved extensively in work-related activities.

In response to the statement, "The quality of our family life has improved because of diaconate ministry," the majority of both husbands (69 percent) and wives (56 percent) agreed. Wives' responses to open-ended questions included positive replies such as: "Diaconate has helped to center and focus the family," "Kids want to be lectors and altar girls," and "Kids show us more sensitivity." Husbands had very positive responses, including "Diaconate has made me more sensitive to my wife," "Ministry has made me a better listener for my family," and "Ministry has made me more thoughtful."

Personal Boundaries and Ministry

There were situations surrounding the diaconate ministry that made some wives uncomfortable. In one instance, discussed in initial focus groups and later reflected in the survey, a woman in the church was going through a divorce and was seeking aid and counseling from the deacon. The problematic part for the deacon's wife was that this woman was becoming too emotionally dependent upon the deacon and then began to "cross the boundaries," making the wife a little uneasy. The counselee would bring gifts to the deacon and their children. The deacon "of course," the deacon's wife said, did not see anything wrong with this behavior, but it drove the wife "crazy." The deacon's clergy role places him in a position to help people spiritually and emotionally, which can become rather intimate and may infringe on personal boundaries as perceived by the deacon and his wife. Discussion of boundary issues such as this need to be included in the diaconate formation process, so that both deacons and wives can be adequately prepared to respond well in such situations.

Social Interaction with Clergy

There were perceived differences in the way clergy interact in the presence of the deacon's wife. More deacons (66 percent) than wives (57 percent) indicated that there were differences in the way

244

in which clergy socialized in the presence of the deacon's wife. The husbands—who can see the differences firsthand because they spend time with other clergy both with and without their wives— noted that clergy were more reserved when wives were present and that clergy were more uncomfortable and often did not interact with the wives at all. Some husbands noted that the wife seems "invisible" when attending functions. Another wife indicated more tension: "I only get invited to a dinner party if the nuns are invited; why don't just the two of us get invited?" In contrast, another wife said, "My pastor always goes out of his way to make sure that I know that I am invited." Overall, the relationship that the wives have with their parish pastors is very important. Despite other very positive relationships with the bishop and other priests, if the relationship with their pastor was tenuous, then the wives' overall ministry satisfaction was compromised. Some wives detailed that their pastor excluded them from events to which their husbands were invited, or that the pastor felt uncomfortable and simply never spoke with the wife when she *was* invited to such events. In other circumstances, the pastor wanted more participation from the wife than she desired.

These kinds of imbalances and miscommunications between pastors and wives can be problematic and need to be addressed. For example, as dioceses require the deacon's wife to be part of the formation process, priests and bishops should be more systematically informed about the wife's involvement. Beyond the slight recognition given to the wives at the deacon's ordination, there should be ongoing interaction and communication between deacons' wives and pastors. This could be accomplished through quarterly meetings, or creating social events for deacons and their spouses to attend with parish pastors and the bishop. The Cleveland diocese, as well as others around the country, has used the term "diaconate couple." The more this language can be integrated into church protocol and everyday use, the more the church may be able to distinguish a presence and contribution of the wife.

Conclusion

Through the restoration of the permanent diaconate ministry, the Catholic Church has created a *married* ministry. It has not, however, ameliorated the problems that arise when there are no official guidelines for the wife's participation in the ministry. Those involved all have different expectations of what the deacon's wife should do. Over the past twenty years, the trend has been to involve the wife in the formation or training process, because it helped marriages and strengthened ministry after ordination. Because of a lack of communication, however, and lack of education about the diaconate ministry overall, some parish pastors, deacons, and wives have mismatched expectations of each other, leaving fertile ground for ambiguity and discontent. Through dioceses' decision making about involving the deacon's wife more in the formation program and in the ministry, there is ample opportunity for the contributions of deacons' wives. To provide the best opportunity for the wife's full contribution to the diaconate ministry, it is imperative to create formalized and meaningful methods of recognition for wives' participation in formation programs (for example, wives earning college credit hours for participating in the Cleveland diocese formation program).

As the diaconate is still relatively new in the Catholic Church today, parishioners and the greater church community may have difficulty accepting and interacting with the deacon, let alone his wife. My recommendations for developing the role of the deacon's wife in the ministry include: First, bishops and parish pastors must communicate to their parishes and to each other about the legitimacy of the wife's role through her current work and her involvement in a four-year formation process. Second, the church must formalize the requirements of deacons' wives in the "official guidelines" of the diaconate ministry. Third, deacons need to involve their wives in parts of their own ministry to create an opportunity for ministry by the diaconate couple. Fourth, dioceses should utilize the language of "diaconate couple" so as to normalize the involvement of the wife to the greater parish community. Finally, the wives themselves need to be comfortable with the way in which they choose to occupy a role in the diaconate ministry. Once there is a comfort level, their wishes can be more succinctly communicated to the parish community and a "negotiation" will begin. When any new social role is created there is typically a process of negotiation among others in the community, and because the roles of the permanent deacon and his wife are so new in the church, there will be a host of thoughts, opinions, and reactions to their presence. To strengthen, maintain, and allow the newly restored diaconate ministry to thrive, it is imperative for the church to recognize the deacons' wives for their ongoing contributions as well as the unlimited potential for a ministry of the diaconate couple.

The role of the deacon's wife in the Catholic Church is participatory and supportive. It is *not* a passive role in which a wife can have little to no involvement from start to finish. This can be an area for the church to deepen its formal recognition of the contributions of women. The wives are already expected to give of themselves in terms of their participation in the formation process, as well as in the subsequent ministerial lives of their husbands; they may also have their own informal ministry as half of a diaconate couple. Recognizing the work of these wives, and integrating their role into the everyday experience of the parish community, can only stabilize the diaconate ministry and allow it to continue successfully. Deacons and deacons' wives are part of an exciting time in which their actions and sentiments are helping to shape a new part of the church. They are broadening the creativity and ministerial contributions of all people within the Catholic community

The Kenotic Leadership of Deacons

Dcn. William T. Ditewig, PhD

Introduction: Christ, *Kenosis,* and the Contemporary Diaconate

Let the same mind be in you that was in Christ Jesus,
who, though he was in the form of God,
    did not regard equality with God
    as something to be exploited,
but emptied himself,
    taking the form of a slave,
    being born in human likeness.
And being found in human form,
    he humbled himself,
    and became obedient to the point of death—
    even death on a cross. (Phil 2:5–8)

In this hymn we encounter the profound and theologically rich mystery of *kenosis,* of Christ's self-emptying love. In *Christ: The Self-Emptying of God,* Lucien Richard, OMI, writes that the Philippian hymn "presents Jesus as recognizing that being equal with God means most profoundly to be 'not grasping.' The self-emptying of Jesus unto death—and death on the cross—is the revelation that to be God is to be unselfishness itself."[1] Richard continues by citing

---

1. Lucien Richard, OMI, *Christ: The Self-Emptying of God* (New York/Mahwah, NJ: Paulist Press, 1997), 22. Although this great christological hymn balances its kenotic

Hans Urs von Balthasar: "It is precisely in the kenosis of Christ (and nowhere else) that the inner majesty of God's love appears, of God who 'is love' (1 John 4:8) and a 'trinity.'"[2] John Paul II affirmed these insights in his 1998 encyclical *Fides et Ratio,* writing that "the prime commitment of theology is seen to be the understanding of God's *kenosis,* a grand and mysterious truth for the human mind, which finds it inconceivable that suffering and death can express a love which gives itself and seeks nothing in return."[3]

It is against this backdrop of Christ's own kenosis that this epilogue considers the ministry of the deacon in the contemporary church. Through sacramental initiation, all disciples of Christ are called to be kenotic, to empty themselves in imitation of Christ. Those disciples who are subsequently ordained into a participation in the apostolic ministry take on permanent and public leadership responsibilities for the communities of disciples they serve. Therefore, one might easily speak of "the kenotic leadership" of bishops and presbyters as well as deacons. Deacons have no more a monopoly on *kenosis* than they do on *diakonia.*[4] Given the focus of the current project on the sacramental diaconate, however, I consider how something I am referring to as "kenotic

dimension with the theotic "exaltation" of Christ in v. 9 ("Therefore God also highly exalted him and gave him the name that is above every name"), Christ's *kenosis* is the necessary first movement. As such, this becomes the primary focus of this epilogue.

2. Ibid., citing Hans Urs von Balthasar, *Love Alone* (New York: Herder & Herder, 1969), 15.

3. John Paul II, *Fides et Ratio* (Faith and Reason, 1998), no. 93.

4. One of the great insights of the Second Vatican Council was its identification of the church-as-servant. Paul VI proclaimed in his homily at the last general session on December 7, 1965: "We stress that the teaching of the Council is channeled in one direction, the service of humankind, of every condition, in every weakness and need. The Church has declared herself a servant of humanity at the very time when her teaching role and her pastoral government have, by reason of this Church solemnity, assumed greater splendor and vigor. However, the idea of service has been central" (Paul VI, *Hodie Concilium, AAS* 58 [1966]: 57–64). John Paul II later remarked, "The service of the deacon is the Church's service sacramentalized....You [deacons] are meant to be living signs of the servanthood of Christ's Church (John Paul II, *Allocution to the Permanent Deacons* [Detroit, MI, September 19, 1987], *Origins* 17 [1987]: 327–29). Similarly, in addressing the deacons of the Archdiocese of Chicago, Joseph Cardinal Bernardin wrote, "This does not mean that the deacon has a monopoly on service in the Church.

leadership" might be particularized in the sacramental nature and ministry of deacons.

Both Paul VI and John Paul II spoke of the *novus mentis habitus* reflected in the discussions and documents of the Second Vatican Council. During the preparation of the 1983 *Code of Canon Law,* for example, Paul VI reminded the Code Commission that this new way of thinking provided by the council was to be reflected not only in the practical applications of the law but in the very structures and processes of the code itself. In promulgating the finished product, John Paul II reaffirmed that what is *new* in the new code is more than a few practical adjustments; it is the newness of Vatican II itself.[5]

As is well known, of course, critical components of the council's new way of thinking involved the way we describe the very nature and mission of the church herself. This is illustrated through any number of examples from the council and its documents; however, one particular event at the council seems to illustrate this vision quite powerfully and succinctly. On December 7, 1965, the day before the solemn closing of the Second Vatican Council in St. Peter's Square, the council fathers celebrated Mass together with Pope Paul VI in St. Peter's Basilica. In this fraternal setting, the pope offered his own reflection on the ultimate significance of the council's work in these words:

Others can carry out many tasks he performs in the community, and his ordination is not intended to exclude others from performing those tasks. *All* in the Church are to serve but by his liturgical consecration and empowerment of *some* of us, that is, the deacons, this call and response to serve is made visible and effective. So, the deacon is a sign and instrument of that manifold service without which the Church cannot be the sign and instrument of the risen Lord Jesus. In other words…[the deacon] is meant to be an eloquent reminder to each of us of what we, too, should be doing, what we must continually strive to become, in accord with our own God-given gifts" (Joseph Bernardin, "The Call to Service: Pastoral Statement on the Permanent Diaconate" [Chicago: Archdiocese of Chicago, 1993], 5, emphasis in the original).

5. James H. Provost, "Canonical Reflection on Selected Issues in Diocesan Governance," in *The Ministry of Governance,* James K. Mallet, ed. (Washington, DC: CLSA, 1986), 211, citing Paul VI, *Allocution to Code Commission* (November 20, 1965), *AAS* 57 (1965): 988.

> We stress that the teaching of the Council is channeled in one
> direction, the service of humankind, of every condition, in
> every weakness and need. The Church has declared herself a
> servant of humanity at the very time when her teaching role
> and her pastoral government have, by reason of this Church
> solemnity, assumed greater splendor and vigor. However, the
> idea of service has been central.[6]

In short, the "new way of thinking" proposed by the council is
reflected in a servant-ecclesiology. This servant-ecclesiology permits a new way of thinking about many things: about the meaning
of sacramental initiation; about the resulting nature of ministry in
general and ordained ministry in particular; about the multifaceted
and multidimensional relationships that are involved in lives of
Christian discipleship and ministry; about the nuances that exist
within the sacrament of orders itself.

A significant difficulty exists in understanding the contemporary
diaconate as a proper and permanent order precisely because much
of the theological and canonical language that has developed concerning the ordained ministries emerged subsequent to the decline of
the diaconate as a permanent order. While it is sometimes said that
the diaconate had disappeared by the end of the patristic era, and that
it was restored by the Second Vatican Council, these characterizations
are inadequate in that they miss a significant paradigm shift. The diaconate never disappeared; rather, it was transformed and redefined
into a transitory stage on the way to ultimate ordination into the presbyterate.[7] The diaconate ceased being described on its own terms
and began being defined and described by its relationship to the
presbyterate. The paradigm for discussions of ordained ministry,

---

6. Paul VI, *Hodie Concilium,* 57–64.

7. Consider the codification of this theological understanding in canon 973 of the
1917 *Code of Canon Law:* "First tonsure and orders are to be conferred only on those who
are proposed for ascending to the presbyterate and who seem correctly understood as,
at some point in the future, being worthy priests." *Codex Iuris Canonici* (Vatican City:
Typis Polyglottis Vaticanis, 1924). English translation from Edward N. Peters, *The 1917
Pio-Benedictine Code of Canon Law in English Translation with Extensive Scholarly Apparatus*
(San Francisco: Ignatius Press, 2001).

therefore, has been primarily sacerdotal, and in particular, pres-byteral, ministry. Other ministries, including the episcopate and dia-conate (as well as various forms of lay ecclesial ministry), are often still measured against this paradigm.[8] Using such a frame of refer-ence, ministries other than the presbyterate are often described in terms of what they are not: the laity are described as "nonordained"; deacons do not "say Mass," do not "hear confessions," do not "give last rites." This method of "negative identification" must be overcome if the diaconate is to develop into the "proper and permanent" order described by the council.

Lumen Gentium paragraph 29 shifted the paradigm vis-à-vis the diaconate. First, the paragraph begins by recalling the patristic dis-tinction between "priesthood" and the "ministry" for which the deacon is ordained. Later in the same paragraph, the council fathers refer to the diaconate and its functions as "extremely nec-essary" for the life of the church, and they note that these functions are "difficult to fulfill" because of the current laws and customs of the Latin church. It is for this reason that the diaconate may be restored "as a proper and permanent rank of the hierarchy." While the diaconate is to function in communion with the presbyterate, it has an identity unique in itself. Contemporary attempts in theol-ogy and canon law to define and describe the nature and functions of the diaconate must be examined critically. Certain terms may have relevance only for the sacerdotal orders; others may have rel-evance only for the diaconate; still others may apply to all the ordained.[9] This is seen in a particular way when discussing issues of pastoral leadership.

---

8. This may be seen in recent statements from the Holy See, such as the interdi-casterial *Instruction on Certain Questions Regarding the Collaboration of the Non-Ordained Faithful in the Sacred Ministry of the Priest* (Vatican City: Libreria Editrice Vaticana, 1997). Notice that even in the title, the laity are not referred to according to their baptismal status but rather according to what they are not.

9. James H. Provost once observed, when writing about the diaconate in the 1983 *Code of Canon Law,* "There is still no coherent treatment of permanent deacons as a 'proper and permanent rank of the hierarchy' comparable to the treatment given pres-byters and bishops in the code; rather, they are treated as exceptions to the norms for

This epilogue is organized around four sections: a *kenotic* view of Christ's mission and its relationship to apostolic ministry; an overview of issues related to the deacon and the *episkopē* of the bishop; the exercise of the ancient diaconate with regard to functions of leadership, governance, and oversight; and, finally, a look to the future possibilities of diaconal leadership in the contemporary church.

Christ, Apostolic Ministry, and the Deacon: Through the Lens of *Kenosis*

A powerful witness to the link between the disciples' exercise of authority and kenotic self-sacrifice in imitation of Christ is found in Christ's washing the disciples' feet in the Gospel of John. Raymond Brown has written:

> In demeaning himself to wash his disciples' feet Jesus is acting out beforehand his humiliation in death....The foot washing is an action of service for others, symbolic of the service he will render in laying down his life for others; that is why Jesus can claim that the foot washing is necessary if the disciples are to share in his heritage and that it will render the disciples clean.[10]

The implication of this passage for the identity and ministry of the apostles is profound, since it links the kenotic self-sacrifice of Christ to the life of the disciple. "To 'have part with Jesus' through washing means to be part of the self-giving love that will bring Jesus' life to an end, symbolically anticipated by the foot washing."[11] Furthermore, those who would be leaders in the community of disciples are to be

---

presbyters." James H. Provost, "Permanent Deacons in the 1983 Code," in *Canon Law Society of America Proceedings* 46 (1984): 175.

10. Raymond Brown, *The Gospel According to John* (New York: Doubleday, 1966–70), 562.

11. Francis J. Moloney, SDB, *The Gospel of John* (Collegeville, MN: Liturgical Press, 1998), 375.

identified by their own self-sacrificing love in imitation of the *kenosis* of Christ.

> The theme of death is behind the use of the word *hypodeigma* [v. 15]. This expression, found only here in the [New Testament]…is associated with exemplary death. Jesus' exhortation is not to moral performance but to imitation of his self-gift….Entrance into the Johannine community of disciples meant taking the risk of accepting the *hypodeigma* of Jesus, a commitment to love even if it led to death.[12]

Apostolic ministry, fully expressed sacramentally in the episcopal order, is to be characterized by an emptying of self for others. This is a ministry, like Christ's, of total self-sacrifice on behalf of others. Those who have a share in the apostolic ministry freely accept this aspect of Christ's identity as part of their own. Apostolic ministry is centered on the Eucharist: It flows from the minister's participation in Christ's own sacrifice of himself, celebrated within the form of a sacred memorial meal. The *diakonia* of apostolic ministry is eucharistic, a breaking and sharing of one's life for the building up of the body in memory of Christ.

Edmund Hill has related the nature of authority as found in the New Testament with the language of power. He describes the nature of "ministerial authority" as described by Jesus as an "absurd paradox."

> Authority ordinarily means the power to give commands and to enforce them; to lay down the law with little expectation of being gainsaid; to wield influence, to control, to rule, to guide effectively. Ministry, if we stick to the real meaning of the word, which perhaps is still more evident in the Greek equivalent *diakonia*, means simply to serve. In fact it means the opposite of authority; it means carrying out commands, accepting law as laid down by others, being ruled, controlled, influenced, or at most being an instrument through which the possessor of authority exercises influence, control and rule.

---

12. Ibid., 376.

So, "ministerial authority" looks like a contradiction in terms. If it is not to be that, then it has to involve either a radical, revolutionary recasting of the idea of authority, or an evaporation of the idea of ministry, of service. There can be no doubt which of the two is involved when Jesus combines the two terms, not only in the gospel texts but in his own person. There we see that the notion of authority is radically recast, while the idea of service is rigorously maintained in all its crude literalness. The authority of Christ himself, and therefore of all who share in it, is an authority *only* for the sake of service; an authority to wash the feet of the disciples; an authority to care for others, to consider their interests; an authority to give his life as a ransom for many.[13]

God is the source of all power, and in the Christian tradition "the sources of power derived from God are manifested historically through Jesus Christ and through the Holy Spirit."[14] This means that the church, in developing its own application and exercise of the ongoing presence and action of God's power, must do so in light of Christ's leadership and example. Given Christ's command to lead in a new way, a way that is radically countercultural, those who would presume to lead must do so in a way that serves the greater good of the community. James Coriden puts it quite succinctly: "Power in the Church is power to serve."[15] One way to describe the deacon's unique participation in sacred power would be to refer to it as *kenotic* power.

Ordination to the diaconate involves a sacramental empowerment of the church and the ordinand. The church is empowered by the Spirit with the particular gifts of the ordinand now being placed at the permanent and public service of the church herself. The deacon is likewise empowered, not with the *sacra potestas* of the sacerdotal orders, but with a *kenotic power,* a power or strength

---

13. Edmund Hill, OP, *Ministry and Authority in the Catholic Church* (London: Geoffrey Chapman, 1988), 11–12.

14. James A. Coriden, *Canon Law as Ministry: Freedom and Good Order for the Church* (New York/Mahwah, NJ: Paulist Press, 2000), 108.

15. Ibid., 112.

to empty himself in service to the church. This kenotic power reflects the model of *diakonia,* Christ, as found in the aforementioned Philippian hymn.

Through sacramental ordination, the deacon celebrates a new sacramental relationship with the Christ who came to serve and not be served. "A deacon is a member of the Church who, in response to God's perceived election and call, reaches out to be of service in the Church, and, in this way, incarnates the presence of Jesus, who is the deacon of the presence of God."[16]

Kenotic power is not the exclusive province of the deacon, but it is the deacon who serves as the sacramental focus for the *diakonia* of the entire community. That is why Patrick McCaslin and Michael Lawlor can say, "A parish, which is a local incarnation of Church and of Jesus, is not sacramentally whole if it is without either priest or deacon."[17] Just as the presbyter shares in the sacred power of the priesthood with the bishop, so too does the deacon share in the kenotic power of the diaconate with the bishop. In other words, I am suggesting that *sacra potestas* may be reflected in two ways: *sacerdotal* and *kenotic.* In the same way that *Lumen Gentium,* paragraph 10, orders the common priesthood of the baptized to the ministerial priesthood, it may be said that the common *diakonia* of the baptized is ordered to the ministerial diaconate. The ministerial diaconate sacramentalizes the self-emptying love of Christ on behalf of others, to which the entire community of disciples is called. It does not supplant, it does not replace, it does not subsume; through the "sacramental grace" received at ordination,[18] the deacon receives the strength to empty himself in the service of others through official ministry in word, sacrament, and charity.

Describing *kenotic power* in terms of a polarity between *power* and *kenosis* helps define the sacramentality of *diakonia,* both within

---

16. Patrick McCaslin and Michael G. Lawlor, *Sacrament of Service: A Vision of the Permanent Deacon Today* (New York/Mahwah, NJ: Paulist Press, 1986), 41.

17. Ibid., 62–63.

18. See Vatican Council II, *Lumen Gentium* (Dogmatic Constitution on the Church, 1964), no. 29, in Walter M. Abbott, SJ, ed., *The Documents of Vatican II* (New York: America Press, 1966).

the church herself and in those who share in apostolic ministry. The tension between power and powerlessness reflects a continuum from power-*full*-ness to power-*less*-ness. As Christ demonstrated in his own life and through his teaching about leadership to his disciples, the one who would be a leader in Christ's image must first surrender power and take the position of a servant, one without power. What is critical in this understanding for our study is the fact that a kenotic empowerment represents a dynamic reality that may be a source of creative energy, a real strengthening, a true force for service. *Kenosis* moves beyond simply giving up power. It is an active emptying, not simply the acceptance of powerlessness.

This idea of kenotic empowerment returns us to Karl Rahner, who wrote:

> By willing itself, power wills what is other than itself. The transition to the other, to allowing the will of others, to unconditional consent to the generosity of the divine will, demands of the finite will, which is not the source of its own power, a self-abandonment, self-sacrifice, self-mediation through weakness, by questioning its own....The redemption of power is the cross....The cross of power involves for the Christian not only readiness for self-sacrifice, but willingness to accept power in its vulnerable earthly conditions. But even then it will only be accepted with detachment and will be valid only because it comes from God.[19]

---

19. Karl Rahner, s.v. "Power," in *Sacramentum Mundi: An Encyclopedia of Theology,* ed. Karl Rahner et al. (New York: Herder & Herder, 1970), 72.

Issues Related to Pastoral Leadership and Deacons

By sacramental initiation, human beings are immersed in the life of the Trinity and are anointed to participate in Christ's own ministry of "priest, prophet, and king."[20] Those Christians subsequently ordained deacons "within the ministry of the Bishop"[21] are consecrated in a distinct sacramental way to the bishop's own exercise of the apostolic ministry of word, sacrament, and charity.

In beginning its own treatment of the hierarchical nature of the church, the Second Vatican Council taught, "For the nurturing and constant growth of the People of God, Christ the Lord instituted in His Church a variety of ministries, which work for the good of the whole body."[22] The paragraphs of this section of *Lumen Gentium* go on to describe the ministries of the bishop (paragraphs 18–27), priests (paragraph 28), and deacons (paragraph 29). From the outset, therefore, the council saw the diaconate as one of these divinely instituted offices intended to "shepherd" the church.

Deacons are specifically mentioned for the first time in this regard two paragraphs later, when the council fathers speak of the relationship of both deacons and priests with the ministry of the bishop. "With their helpers, the priests and deacons, bishops have therefore taken up the service of the community, presiding in place of God over the flock whose shepherds they are, as teachers of doctrine, priests of sacred worship, and officers of good order."[23] Walter Cardinal Kasper echoes this passage when he writes, "The gradations in participation in the bishop's ministry thus denote two different

---

20. As the newly baptized person's head is anointed with sacred chrism, the minister says, "As Christ was anointed Priest, Prophet, and King, so may you live always as a member of his body, sharing everlasting life."

21. Hippolytus, *Traditio Apostolica,* 8, cited in the *Rite of Ordination of a Bishop, Priests and Deacons,* 179.

22. Vatican Council II, *Lumen Gentium,* no. 18.

23. Ibid., no. 20.

structures: the bishop is aided by two separate arms (so to speak), which have differing tasks but must collaborate with one another."[24]

While leadership in general may be exercised by many in the church, ordination itself involves a variety of sacramental participations in the pastoral leadership of the bishop. Nathan Mitchell has written, "The restoration of the diaconate is thus important not because it resurrects an ancient order that had all but faded in the West, but because it affirms the principle that *recognition of pastoral leadership is the fundamental basis for calling a Christian to ordained ministry.*"[25] This ministry of pastoral leadership or supervision, which is expressed fully in the ministry of the bishop, is often referred to by the Greek *episkopē* ("oversight"), which is related directly to the *episkopos* ("one who watches over"; and in modern usage, "bishop"). Scripture scholar Raymond Brown once described *episkopē* as "supervision in matters pastoral, doctrinal, and sacramental....If one considers the Greek vocabulary most directly expressing the idea of supervision in the [New Testament], it is obvious that those called *episkopoi* exercised some form of *episkopē*; but so did others."[26] After tracing the supervision exercised by these "others"—the Twelve, the seven Hellenist leaders of Acts 6, James of Jerusalem, and others—Brown concludes, "This survey shows that the manner and exercise of supervision varied greatly in the different places and different periods within the first century or [New Testament] era."[27]

---

24. Walter Kasper, *Leadership in the Church: How Traditional Roles Can Serve the Christian Community Today* (New York: Crossroad, 2003), 18. Originally a paper presented to a study conference of the International Diaconate Center, this essay first appeared as "Der Diakon in ekklesiologischer Sicht angesichts der gegenwärtigen Herausforderungen in Kirche und Gesellschaft," *Diakonia* 32, nos. 3–4 (1997): 13–33; also in Walter Kasper, *Theologie und Kirche* (Mainz: Matthias-Grünewald, 1999), 2: 145–62.

25. Nathan Mitchell, OSB, *Mission and Ministry: History and Theology in the Sacrament of Order* (Wilmington, DE: Michael Glazier, 1982), 304 (emphasis in the original).

26. Raymond E. Brown, "*Episkopē* and *Episkopos:* The New Testament Evidence," *Theological Studies* 41, no. 2 (June 1980): 322–23.

27. Ibid., 338.

The fact that many persons, including deacons, might participate in various ways in the *episkopē* of the bishop seems strongly
supported to this point. More recent literature on the sacramental
nature of ordained ministry, however, would seem to deny such
participation, limiting *episkopē* to those in the sacerdotal orders of
bishop and presbyter. Consider the following from theologian
Richard Gaillardetz:

> In the early Church the privileged role of the bishop lay in his
> unique ministry of *episkopē,* the pastoral oversight of a
> eucharistic community in which the bishop functioned as the
> chief judge and witness to the apostolic faith, the servant of
> the unity of that community and the agent for bringing that
> community into communion with other communities. By the
> third century the presbyter gradually was given a share in this
> ministry of apostolic oversight, though limited to oversight of
> a particular community.[28]

Notice that Gaillardetz refers to the "privileged role" of the bishop
and his "unique" ministry of *episkopē*, which was eventually shared in
a limited way with presbyters. Certainly these insights are consistent
with the scriptural evidence and the tradition of the church. In particular, as David Power notes, "Safeguarding the unity of the Church
in the one apostolic tradition, presiding over its essential unity, and
presiding over its Eucharist all go together."[29] This particular exercise
of the *episkopē*, linking as it does leadership of the community and its
Eucharist, is clearly the province of the bishop and his presbyters.
Professor Gaillardetz takes a further step, however, and describes an
exclusivity to this *episkopē*. In this regard he seems to be echoing certain official statements, such as the interdicasterial instruction cited

---

28. Richard R. Gaillardetz, "Reflections on the Theological Integrity of the
Diaconate," in Owen Cummings, William T. Ditewig, and Richard R. Gaillardetz,
Theology of the Diaconate: State of the Question (New York/Mahwah, NJ: Paulist Press,
2005), 86.

29. David N. Power, "The Basis for Official Ministry in the Church," in James H.
Provost, ed., *Official Ministry* (Washington, DC: Canon Law Society of America, 1981),
66.

previously, in which bishops and (to a limited degree) presbyters share in apostolic oversight, while deacons and laypersons assist those who exercise such oversight.

> The diaconate presented a somewhat different situation because the deacon's sacramental relationship within the life of the Church was not constituted by the ministry of apostolic oversight (*episkopē*), as with the bishop or local pastor. However, and I take this to be decisive for understanding the diaconate, the deacon was ordained *to serve* the ministry of apostolic oversight....For both the presbyter and bishop, ordination introduces them into a new relationship within the Church characterized by pastoral oversight (*episkopē*) and ritualized, as it were, in their presidency at the celebration of the Eucharist....The deacon is also ordained into apostolic office, but his share in this office is not by way of *exercising* pastoral oversight (the ministerial province of the bishop and pastor) properly speaking, but of *assisting or serving the needs of pastoral oversight* as determined by the one who exercises that oversight.[30]

In summary, then, we find two contrasting positions: that represented by Brown, which, while acknowledging the unique role of *episkopoi,* finds scriptural evidence that *episkopē* was exercised by many; and that represented by Gaillardetz, which seems to restrict the exercise of *episkopē* to those in sacerdotal orders. To pursue the matter further, I turn our attention to the so-called Golden Age of the diaconate and examine briefly the functions of deacons related to pastoral leadership and governance.

Leadership and the Ancient Diaconate

The study of the ancient diaconate has become quite extensive over the past forty years.[31] An examination of the patristic diaconate

---

30. Gaillardetz, "Reflections," in Cummings et al., *Theology of the Diaconate,* 86.
31. See, for example, Bernard Cooke, *Ministry to Word and Sacrament* (Philadelphia:

reveals that, while deacons always served in an assisting capacity, they had authority in many areas, either through their participation in the order of deacons or because of particular delegation by the bishop. Several sources reveal that deacons in some areas served in a variety of roles related to judicial functions, in this sense understood as part of the governing body of the community; that is, an entity empowered to make decisions on behalf of the community for its efficient and orderly functioning. This is suggested in Ignatius, Polycarp, the *Didascalia Apostolorum,* the *Apostolic Constitutions,* and possibly the *Apostolic Church Order.* Some deacons served in various functions of administration, serving as emissaries, administrators of church property and goods, and as leaders of remote communities.

Ignatius, the bishop-martyr of Antioch, was concerned with "order" and unity in the Christian community.[32] Written toward the end of Trajan's reign (AD 98–117), the letters of Ignatius "witness to a unique understanding of the office of bishop."[33] From his letters we see the emergence of a monoepiscopate and a clearly defined tripartite hierarchy of bishop, with priests and deacons assisting, each in their proper roles. Ignatius compares the bishop to God the Father, presbyters to the College of the Apostles, and the deacons to Jesus Christ: "Correspondingly, everyone must show the deacons respect. They represent Jesus Christ, just as the bishop has the role of the Father, and the presbyters are like God's council and an apostolic band. You cannot have a Church *(ecclesia)* without these."[34] "Let the

---

Fortress, 1976); Kenan B. Osborne, *Priesthood: A History of the Ordained Ministry in the Roman Catholic Church* (NewYork/Mahwah, NJ: Paulist Press, 1988); Kenan B. Osborne, *The Diaconate in the Christian Church* (Chicago: National Association of Diaconate Directors, 1996); Nathan Mitchell, *Mission and Ministry: History and Theology in the Sacrament of Order* (Wilmington, DE: Michael Glazier, 1982); James M. Barnett, *The Diaconate: A Full and Equal Order,* rev. ed. (Valley Forge, PA: Trinity Press International, 1995).

32. See, for example, Edward P. Echlin, *The Deacon in the Church: Past and Present* (Staten Island, NY: Alba House, 1971), 19.

33. Graydon F. Snyder, "Ignatius of Antioch," in Ferguson, 559; see also, F. R. Prostmeier, "Ignatius of Antioch," in *Dictionary of Early Christian Literature,* ed. Siegmar Döpp and Wilhelm Geerlings (NewYork: Crossroad, 2000), 297.

34. Ignatius, *Trallians,* 3:1, in *Early Christian Fathers,* ed. Cyril C. Richardson (NewYork: Collier Books, Macmillan Publishing Co., 1970), 99.

deacons (my special favorites) be entrusted with the ministry of Jesus Christ who was with the Father from eternity and appeared at the end of the world."[35]

Ignatius is interested in promoting the unity and harmony of the church; his call for the respect to be shown to the community's ministers should be seen in this light. In his letter to the church in Smyrna, Ignatius writes:

> Flee from schism as the source of mischief. You should all fol-low the bishop as Jesus Christ did the Father. Follow, too, the presbytery as you would the apostles; and respect the deacons as you would God's law. Nobody must do anything that has to do with the Church without the bishop's approval.[36]

Such a reference leads Barnett to conclude, "It is because of the high esteem in which the deacon was held that he may have been included in the governing council."[37] While this conclusion is not readily sustainable, clearly deacons are seen as ministers exercising a responsibility for the governance of the community.

Ignatius also spoke of the deacon as a legate of the commu-nity. In his letter to the Philadelphians he wrote:

> I feel that you ought, as a Church of God, to choose a deacon to go there [Antioch] as an ambassador of God, for the glory of the Name and to congratulate them when they assemble together. Blessed in Jesus Christ is the man who is to be found worthy of this ministry. All praise to you, too, who send him. You can do this for the Name of God if only you choose to; just as the Churches which are near neighbors sent deacons or priests and, some of them, bishops.[38]

The deacon's leadership role in the community becomes increas-ingly clear. Polycarp, an *episkopos* of Smyrna martyred around 156,

---

35. Ignatius, *Magnesians,* 6:1, in Richardson, *Early Christian Fathers,* 95.

36. Ignatius, *Smyrneans,* 8, in Richardson, *Early Christian Fathers,* 115.

37. Barnett, *Diaconate,* 52.

38. Ignatius, *Philadelphians,* 10, in *The Fathers of the Church,* vol. 51, ed. Ludwig Schopp, trans. Gerald G. Walsh (New York: CIMA Publishing, 1947), 117.

refers to presbyters and deacons in his letter to the Philippians (about 117)[39]:

> Likewise the deacons should be blameless before his right-
> eousness, as servants of God and Christ and not of men; not
> slanderers, not double-tongued, not lovers of money, tem-
> perate in all matters, compassionate, careful, living according
> to the truth of the Lord, who became a "servant of all."…It
> is necessary…to be subject to the presbyters and deacons as
> to God and Christ.[40]

Kenan Osborne notes a tone reminiscent of 1 Timothy in this description, and, consistent with Ignatius, the deacon is compared with Christ, specifically Christ the servant.[41] No precise information is given concerning the functions of deacons, but the people are to be subject to the authority shared by presbyters and deacons, suggesting to some that deacons were part of the ruling church council at Philippi.[42]

The *Didascalia Apostolorum* was composed in Syria during the early to middle years of the third century.[43] Probably no other ancient source is more descriptive of the relationship of bishop to deacon, of the source of the deacon's authority, of the deacon's responsibility to the poor, and of the deacon's exercise of governance.

> Let the bishops and the deacons, then, be of one mind; and do
> you shepherd the people diligently with one accord. For you
> ought both to be one body, father and son; for you are in the
> likeness of the Lordship. And let the deacon make known all
> things to the bishop, even as Christ to His Father. But let him

---

39. "Polycarp makes no mention of a bishop of Philippi but he does speak of the obedience due to presbyters and deacons" (Johannes Quasten, *Patrology*, 4 vols. [Allen, TX: Christian Classics, n.d.], 1:80).

40. Polycarp, *The Letter of Polycarp to the Philippians*, 5:2, in Richardson, *Early Christian Fathers*, 133.

41. See Osborne, *Priesthood*, 103.

42. See Barnett, *Diaconate*, 53; Osborne, *Diaconate*, 30.

43. See B. Steimer, "Didascalia," in Döpp and Geerlings, *Early Christian Literature*, 171–72.

order such things as he is able by himself, receiving power from the bishop, as the Lord did from His Father....But the weighty matters let the bishop judge. Yet let the deacon be the hearing of the bishop, and his mouth and his heart and his soul; for when you are both of one mind, through your agreement there will be peace in the Church....

Let the deacon be ready to obey and to submit himself to the command of the bishop. And let him labor and toil in every place whither he is sent to minister or to speak of some matter to anyone. For it behooves each one to know his office and to be diligent in executing it. And be you [bishop and deacon] of one counsel and of one purpose, and one soul dwelling in two bodies.[44]

According to the *Didascalia,* deacons participate in a variety of functions associated with the good order, discipline, and administration of the community: among them, the deacon assists in the administration of justice. The author exhorts bishops, "Let your judgments be held on the second day of the week....Let also the deacons and presbyters be ever present in all your judgments, to judge without acceptance of persons, as men of God, with righteousness."[45] Another function performed by the deacon will be echoed in later developments: namely, the welcoming and "certification" of new members of the community.

If anyone come in from another place, bringing recommendatory letters, let the deacon be the judge of the affair, inquiring whether they be of the faithful, and of the Church, whether they be not defiled by heresy, and besides, whether the party be a married woman or a widow. And when he is satisfied in the things of the Lord, let him conduct everyone to the place proper to him.[46]

The deacon does all this because of the power received from the bishop, both through the laying on of hands and also by specific

---

44. R. Hugh Connolly, *Didascalia Apostolorum: The Syriac Version* (Oxford: Clarendon Press, 1929), 109, 148.
45. Ibid., 111.
46. Ibid.

assignments given to him by the bishop. The *Didascalia* echoes Ignatius in describing the deacon in terms of Christ: "The bishop sits for you in the place of God Almighty. But the deacon stands in place of Christ."[47] Similarly, "If then our Lord did thus, will you, O deacons, hesitate to do the like for them that are sick and infirm, you who are workmen of the truth, and bear the likeness of Christ."[48]

The *Apostolic Constitutions*, dated AD 375–400,[49] repeats points already noted: that deacons were to be a part of the bishop's "judgments" on the second day of the week, and that the deacon was responsible for welcoming new members (at least lay persons and other deacons) into the community after assessing their "references." Finally, the *Apostolic Church Order*, most probably written in Egypt at the beginning of the fourth century,[50] directs that three deacons were to be appointed for legal reasons: "There shall be three deacons for 'by three shall every matter be established.'"[51] These deacons are appointed "in order that they may be able to bear an effective witness in cases of complaint before the disciplinary judgment."[52]

Deacons served a variety of administrative or executive functions, whether as a representative of the bishop (or the entire community), or in supervising the care of those in need. As seen in the letter of Ignatius to the Philadelphians, there is evidence that some deacons served as emissaries or legates of bishops and their communities. *The Shepherd of Hermas*, dated approximately 140, "consists of a sermon on penance, apocalyptic in character, and, all in all, curious in form and subject."[53] Deacons are referenced in one

---

47. Ibid., 88.

48. Ibid., 150.

49. See Steimer, "Apostolic Constitutions," in Döpp and Geerlings, *Early Christian Literature,* 44, for date.

50. See Steimer, "Apostolic Church Order," in Döpp and Geerlings, *Early Christian Literature,* 44, for date and location.

51. Adolf Harnack, *Sources of the Apostolic Canons,* trans. John Owen (London: F. Norgate & Co., 1895), 17.

52. Ibid., 39.

53. Quasten, *Patrology,* 1:93. See also David E. Aune, "Hermas," in Ferguson, *Encyclopedia of Early Christianity,* 521, and N. Brox, "Hermas," in Döpp and Geerlings, *Early Christian Literature,* 277–88.

of the visions, in which the growing church is described in terms of a tower under construction, and in one of the parables, which identifies sinners in need of repentance. In the vision is this reference: "The stones that are square and white and fit their joints are the apostles and bishops and teachers and deacons who have lived in the holiness of God, and have been bishops and teachers and deacons for God's chosen in purity and reverence."[54] In the parable, however, among the sinners in need of repentance are found "deacons who served badly and plundered the living of widows and orphans, and made profit for themselves from the ministry they had accepted to perform."[55] Deacons are identified through their direct care of the poor, in this case widows and orphans.

While the exact dating of the *Apostolic Tradition* remains disputed, it has most often been dated approximately 215, and it is frequently (but not definitively) attributed to Hippolytus of Rome.[56] The document begins with directions for the ordination of bishops, presbyters, and deacons. A deacon is to be ordained after he is selected "after the fashion of those things said above,"[57] referring back to the instructions concerning the ordination of the bishop, who is chosen by all the people.

Unlike the ordination of a bishop, in which *all* bishops present lay hands on the new bishop, and the ordination of a presbyter, in which *all* presbyters present "touch the one to be ordained," *only* the bishop lays hands on the deacon.

> When the deacon is ordained, this is the reason why the bishop alone shall lay his hands upon him: he is not ordained to the priesthood but to serve the bishop and to carry out the

---

54. Hermas, *Shepherd,* Vision 3.5.1, in Goodspeed, Edgar J., *A History of Early Christian Literature* (Chicago, IL: University of Chicago Press, 1942), 112.

55. Ibid., Parable 9.26.2, in Goodspeed, 193.

56. Everett Ferguson, "Hippolytus," in Ferguson, *Encyclopedia of Early Christianity,* 531–32; B. R. Suchla, "Hippolytus," in Döpp and Gerrlings, *Early Christian Literature,* 287–89.

57. Burton Scott Easton, trans. and ed., *The Apostolic Tradition of Hippolytus: Translated into English with Introduction and Notes* (Cambridge: Cambridge University Press, 1934), 38–39.

bishop's commands. He does not take part in the council of the clergy; he is to attend to his own duties and to make known to the bishop such things as are needful. He does not receive that Spirit that is possessed by the presbytery, in which the presbyters share; he receives only what is confided in him under the bishop's authority.[58]

The text describes the following duties that might be assigned to the deacons. "Let each of the deacons with the subdeacons attend upon the bishop; and let it be reported to him who are sick, that if it seem good to the bishop he may visit them."[59] Also, deacons are part of a daily "staff meeting": "Let the deacons and presbyters assemble daily at the place which the bishop shall appoint for them. And let not the deacons especially neglect to assemble every day unless sickness prevents them."[60] This passage is interesting, especially in light of the earlier observation that deacons do not share in the "council of the clergy." In this passage, however, both presbyters and deacons are present, with a special emphasis on the participation of the deacons. Easton concludes, "At these gatherings the clergy received assignments for their duties of that day; in these latter the deacons were more important than the presbyters and their absence a more serious fault."[61]

Fabian, the bishop of Rome who was martyred in 250, divided Rome into seven districts, with each district assigned to one of the seven Roman deacons, who exercised administrative governance over their respective "deaconries."[62] The well-known legend of the deacon Lawrence (d. 258) gives an insight into the role of the deacon in Rome during this period.[63] After the arrest and martyrdom of his bishop, Lawrence himself was arrested and ordered to hand over the treasures of the church—at the appointed time, Lawrence brought the poor of the Christian community. Again the deacon is

---

58. Ibid.

59. Gregory Dix, *The Treatise on the Apostolic Tradition of St. Hippolytus of Rome* (London: SPCK, 1968), 57.

60. Ibid., 60.

61. Easton, *Hippolytus,* 102.

62. Barnett, *Diaconate,* 65.

63. See, for example, Barnett, *Diaconate,* 65–66.

linked with his bishop in his service to the poor, and the deacon is the Christian official who was expected by the authorities to be responsible for the goods of the Christian community.

This sketch of diaconal functions related to governance has centered on the *ordinary* exercise of such functions: the kinds of governance that might have been expected of most deacons simply by virtue of their ordination into the order of deacons.[64]

To summarize: Notice must be taken of the remarkably consistent connection between bishop and deacon. Even as the deacon gradually and increasingly became associated with and subordinate to the presbyters, the connection with the bishop never disappears. It is the bishop who ordains the deacon, not the presbyter, and it is on behalf of the bishop that the deacon acts. A particularly telling historical fact that underscores the close connection between deacon and bishop is that in many documented instances, it is the deacon that is elected to succeed the bishop. "The selection of deacons rather than presbyters oftentimes to fill vacancies in the bishop's office was logical, since many of the bishop's duties were administrative, as were the deacon's, following the emergence of the monoepiscopate and later the monarchial episcopate."[65] The diaconate was perceived as a powerful administrative ministry that worked intimately with the bishops—so closely that the deacon was often the most qualified successor to the bishop. As vicars of the bishop, deacons exercised a share in his responsibilities in governance as the bishop deemed proper. In short, the deacon in this period seems to have exercised significant administrative governance functions, clearly a participation in the bishop's own administrative responsibilities.

In considering the nonliturgical functions of the deacon throughout this period, we have seen the deacon emerge as an office holder in the ancient church, a person who shared in the responsibility of good order within the Christian community, a person who,

---

64. Three additional *extraordinary* sets of functions also suggest themselves: the deacon as an extraordinary minister of reconciliation (Cyprian), the deacon leading remote communities in the absence of presbyters or bishops, and the powerful role of the archdeacon.

65. Barnett, *Diaconate,* 66.

on behalf of the community and in the name of the bishop, had a particular role in being responsible for those in need. The deacon took on various roles as catechist, member of the community's ruling council, and legate. Always closely associated with his bishop, the deacon was often the bishop's successor, and some deacons served in the extremely powerful office of archdeacon, with responsibilities over the rest of the clergy (including presbyters), with fiscal and judicial oversight. Given the radical and unique sacramental relationship between the bishop and his deacons (reflected in the bishop's sole laying on of hands at diaconal ordination), it seems inescapable to conclude that the deacon shared in the bishop's own *episkopē* for the good of the church. Such a participation in the bishop's *episkopē* continues today, not in a sacerdotal way as enjoyed by the bishop's *presbyterium,* but in a uniquely diaconal way, which is no less tied sacramentally to the bishop's apostolic ministry of oversight.

Diaconal Leadership

This section suggests additional leadership initiatives that might be undertaken by deacons in several venues in the contemporary church: parish-based ministry, regional diocesan ministry, and community-based ministry. Paul Philibert has written that the priest today is probably best described as "a generative mentoring pastor—one whose responsibility is to maintain harmony while bringing into cooperation the rich and diverse gifts of all the members of the community."[66] Furthermore, I affirm that the deacon is the animator of the church's *diakonia.* Interestingly, Philibert picks up on this connection between generativity and animator when he writes, "The role of pastor and animator of the local church's varied charisms is far more demanding than the role of liturgical presider alone."[67] The same could be said, with only minor revision,

---

66. Paul Philibert, OP, "Issues for a Theology of Priesthood: A Status Report," in *The Theology of Priesthood,* Donald J. Goergen and Ann Garrido, eds. (Collegeville, MN: Liturgical Press, 2000), 3–4.

67. Ibid., 4.

of the deacon. Therefore, what follows is a suggestion of what might be done by deacons as "generative animators" of the diocesan church. Helmut Hoping has written:

> The presbyter represents the bishop *in situ,* that is, in the parishes, where they have governance of the parishes to which they have been assigned, and where they are responsible for presiding at the Eucharist....The deacon also has a share of the apostolic mission of the bishop. The deacon represents the bishop *in situ* in *diakonia,* which—as has become clear—is at the direct disposal of the bishop. As a function of the Church's governance, the diaconate highlights the *diakonia* of every single Christian.[68]

Parish-Based Ministry

The Second Vatican Council referred to the parish as being "a kind of cell" *(velut cellula)* of the diocese, a basic community that "brings together the many human differences found within its boundaries and draws them into the universality of the Church."[69]

> As sharers in the role of Christ the Priest, the Prophet, and the King, the laity have an active part to play in the life and activity of the Church....
> The laity should accustom themselves to working in the parish in close union with their priests, bringing to the church community their own and the world's problems as well as questions concerning human salvation, all of which should be examined and resolved by common deliberation. As far as possible, the laity ought to collaborate energetically in every apostolic and missionary undertaking sponsored by their local parish.[70]

---

68. Helmut Hoping, "Diakonie als Aufgabe des kirchlichen Leitungsamtes," *Dokumentation 13–Jahrestagung 1996* (Tübingen: Arbeitsgemeinschaft Ständiger Diakonat, Bundesrepublik Deutschland, 1996), 34.

69. Vatican Council II, *Apostolicam Actuositatem* (Decree on the Apostolate of the Laity, 1965), no. 10.

70. Ibid.

These challenging words of the council have yet to be realized in many parish communities. Faced with shifting population centers— creating rapid growth in some parishes and an exodus from others— many parishes are simply struggling to survive. Coupled with this situation, the growing shortage of presbyters in many areas creates even more intense stress on some communities. As many dioceses develop strategies for closing, merging, and clustering parishes, some parishioners wonder if their parish will continue to exist in *any* form. This leads many to think about parish-as-church in a minimalist mode: What is absolutely necessary (contrasted with what would be "nice to have") if they are to survive as a Catholic parish? The answers quite naturally focus on the Eucharist and the community's ability to have someone present who can preside at the Eucharist. In such a view, having deacons or lay ecclesial ministers, who cannot "say Mass" or "hear confessions," seems far less critical. The result of this popular perspective is that the ordained ministry of the deacon (and even the bishop) is perceived as of much lesser significance in the life of the parish. The value of a deacon is often characterized merely by those functions in which he is perceived as being able "to help Father" in the performance of certain "priest"-like ways. In addition, the church's social justice ministry at the parish level, even if a deacon is involved, is usually not seen as the responsibility of the entire parish. Rather, involvement in social justice ministries is more often than not the province of a handful of volunteers who take them on as personal ministries.

It is at this point that the ministry of the deacon could be critical, and yet it remains largely unrealized. As the church's sacramental icon of *diakonia,* it should be a primary duty of the deacon to build up diaconal parishes, communities that realize and live their own diaconal responsibilities. Cardinal Kasper writes:

> Each parish has to make sure that *diakonia* is realized. This means that faith and preaching, as well as the Eucharist and liturgy must be oriented to *diakonia*. Faith without *diakonia* is not a Christian faith. Preaching without *diakonia* is not Christian preaching. A non-diaconal parish celebrating the Eucharist may express its faith, but its faith remains dead; in

the final analysis it cannot find God, as they miss the point that God reveals himself in the people, especially in the poor.

The Church lives wherever the corporal works of mercy are practiced: feeding the hungry, giving drink to the thirsty, clothing the naked, giving shelter to strangers, liberating prisoners, visiting the sick and burying the dead. The Church also lives wherever the spiritual works of mercy are practiced; correcting sinners, teaching the ignorant, giving counsel to the doubters, comforting the distressed, enduring the troublesome, forgiving those who offend us, praying for the living and the dead.[71]

The deacon as community builder can inspire, motivate, encourage, and assist the parish in its pastoral planning efforts. Many deacons bring a variety of community-building and planning skills to ministry from their professional and family life. The deacon can also exercise leadership through sacramentalizing the links between word, sacrament, and charity *(martyria, leitourgia, diakonia),* which are the constitutive elements of church life. In these and similar ways, the deacon fulfills duties of administration that have been associated with the diaconate since the patristic era. The deacon also serves again as a visible link between the love and worship of God and the love and care of neighbor that were so prevalent in the patristic heritage.

Specifically, the deacon can provide apostolic leadership in addressing the great needs of the contemporary world. The "issues of special urgency" identified by *Gaudium et Spes* may serve as an agenda of opportunities for diaconal leadership. The deacon, most often operating within the context of family and work, brings special sensitivity to such issues as the dignity of marriage and the family; the proper development of culture; economic and social life; the political community; and the fostering of peace and the establishment of a community of nations. The first venue of leadership in these issues is—or ought to be—the parish.

---

71. Kasper, *Leadership,* 23.

The Kenotic Leadership of Deacons

The deacon is not only suited for such leadership in virtue of life experience, but through sacramental ordination as well. The deacon stands empowered as a sign of Christ's own *kenosis,* a sign that human life is not about seeking material wealth, possessions, and positions of power and domination. Rather, the communion of disciples is called to empty themselves in addressing the needs of others.

Regional Diocesan Ministry

While most deacons exercise ministry within parish settings, they remain ministers in service to the entire diocese. Through ordination and incardination, deacons are responsible for building up the community, often through diocesan structures. Given the impact of current demographics and other factors of parish life, many dioceses are approaching pastoral planning and ministry from a regional or even diocesan-wide basis. Unfortunately, as documented in the most recent national survey on the diaconate, too often deacons are perceived as parish-based ministers. The central finding of the study was

> The restored Order of the Diaconate, largely parish-based, has been successful and increasingly important for the life of the Church. The primary challenges of the diaconate for the future are to broaden its ministries beyond its largely successful and increasingly indispensable adaptation to parish life and to emphasize more strongly that deacons, through ordination, are called to be model, animator, and facilitator of ministries of charity and justice within the local church.[72]

Qualified deacons may be given assignments to coordinate outreach ministries throughout the deaneries or diocese, strategic planning efforts or other diocesan or interdiocesan initiatives. Once again we turn to Kasper:

---

72. National Conference of Catholic Bishops, *A National Study on the Permanent Diaconate of the Catholic Church in the United States, 1994–1995* (Washington, DC: United States Catholic Conference, 1996), 13.

> I am thinking here of hospitals, homes for the elderly, spiritual care in places of work, in prisons, in refugee shelters, etc. I also include co-operation in the leadership of a diocese in those regions, where the main question is that of diaconal leadership. In this context, I would like to point out that for the bishop the community of deacons of a diocese can be a welcome panel of advisors. The deacons can act as the eyes and ears of the bishop in identifying areas of need and can help him in his task of being father to the poor.[73]

Such a vision restores some of the ancient responsibilities of the deacon, and the challenges it embodies would be profound, especially in the formation of deacons. Increasingly, ministries involving health care, prisons, and other areas of social concern are becoming more specialized, with stringent professional standards for their practitioners. Deacons assuming leadership roles in such areas not only need the personal gifts and talents to serve in these areas, but also often need diocesan support to attain the appropriate professional credentials to enable their participation in them.

Community-Based Ministry

"A deeply felt need in the decision to re-establish the permanent diaconate was and is that of greater and more direct presence of Church ministers in the various spheres of the family, work, school, etc., in addition to existing pastoral structures."[74] Deacons can and should exercise leadership in community-based service initiatives. Conformed in a special way to Christ the Head and Servant, the deacon imitates Christ in reaching out beyond the limits of the church. Such service can take many forms, defined by the deacon's own skills and qualifications, the sociopolitical structures of the society in which he lives, and the needs to be met.

Furthermore, in terms of canon law, the deacon is the *only* cleric who may participate in various offices of public life, always

---

73. Kasper, *Leadership,* 27.

74. John Paul II, *Deacons Serve the Kingdom of God* (catechesis at the General Audience of October 6, 1993), no. 6, in *Insegnamenti* XVI, no. 2 (1993): 954.

with the permission of his bishop. While this does not exhaust the possibilities of community-based ministry, it remains largely unexamined. While canon 285, paragraph 3, prohibits clerics from assuming "public offices which entail a participation in the exercise of civil power," canon 288 exempts permanent deacons from this and other canons. In response to the canons, the 1984 guidelines state, "While the Code of Canon Law permits permanent deacons to hold political office, a deacon should consult with his bishop before seeking or accepting such an office. In particular cases, the bishop may forbid such an undertaking."[75]

While precise data are unavailable, some deacons are serving as judges in civil and criminal courts, elected members of local governments, and even in positions of military authority. Such participation by deacons in offices of public life is unexplored territory, for many reasons. Certainly there is concern that some forms of public life may be inappropriate for an ordained minister. Still another factor is the risk that the level of public scrutiny on the lives of its officials may be detrimental to the deacon and his role in the church. For these and similar reasons, the participation of a deacon in offices of public life is often an extraordinary, ad hoc matter between the deacon and his bishop. Nonetheless,

> It must not be forgotten that the object of Christ's *diaconia* is mankind. Every human being carries the traces of sin but is called to communion with God. "God so loved the world that He gave His only Son, so that all who believe in Him might not die but have eternal life" (John 3:16). It was for this plan of love, that Christ became a slave and took human flesh. The Church continues to be the sign and instrument of that *diaconia* in history....

---

75. National Conference of Catholic Bishops, Committee on the Permanent Diaconate, *Permanent Deacons in the United States: Guidelines on Their Formation and Ministry* (1971; Washington, DC: United States Catholic Conference, 1985), no. 131.

Growth in imitation of Christ's love for mankind—which surpasses all ideologies—is thus an essential component of the spiritual life of every deacon.[76]

How the deacon, as a minister of the church in the world and as a leader in the church's *diakonia,* may best carry out these responsibilities in community-based ministries is an area that needs much greater examination. Opportunities for such service ought to be the subject of intense and intentional scrutiny by bishops, deacons, and those responsible for the formation of deacons.

Conclusion

The challenge for the contemporary diaconate is to realize the ramifications of *kenotic* power, a power that is given to be given away, a totally self-sacrificial strength for leadership through service. In real terms this means that deacons divorce themselves from any expressions, attitudes, or behaviors that smack of clericalism or the acquisition of power and authority for its own sake. This means that there should be something unique in the ways in which deacons lead in and through service that demonstrates this kenotic dimension. The deacon should always bring a uniquely diaconal and kenotic quality to any assignment: his sacramental extension of and participation in the ministry of the bishop, his witness and dedication to the church's inherent *diakonia,* and his commitment to the entire diocesan church and the community in which he lives and serves.

---

76. Congregation for the Clergy, *Directory for the Ministry and Life of Permanent Deacons* (Washington, DC: United States Catholic Conference, 1998), no. 49.

Select Theological Bibliography

Barnett, James Monroe. *The Diaconate: A Full and Equal Order,* rev. ed. 1981; Valley Forge, PA: Trinity Press International, 1995.

Borgegard, Gunnel, and Christine Hall, ed. *The Ministry of the Deacon.* Uppsala: Nordic Ecumenical Council, 1999.

Brockman, Norman. *Ordained to Service: A Theology of the Permanent Diaconate.* Hicksville, NY: Exposition Press, 1976.

Center for Applied Research on the Apostolate (CARA). "Profile of the Diaconate in the United States," CARA Working Papers Series 6. Washington, DC: Georgetown University, 2004.

Collins, John N. *Deacons and the Church: Making Connections between Old and New.* Harrisburg, PA: Gracewing, 2002.

————. *Diakonia: Re-interpreting the Ancient Sources.* New York: Oxford University Press, 1990.

Cummings, Owen F. *Deacons and the Church.* Mahwah, NJ: Paulist Press, 2004.

Ditewig, William T. "The Deacon as a Voice of Lament and Link to Thanksgiving and Justice." *Liturgical Ministry* 13 (Winter 2004): 24–28.

————. "The Exercise of Governance by Deacons: A Theological and Canonical Study." PhD diss., Catholic University of America, 2002.

————. "From the Ashes of Dachau: The Contemporary Diaconate." *Seminary Journal* 10, no. 3 (Winter 2004): 10–14.

————. "The Once and Future Diaconate: Notes from the Past, Possibilities for the Future." *Church* 20, no. 2 (Summer 2004): 51–54.

————. *101 Questions and Answers on Deacons.* New York: Paulist Press, 2004.

Echlin, Edward P. *The Deacon in the Church: Past and Present.* Staten Island, NY: Alba House, 1971.

Fichter, Joseph. "Wives of Catholic Deacons." In *Wives of Catholic Clergy.* Kansas City, MO: Sheed & Ward, 1992.

International Theological Commission. *From the Diakonia of Christ to the Diakonia of the Apostles.* Chicago: Hillenbrand Books, 2004.

John Paul II. "Deacons Are Configured to Christ the Servant" (November 30, 1995). Available at: www.ewtn.com/library/ PAPALDOC/JP951130.HTM.

Kasper, Walter Cardinal. *Leadership in the Church: How Traditional Roles Can Serve the Christian Community Today.* New York: Herder & Herder, 2003.

————. "The Ministry of the Deacon." *Deacon Digest* (March/ April 1998): 19–27.

Latcovich, Mark A. "The Effects of the Ministerial Environment on Roman Catholic Permanent Deacons and Their Spouses." PhD diss., Case Western Reserve University, 1995.

LeClair, Douglas M. *The Deacon as Icon of Christ.* Phoenix, AZ: Catholic Sun Publishing, 2001.

McCaslin, Patrick, and Michael G. Lawlor. *Sacrament of Service: A Vision of the Permanent Diaconate Today.* New York: Paulist Press, 1986.

McKnight, William S. "The Latin Rite Deacon: Symbol of Communitas and Social Intermediary among the People of God." STD diss., Pontificium Athenaeum S. Anselmi, 2001.

Nowell, Robert. *The Ministry of Service: Deacons in the Contemporary Church.* New York: Herder & Herder, 1968.

Osborne, Kenan B. *The Diaconate in the Christian Church: Its History and Theology.* Chicago: National Association of Diaconate Directors, 1996.

Paul VI. *Sacrum Diaconatus Ordinem,* General Norms for Restoring the Permanent Diaconate in the Latin Church. Washington, DC: United States Catholic Conference, 1967.

Pontifical Biblical Commission. *The Interpretation of the Bible in the Church.* Rome: Libreria Editrice Vaticana, 1993.

Ratigan, V., and A. Swidler, eds. *A New Phoebe: Perspectives on Roman Catholic Women and the Permanent Diaconate.* Kansas City, MO: Sheed & Ward, 1990.

Shugrue, Timothy. *Service Ministry of the Deacon.* Washington, DC: Bishops' Committee on the Permanent Diaconate, National Conference of Catholic Bishops, 1988.